JIM MATHIS

REINVENTION MADE EASY:

Change Your Strategy,
Change Your Results

NEW YORK

REINVENTION MADE EASY:
Change Your Strategy, Change Your Results

Published in New York, New York, by Morgan James Publishing. Morgan James and The Entrepreneurial Publisher are trademarks of Morgan James, LLC.
www.MorganJamesPublishing.com

The Morgan James Speakers Group can bring authors to your live event. For more information or to book an event visit The Morgan James Speakers Group at
www.TheMorganJamesSpeakersGroup.com.

A **free** eBook edition is available
with the purchase of this print book.

CLEARLY PRINT YOUR NAME ABOVE IN UPPER CASE

Instructions to claim your free eBook edition:
1. Download the BitLit app for Android or iOS
2. Write your name in **UPPER CASE** on the line
3. Use the BitLit app to submit a photo
4. Download your eBook to any device

ISBN 978-1-61448-091-4 paperback
Library of Congress Control Number:
2011934591

Cover Design by:
3 Dog Design
www.3dogdesign.net

Interior Design by:
Bonnie Bushman
bonnie@caboodlegraphics.com

Editor – Mike and Cindy Pfeiffer,
Colin Bosler

In an effort to support local communities, raise awareness and funds, Morgan James Publishing donates a percentage of all book sales for the life of each book to Habitat for Humanity Peninsula and Greater Williamsbu--

Get involved today, visit
www.MorganJamesBuilds.com

Habitat
for Humanity®
Peninsula and
Greater Williamsburg
Building Partner

DEDICATION

This is dedicated to the one I love... my wife, Laura. We met in the youth program at Wieuca Road Baptist Church in 1970. We went on choir tours to Boston and Hawaii. Your mother, Gini, made an early impression on me. You and I were friends then, became best friends several years ago and finally husband and wife (even though it took 43 years for that to happen!). God has shown His Grace to me through you and continues to every day. You help me reinvent myself continually and I can't imagine how I made it this far without you, my best friend, at my side. It took almost 40 years for us both to see that, but I look forward to many more years as we grow spiritually, emotionally and romantically together. I love you!

ACKNOWLEDGMENTS

I am most appreciative of the many people who have offered stories and ideas to make me the person that I am and this book what it is. I am a compilation of everyone I have ever met, for good or bad. Each person and relationship has come into my life for a reason. The positive ones and the negative ones all shaped my destiny. They have each reinvented me many times over.

Thank you to Mike and Cindy Pfeiffer who edited this book and went through so many revisions that I wondered if you had a life aside from this project. Mike is my best friend and we have known each other long enough to know what that truly means.

My family means the world to me. Thank you to Laura, Faith, Mom, Chris, Corey, Cody and Wiley for your support. I love you all.

Finally, thank you God for blessing my life and bringing people into it people who have shaped me. All along You were there. You have guarded me, protected me and shown me your mighty hand and heart so many times. When I look back on my life, I can see your guidance in it all the way. To quote the hymn: "Through many dangers, toils and snares I have already come. Grace has brought me safe thus far, and grace will lead me home…"

TABLE OF CONTENTS

"I like people who shake other people up and make them feel uncomfortable."

— Jim Morrison

INTRODUCTION

I am not the person I used to be...something changed.

When I first became a professional speaker, I wanted to motivate people to take action. I embraced my Southern heritage and my accent and billed myself as "Dr. Phil meets Jeff Foxworthy." I was very entertaining and enjoyed making people laugh. I still do. But something changed... the economy changed. Meetings changed. The world changed. My clients and customers changed. I found that no one wanted to buy the fluffy, feel-good, down-home-spun humor. People were hurting and wanted relief from their pain. They were sitting in their seats and listening (most were) to speakers who would come in, do their traveling dog-and-pony show and leave. The feel-good feelings would linger a short while and then it was back to the workplace and the same headaches that plagued them before the meeting.

Then it occurred to me that every speaker was doing the same thing. A lady who was on the same program with me in Philadelphia came up to me and said, "Well, I guess it's our job to pump them up, motivate them, give them a laugh or two then send them out ready to take charge." That stuck with me. She was right... that was exactly what they were expecting us to do. That is what almost every speaker does. And from that point on I didn't want to do that anymore. I wanted to use the skills that I had used in my previous occupation in the church to challenge people in their seats and get them thinking. I didn't want to "leave them pumped up." I wanted to "leave them wanting more," as P.T. Barnum, a master marketer, would say.

So when I took the platform that day, I had a different message (you will find in this book that I don't have a problem with changing what I am going to say on the spot). I opened by telling everyone that this program was going to be different than what they expected. I said that I USED to be "Dr. Phil meets Jeff Foxworthy," but that is not who I would be for them that day. "Today I am probably going to say some things that might upset you. They might frustrate you. They will leave you unsettled. In fact, I wouldn't be surprised if you are challenged by my presentation so much that you have an uncomfortable time for the rest of this conference." They were stunned – and so was I. Did I say that? I loved it. I decided to "tell it like it is" and leave no holds barred with them. I wasn't going to sugar-coat things.

And I didn't. I told them the realities that no one else on the program that day was willing to face. Was it all bad news? No, they were in an industry hit hard by the recession, but were facing some of the best opportunities in their industry in years. They just hadn't rotated around the opposite side of the problem and seen it from the right perspective. No matter what you do, you are faced with difficulties every day that by your choice you run from, hide from or deny; OR that by your alternative choice you embrace, tackle and conquer. It has nothing to do with what is going on around you, but what is going on INSIDE of you. Now I know that may sound to some folks like motivational garbage, but hear me out.

I won't argue with you that these times are tumultuous for business. They are rough and many people have found themselves out of work, out of business and out of luck. I meet them every day. I can also tell you that many people have had to face challenges that they would have never had to face had things remained unchanged. I can say without any doubt that had I not had the difficult times in my life, I wouldn't be the strong person I am today. Had I not changed colleges, I wouldn't have met the people I know now who are major influences in my life. Had I not decided to quit my occupation in the church, I wouldn't be enjoying what I now do for a living. Had my business not fallen apart, I wouldn't be The Reinvention Professional. You get the idea…

Every one of those changes was traumatic in my life. I could have buried my head in the sand and pretended they weren't there, but that wouldn't make them go away. I could have sat around in a funk of depression for months on end, but that wouldn't have made me or my situation any better. You choose how you react to what is going on in your environment. You either choose to act positively or negatively. Either way, it's all your choice.

Don't misunderstand me; I am still in the business of making people's lives better. I just got tired of doing all the work for people who didn't want to change. So I changed my focus. I only work with people who want to reinvent themselves in a challenging economy. And fortunately for me, every economy has challenges in it.

About the economy: The US and world economy have taken a beating over the last few years. They have been at the brink, recovered then wandered more into uncertainty. This morning as I wrote this section, it was announced that several major corporations are reporting profits for the first time in many quarters, but unemployment statistics in the United States (and the world) are still at all-time highs. No one is ready to declare the recession over. You choose how you react to that news. You can either wait, wait and further wait for the economy to come back to where it was two years ago (it won't) or you can choose to act on what is different about it now and make your own difference. It's all your choice. Oh, and for those who opt to wait, you should know that the economy won't return to its previous state.

This book is not designed to make you comfortable, feel good or give you that "rah-rah" feeling you might seek to make it a great day. That isn't my job anymore. You must generate that on your own. This book is designed to do what I do every day. It is designed to make you feel uncomfortable. It is designed to not give you answers as much as give you better questions to ask. It is designed to frustrate you and to make you unsettled. It is designed so that you will have to think your way to the last page. I want you to feel uncomfortable after reading this. I want you to be so upset with the way you are doing business and dealing with customers, clients and prospects that you never want to return to work the same way again.

You will read some very provocative statements here: "The recession will never end." "The economy isn't down; it's different." "People don't buy what you think you sell." "If you want to be unique in your industry get away from it." "Your people don't always work better together." "If you don't reinvent yourself in the next year, you may be extinct in two years." It can happen. It already has to Circuit City, Pontiac, Schlitz, Gateway computers, Aloha Airlines, Palm and many others. The vultures are gathering for Blackberry, Radio Shack Aeropostale, Sears and suburban malls. It's a competitive world and just as you were reading this, many other businesses closed their doors for the last time. They couldn't adapt to a challenging economy and they got swept away with no loyal customer base to support them or their brands. They failed to create a culture that would stand the test of change or the test of time.

Many more organizations have changed successfully. They were faced with a choice and they chose reinvention over extinction. Companies like Motorola, Novell, Western Union, Domino's, IBM, Nintendo, Jim Mathis (me, of course) and many, many more reinvented themselves and carved out new industries and market niches. As you read these pages, look for the stories of organizations who changed (and the ones who didn't). Look for ways you can adopt their ideas, methods and concepts. Their techniques aren't very deep or difficult. In fact you might be surprised at how simple and easy they are. Most will seem like common sense. They will be so easy, in fact that they will make you angry at yourself for not thinking of them on your own. They are so obvious that they will make you frustrated that you didn't see them and act before now. They are so simple that they will make you uncomfortable with the way you are living and running your business. Good. My work will not have been in vain.

Enjoy the journey. Find a comfortable place to sit and prepare to become UNcomfortable as you read and apply!

Chapter 1

WELCOME TO THE
NEW WORLD OF WORK!

"The best way to predict the future is to create it."
– Peter Drucker

Old World Meets New World

If you were a merchant or part of the upper class living in Western Europe in 1550, the buzz would've been about the latest discovery – the New World. A crazy radical had raised the money to disprove the "flat-earth sail-til-you-drop-off-the-edge" theory. In the process, Columbus discovered a New World, an unknown continent and revealed new challenges, possibilities and opportunities forever changing their Old World. Though the initial discovery occurred 58 years before, there was yet so much to be discovered. Imagine the untapped resources. Why, could you have resisted the temptation to wonder what it would be like to get there first and bring home the riches? The rumor had it that the natives possessed enormous caches of gold. With minimum investment and shrewd trading on your part – trading mere trinkets - you could own all of that wealth. It was all there for the taking.

The old paradigm of trading and bargaining was being overwhelmed by the promise of untold riches that lay ahead. Everyone wanted in on the deal. Each principality - from Spain, to Portugal, to England, to France

- wanted to capitalize on the vast expanse of land and resources that stretched just across the ocean. Gone were the days of traversing East across hostile lands to India and China. Now all that was needed were a few ships and the backing of over-eager royalty wanting to corner the new market. Even the church maneuvered for a hand in the arrangements and profits. Imagine that moment in history. The New World meant that everything changed.

Now look around and you'll agree that today is much the same. A New World of business is sweeping across the landscape. The old ways of work are almost gone, or they will be within the next few years. The Third World nations that once seemed backward and uneducated are now taking front seats to North America, England, Japan and Russia. A mere twenty years ago, items bearing the stamp "Made in China" were commonly thought to be cheap and shoddy. Likewise in the 1950's the brand: "Made in Japan" was similarly snubbed. Since then, Japan and now China has each taken its place as the industrial leader to beat, with India coming in close behind. Goods manufactured there are now being marketed in the United States to add to an already hefty product profit margin.

The currency of the old world was the US Dollar. It was sound and stable. Everyone who did business sought to trade in US Dollars. But look at today. Rap singers now flaunt Euros in their music videos. Disney now trades in its own currency within the theme parks. Since the market tumble of 2009 the most stable and sought after currency is the South African Rand. All over North America, banks which were once the only place to deposit and save money are now in heavy competition with community chartered credit unions. Even Wal-Mart is trying its hand at the banking business. Credit cards are being offered with as much value as those who once were only issued by banks. Banks are offering to allow customers to transfer funds to other customer accounts from their smart phones. Who could have seen this coming?

I recently had a telephone conversation with my mega-lending bank. I had a concern for the lack of professional courtesy being extended by the untrained individual on the phone. So I asked to speak to their supervisor. After a long wait on hold I was allowed a conversation with their supervisor.. When I mentioned the lack of courtesy in the earlier conversation with their subordinate, the supervisor said that "it was not their policy to act in any other manner." "Don't you think it should be your policy to treat customers with respect?" I asked. The answer was predictably 'old world.' "This is a big bank, which has been very successful. We don't need to take advice from customers like you on the phone", whereupon he hung up." I wanted to ask him, "Why, then, if you are so successful, did another mega-bank just buy you out ahead of certain bankruptcy?" I never got to ask that question, but I'm sure I'd have gotten another smart come-back.

The recession of 2008-2009 forever changed the perception that large banks are unshakeable places to save, invest or borrow. Small community banks are rapidly becoming preferred by consumers who want a relationship built on trust, stability and personalization. The greater business priority is now with the individual depositor. The large, overextended business is no longer a banker's prime target. When the Continental Army of the fledgling United States of America accepted the surrender of General Cornwallis at Yorktown in 1781, the British band played a familiar tune of the day, "The World Turned Upside Down." It happened then and it is happening now.

Financial institutions once thought to be the bedrock of stability are receiving bailouts from the United States government at taxpayer expense. Many banks once thought to be successful because of their enormous size now have been bought out in the diminishing hope they can stay in business. People like the rude supervisor at the mega-bank will have to change their attitude, their practices and their outlook if they want to stay in business in the next few years. It's not the same way it was by any stretch of the imagination. The playing field has changed. What was once thought of as safe ground is now unstable and shifting.

The change started before the recession with tremors in the housing markets, the lending markets and the change in buying practices among consumers. Remember the great tsunami of March 2011? An earthquake event off the coast of Japan triggered a giant wave that swept across the Pacific Ocean, finally washing ashore thousands of miles away. The surge took homes, property, lives and everything in its path, leaving destruction in its wake. For these communities, their geographic landscape and quality of life will never be as it was before. When AIG was bailed out by the United States government and the stock market soon afterwards began to tumble, the financial landscape changed forever. It's as if a giant tsunami swept across the banking world and nothing will ever be the same again.

Some already know how to take advantage of the opportunities that abound in a crisis. In a letter to his shareholders in February 2010, iconic American investor Warren Buffett wrote, "We've put a lot of money to work during the chaos of the last two years. It's been an ideal period for investors. The climate of fear is our best friend." As the so-called Sage of Omaha, Buffet is America's most listened-to investor. His annual letter is scrutinized by the street for a frank assessment of his own businesses and of the general economy. Warren knows the investors secret: <u>a shrewd investor can take the worst of an economic crisis and turn it into a huge advantage.</u> Said another way,

There is no better time to seize the moment
than when the world is in a fetal position.

Life in Competition

In the Old World of work, employers dominated their workers. Please the boss. Do what he says. Look busy when he enters the room. Employees were grouped in teams to accomplish tasks, compete with each other in performance and beat the competition in sales or productivity. The focus was on what the competition was doing. Study the competition and find out what they are doing. How can we replicate it here? How can I be a compliant follower? Like individual employees, entire businesses can fall into this pattern.

My background is in local church ministry. You can search the world over and you won't find an institution more steeped in tradition and old ideas than a church. Believe it or not, this description of work in the corporate world depicts working in the church. A pastor who dominates the staff and all decisions come from or must be approved by him. The staff team works together with friendly competition and the goal is to get more people to show up than the church across town or down the street. We constantly studied what was working in one parish to replicate it in our own. As one finance committee chairman told me "The focus is on nickels and noses." If you want to keep getting paid and want your budget to remain intact, you better get more people to show up.

So as ministers pressed to raise attendance and donations, we examined every church that was doing anything successful to get ideas on how to achieve our goals. Maybe if it works there, it will work here. Never mind the fact that it worked there because it was "there" and not "here."

My denomination took pride in their focus on reaching un-churched individuals and families. They taught outreach and witnessing on a professional basis. But I noticed that the people we were attracting were already well-versed in church language and practices. Even the avant-garde churches that claimed to reach only "lost" people were populated with families that had left another congregation for one reason or another and come to the new church. They brought all their problems with them. More importantly, they brought their expectations that church would be just like it was in the former congregation, only without all those "other problem people."

Almost every church was copying each other or perpetuating the traditions that they claimed to be setting themselves apart from. I once had a pastor wanting to raise capital funds in a recession to build a gymnasium. His circular reasoning went something like this: "We are the only large church in our part of town that doesn't have a gymnasium. The Community Center isn't church-based so Christians have no business recreating there. They need a campus like ours to exercise and play." What he failed to see was that there was no demand on the part of his constituents for a new gymnasium. The fund raising campaign did take place. Almost no pledges were turned in.

Once in the business world, I learned there is very little difference. Companies spend more time replicating what works down the street or across the industry than coming up with original ideas. When someone does, they are often initially condemned by their peers. But if the idea takes hold, they are immediately heralded as the great new wave of the future. Just like the churches I observed, they became market followers.

On the other hand, market leaders don't pay as much attention to what their competitors are doing. In the New World of Work, the customer is the focus of attention. What do they want? What are we doing that they like? What are we not doing that they wish we would do?

What if that pastor who wanted to build the activities center had asked the community what it needed? What if he had gone out and mingled with un-churched individuals and families and asked them what our church was doing that they liked, or what it wasn't doing that they wanted? Do you think the story would have changed? I think so. In fact, I know so. When the focus is on your competitors and not your customers, you have more competition and less customers. When you get closer to you customers, you will have more customers. It just makes common sense.

Changing Customers

Your customers have changed. They are the same people they always were, but their buying habits, their expectations, their communication, their access to information, their resources and their needs have changed. They don't buy the way they used to buy. They don't bank the way they used to bank (consider the shift to on-line banking). They have no patience with voice messages. They don't like overseas customer service (calling them "help desks" is a lousy excuse). They use Google and Bing rather than Yellow Pages. They YouTube their experiences with your company for the world - *by the millions* - to watch (any questions United Airlines?). They are using their mobile devices to do almost everything.

In the New World of work, your customer is smarter, faster and pickier about how he (or she) spends their money - and where. He's Wifi-ing in his hotel room, on the plane, in Starbucks, and at home. He knows more about your competition and price differences than you do. He doesn't care how important you say his call is. He buys late at night – in huge numbers. He gets his news from Stephen Colbert, Jon Stewart, Jay Leno, David Letterman, Bill O'Reilly and many others "outside" of the newsroom. He texts - all the time – even in the car (Bad but it's still happening). He can pay right now if you take a credit card online or from your smart phone. He expects someone that can actually help him on 'live chat' with him or answer the phone when he calls; not "feel his pain."

Meanwhile you really don't get it. You still believe your customers should be glad you are doing business with them. You think they are lucky to being working with an organization as large as yours. You think they should wait on hold, wait for an answer, or take a survey after the call for customer service. You think that just because your lame recording says their call is important that they believe it is (and will sit on hold for a longer period of time). You think they don't know as much about your competition as you do. You think they only are interested in your business from 9-5 on weekdays.

Think again. They are way past your "old world" thinking. It's time to move forward. It's time to work in this new decade, not in spite of it. The customer has adapted to his/her changing environment. He checks out your products at night after your customer service lines have shut down for the evening. She checks your prices against your competitor with the click of a button and knows the differences in minutes.

He registers his concerns and complaints on his blog, his Facebook page, his YouTube channel, his Twitter account, Yelp or Trip Advisor for all the world to see and agree. He is better in touch with other customers than you are. And he is getting even better at it at this very moment. She is technologically adept. He is smarter. According to a CNN poll released in March 2010, men and women get more news from the internet than radio and television combined. So where are you investing your energy, your time and your advertising dollars?

Are you using the internet to mesh your sales, service, orders and information? Have you unified your message to make one (and only one) statement as your brand? Are you on Facebook, Twitter, LinkedIn, You Tube or blogging? Are you immersed in social media? Consider that they, your customers are. The most followed man on Twitter is Ashton. In accepting a People's Choice award on live television in January 2010, he filmed himself with his cell phone and "tweeted" it to the world while on stage. He has a following. Do you have a group, a Fan Page or a set group of followers that you communicate with on a regular basis? If you don't, your competitors may already have of these and be several steps (or decades) ahead of you.

The customer today is savvier than ever before. They are more likely than ever before to comparison shop *before* you ever communicate with them. They demand more and expect more. They expect you to provide accurate information regarding your hours of operation. One Sunday when a major sporting event was taking place I noticed an advertisement and went online looking for office furniture. What were you doing with your business that day? Customers will take their business to anyone meeting these expectations SECONDS before you have a chance to respond. What are you doing about it? How are you finding out what your customers want and expect? How are you turning their feedback, blog opinions and impressions into real profits? How are your frontline workers equipped to get closer to these new customers and make more money from them? You need to regularly measure and be poised to reinvent the whole process from start to finish.

Your competitors are growing savvier, too. They are using *"Crowdsourcing"* while you are researching with focus groups, expensive consultants and marketing statistics. They are using idictate.org and elance.com while you are using stenographers and editors. They are publishing their works for Kindles and iPads while you are using same-old bindery book publishing houses. They are advancing their internet presence with video, social networks and live chat while you are thinking about updating your site because it's been unchanged for over two years. More has been invented in the last 20 years than the past 500. What are you doing to keep pace with the rate of change every month?

There is a New World of work that reinvents itself every few months - and that pace accelerates every year. You never get a second chance to make a SPLIT SECOND impression. Do you have to have social media to succeed? Keep this in mind : you won't succeed without it. So do you have to have a great, expensive web site to make a profit? Not necessarily, but it *will* help you look like the ones who do. Do you have to use technology? No, but we'll see what you are doing to stay closer to your people than your competitors are doing. Is reinventing yourself an ongoing process? Yes.

Are Recessions Really Bad for Business?

When the recession of 2008-2009 hit, it caught everyone unawares. It revealed something of incredible importance: *The economy wasn't down; it was different*. A Ford Motors Company advertising executive was quoted several years ago saying: "We had to divert $120 million to online advertising because as much as we tried to discourage it, people kept going online to look at our cars." I said at that time, "Huh? If your customers want something from you that is reasonable and will make you more money, why wouldn't you want to satisfy them?"

But in April 2010, Group VP-Global Marketing at Ford Motor Co. Jim Farley, said that the recession was actually the best thing for automotive marketing, especially on the digital front. "Everything has to work in this economy," says Farley. "If the economy hadn't dropped as it did, we would've been on auto-pilot and not experimenting the way we did. Our production quality online is better than our broadcast." Mr. Farley said the company is also rethinking the way it approaches media planning. Ford executives found themselves in a different world of work and had to make changes. They admitted that without the recession, they wouldn't have been successful going forward.

I was speaking in Canada in early 2008 just as the media was talking about the slowdown in the US economy and the coming recession. I stopped in to see a client in Toronto. I noticed in reading the *Globe and Mail* (Canada's nationwide newspaper) that the Canadian economy was doing much better than the American economy at that time. I asked my friend if Canada was experiencing the same recession fears we were. She responded, "No. Our press isn't *trying to convince us* that our economy is bad." Hmmm.

On May 6, 2010 Wall Street experienced the largest one day drop in history. At one point the DOW Jones Industrial Average was down 998 points. Then they "recovered" - to only lose about 300 points. Nice. What caused this selling frenzy? Panic. Someone, according to the news media, hit the wrong button on a sell order that changed the amount from Million to Billion. From that point on, logic took a back seat. Emotion took over, fear being the most prevalent. The rest is new history. Or is it really "new?"

In my opinion, most economies are driven more by emotion than by fact. Examination reveals they are almost 80% Fiction and 20% Fact. A bear market is called a "recession" or "depression." People panic and sell, often creating a run on the market as we saw in May 2010. History records many recessions that were labeled panics. For instance, the Panic of 1873 occurred when there was a run on American banks and a recession wiped out many wealthy people – Andrew Carnegie being one of them. On the other hand, in a bull market people buy in a "frenzy." Most of the current economic problems experienced by America and the world have been brought on by fear and loss of confidence.

Look how this played out in the US. Our national GDP was growing and we hadn't had one quarter of decline by early 2008. However the media was trumpeting the cover-up of a recession. Then the stock market fell in September 2008 as a direct result of the failure of Lehman Brothers and a week of negative news coverage followed. The story went virally global, and soon thereafter the Canadian economy went into a tumble. As a friend in Toronto told me, "When the US gets the flu, Canada gets a cold." What helped propel the wildest day on Wall Street? According to

Patrick Rizzo and John Schoen writing for MSNBC.com, "Fear that the European debt crisis could spread was a factor." Even now the disaster in the Greek economy is affecting attitudes and markets around the world. Fear is rampant among investors, producers, and consumers today. What can you do in the face of mounting fear and despair?

I like to network and socialize with successful people. I've noticed that they choose not to participate in talk of fear and recession. No, they're not in denial. That's because they are *participating* in the recession - successfully; just not indulging in the talk of fear associated with a recession. I believe that if you work hard there is always enough money circulating and you will receive an ample amount of it. Senior leadership who are motivated by fear and who won't spend money on improving customer service and educating their people will pay dearly when the present "crisis" is over and they find themselves without customers...and a job.

In a recession the economy isn't down; it's different. You are in a different environment than you were just two years ago. The changes are coming faster, too. Price fluctuations at the gas pump occur daily instead of weekly or monthly. The internet has increased business traffic to lightning speeds. The number of people buying, shopping and comparing online has increased dramatically in the past year alone. "American Idol Gives Back" has demonstrated that the number of donations to charitable groups through texting is skyrocketing. Unlike previous generations, our global economy now influences a farmer in North Dakota, a health care worker in Pennsylvania, a "mom and pop" radio station in Michigan, a small community banker in Montana and an office products company in New Brunswick – all at the same time from the same event.

Who's In Your Room?

Have you ever heard the expression: "the elephant in the room"? It can refer to an obvious **truth** that is being ignored or goes unaddressed. It also applies to an obvious **problem** no one wants to discuss. Because an elephant in the room with us would be impossible to overlook, those in the room who pretend the elephant is not there are more likely to be focused on small and irrelevant matters, never coming to terms with the looming big one. Think what's going to happen when that elephant moves!

Archaeologists tell us that the dinosaurs probably died out and became extinct because they weren't equipped to adapt to a changed environment. As the environment became different, they couldn't, or wouldn't become different. But other species on this planet survived because they were able to adapt and they became different with the different environment. It's called survival of the fittest.

Your environment has definitely changed. But there are obvious practices, problems, attitudes, beliefs, employees, inventory, customers and items that you believe are holding you back from changing. They don't allow you to become what you can be. When you resist changing them by refusing to adapt to a changed business environment, global marketplace or economy, they hold you back from making the decision required to move forward. Whatever excuse you choose for avoiding change, it will lead to your extinction.

Sadly, everyone can see it but you. It might be a fashion style you think makes you stand out, but instead is being ridiculed by onlookers. It might be your stubborn belief in a product or item in your inventory that you just know someone will want to buy if you push it hard and long enough. It might be meetings with your employees that are useless, time-wasting, or simply self-aggrandizing. Whatever name it goes by, it is costing you more money to hold on to it than to just get over it and move on.

Steve Jobs, CEO of Apple (and creator of all things technologically wonderful) said, "Get rid of all the crappy stuff, and focus on the good stuff." He was advising Nike president and CEO Mark Parker, but it spoke to items unwanted by the marketplace that Apple tried unsuccessfully to sell. Remember the Newton? Like Steve Jobs and Apple, you have "crappy stuff" too. That stuff has dwindled in importance or function and is no longer profitable for you. Instead of being the elephant in the room, it is really the dinosaur in the room. You need to purge it, release it, free it, let it die and get over it.

Your employees are in the room. Most of them contribute to your profit line. Some make more than others. Some cost you more to retain than if you let them find somewhere else to suck profits from. The few are draining your organization of money, time and energy. They have no intention of making a profit for you. Your ability to work them into your "vision" hasn't gone as well as you planned. Your total team concept and the useless people on your staff are the dinosaur(s) in your room. They have become extinct. You need to get over it and let the concept die.

Your ego is in the room. You are convinced that your methods are tried and true in business, but your bottom line indicates otherwise.

I saw an ad for a car dealer on television. All he talked about was how he had more inventory than anyone else in the state. People should buy from him because he had more than all of his competitors. He must have bragged about the inventory surplus for 50 seconds of the 60 second commercial. Then the dealership information followed. The brand on his lot was under investigation for serious safety defects, and instead of confronting his elephant, he cried louder his perceived positive of "Inventory! Inventory! Inventory!" He could not admit that his inventory could not offset his customers' fears. He missed his opportunity to step into their comfort zone. Guess who still has his enormous inventory? You insist that everyone follow your leadership regardless of your wisdom. You feel your eccentricities are unique and that everyone appreciates your uniqueness, even while your employees think otherwise. Your ego is in the room. It is becoming extinct. You need to get over it and let it die.

I realized the same thing a year ago and it became the impetus to reinvent my business. The "Old World" thinking wasn't working for me. At that time, no one was buying what I was selling. I couldn't figure out why. Although I marketed more, it didn't make a difference. Although I talked more about what I did that I thought everyone would benefit from, no one was calling for it. Although I tried to work harder and push what I sold harder, it made no difference and didn't fulfill me at the end of the day. Then one day I realized the truth. I was the dinosaur in the room. I was becoming extinct. I was allowing the recession to get me "down." I wasn't being different.

So I did a lot of soul searching. I asked a lot of questions. I asked my most loyal customers what they wanted. I asked people why they bought from me. I asked customers what they heard me say that affected them the most. I asked clients what they liked best about what I had for them. I asked what they weren't getting from me that they wanted. I asked myself what I needed to let go of that was costing me more in money, time and energy than what it was bringing in. It made me reinvent my business, my appearance, my marketing, my brand, my culture, my customer base, my selling/buying plan and even my personal life and wardrobe. I needed to get Old World thinking out of the room and let it become extinct and die.

The Old World of Work is in the room. It says that if you feed it by doing the same things you used to do, it will reward you with success like you used to have. It promises that the old ways are tried and true. It says that if you push a product or service hard enough, no matter what it is, you will sell it to almost anyone. It affirms that you need to keep the customer at bay, your employees in the dark and everyone else guessing about your next move. It pooh-poohs the internet as a passing fad where no real business takes place. It charms you with leftover inventory, then woos you with the temptation "One day, someone will buy all of this and you will recoup the loss to make a fortune." It says that although Fred doesn't do much work, getting rid of him would cost more in expense and trouble.

This Old World of Work is a dying beast. In the most successful and competitive businesses it has already died, been buried and the funeral held. In your business, you need to do more than let it die of natural causes. You need to proactively exorcize it from your inventory, staff, schedule, to-do list, practices, attitudes, beliefs and expectations. The Old World of Work is the dinosaur in your room. Banish it to extinction.

OK, so you get this. You're saying, "Great points, Jim." You made me think about some things in my business." You're still headed for extinction. You read this and say, "Okay, I get it. But my boss and customers don't.

So what can I do?" You too are still headed for extinction. If you say, "I get it, but I don't have the authority to do anything about all of this," you are headed for extinction. Reinventing yourself begins with your attitude. It isn't *part* of your job; it *IS* your job.

Why Are We Here?

This book is about: *Reinvention Made Easy*. It's about going back to your people and asking, "What are we here for in the first place?" "Why do we exist in the global market?" "Why were we founded?"

Thom Winninger tells the story of how the Kodak Company embraced reinvention several years ago. Their prices were being undercut by other companies. Kodak was faced with the prospect of lowering the price on their film. However their expenses and payroll were too high to lower prices and the corresponding already thin profit margins. No, a price war would put them out of business. So instead of cutting film prices, they searched inward. They asked themselves this question: "What was George Eastman's original intent when he founded Kodak? Was it to sell film?" They discovered the answer was a resounding "NO." The Kodak Company was originally founded to help people capture the precious moments of their lives, thereby facilitating memories and heritage. With this fresh discovery, Kodak embarked on reinventing themselves from the inside out. What resulted was a campaign centered around what customers were really buying.

Kodak customers weren't looking for film. They were looking to preserve the feeling of Johnny's first birthday. They wanted to remember Grandma and Grandpa long after they passed on. They wanted to capture the beauty of the Grand Canyon vacation trip. Kodak's sales skyrocketed as they became the choice for creating magic moments. They sponsored "Magic Moment" spots in Disney theme parks to pose with characters in costume from children's movies. They stopped marketing the film's price and instead marketed what the film does for you. Why? Because what the film does for you *is what people were buying!* People associated Kodak with great memories, and that's what they were buying – not bargain priced film.

This book is filled with stories just like Kodak's that I have witnessed, collected and heard from people strategizing in the New World of Work. It is about how companies and individuals are rediscovering their roots and reinventing themselves for the new decade and the New World. It's about how the traditional Old World of Work is rapidly passing and what is replacing it today. It is a journey that you must make if you want to survive into this second decade of the Twenty First Century. It is fraught with risks and unexpected challenges. Sometimes it's a scary place to go. Many attempting the crossing have failed out of fear of the known and the unknown. Ugly rumor says that if you step outside of your comfort zone your business will die. You'll hit a wall. You'll fall off the edge. Just like in 1492, fear of the unknown is rampant. By 1550 the New World was an opportunity. The same opportunity presents itself to you today.

The New World of Work contains rich resources you can only imagine. But you have to be willing to take the risk. When Cortez landed in what is now Veracruz, Mexico he took everything ashore; men, supplies and horses. Then he burned his ships in full view of his troops. His message was, "We aren't going back, we are going forward. This is where we live now and where we will stay. We can either conquer it or be conquered by it." Come along on this journey as we discover the brave New World of Work. We will explore why we are here in the first place. What purpose were you meant to fulfill? Why was your business conceived? Who are your customers and what do they really want?

Speaking to a group of convenience store owners, I asked what differentiated one store chain from another? They didn't know. Why should I shop at *Valero* instead of *QT* or *7-11*? What is the advantage of buying from *Wawa* over *Circle K*? Does *ampm* have an edge over *Busslers*? These are questions you need to know in your own industry if you are going to run a competitively successful business. Answers to questions like these are at the very root of why you think you are in business. One of the attendees smirked and said simply, "We are better."

I asked why. He shrugged and said, "I don't know, we just are." Then I asked every other owner in the room, who is really the best. Most said themselves. Do you get the picture? Everyone thinks they are the best. Is that their opinion or is that the customer's opinion? Is it the opinion of future potential customers? If everyone looks alike, ask yourself this question: Why do people buy from you?

In the New World of Work market leaders ask different questions like these. They want to know why someone buys. They want to know why a customer comes back. Sales author Jeffrey Gitomer says, "In a down economy, personal motivation is something everyone needs. Unfortunately few people are aware of how to discover it for themselves. They instead focus on the negative news, the state of the economy, business worries, job security and in many cases even personal financial security. Meanwhile corporate leaders are slashing budgets, cutting meetings that they deem unnecessary, and doing their best to communicate as little as possible to their people, until the other shoe drops. And these leaders wonder why morale is down... It's not a matter of shaking it off. It's a matter of looking at your sales (the ones you made), calling the people back, and discovering why they bought from you. Do that a dozen times and you'll uncover genuine motives for purchases."

The New World of Work is there to be discovered and explored. The rewards are plentiful. The risks are high, but not as high as sitting on the sidelines and doing nothing. It takes a strong positive attitude, a commitment to put everything on the table and gamble. Temporary losses may be necessary. I like to play cards with friends. One of my favorite card games is "Texas Hold'em." When you think you have a great hand you can go "All In." This means betting every match stick (or poker chip) you have on winning the pot. Sometimes, though players go All In when they are desperate. The difference is knowing when to bet, when to bluff and when to get out and watch.

My Wish for You

Reinvention Made Easy is your personal and professional guide to knowing how to play the game and win. Expert players select a system they use. You will find many systems here that are tried and successful. You will find stories of people and corporations that went all in and won the entire pot. You will recognize pitfalls to bypass, and see the mistakes made by others - and how to avoid them. In the end you will know what works for you and what doesn't.

In the movie, "One Flew Over the Cuckoo's Nest," the character played by Jack Nicholson is confined to a state mental hospital. He is guilty of a crime and took the mental option for treatment, rather than prison. In one scene, he bets the other patients that he can lift a very large marble sink that is bolted to the floor. No one believes he can accomplish this feat. They debate and bet. When he makes the attempt, he struggles and strains, but to no avail. As he walks away in apparent defeat, they ridicule him for his failure. "At least I tried," he answers. At the end of the movie, inspired by his efforts to motivate the others, the strongest silent character who watched earlier steps forward and lifts the sink, throwing it through a window to escape. Hopefully you will find resources and inspiration from those who tried - and succeeded before you - in reinventing themselves. My wish is that you take what you find here and develop your own system for making the New World of Work a better place, shaped in your image.

There is no single picture of what the New World looks like. Who could have imagined 8-lane expressways, jammed with automobiles moving at 70+ miles per hour in 1550? Who could have seen a traveler boarding an airplane in England and being in America in a mere 4 hours? Who could have seen spending $200 for a small, hand-held device that allows you to speak "live" with almost anyone in the world, play any song you long to hear and store an immense library of information than was even known in the Sixteenth Century? What seer could have peered into the future and observed giant corporations that serve the purpose of supplying food, fun or entertainment for leisure? The city fathers of London couldn't conceive the advent of automobiles and the demise of equine liveries in 1900, but within 10 years, their long-range plans for more riders, carriages, and "honey-bucket" workers was useless and extinct.

It's all about you. Why were you put here on this earth? What is your purpose? Why does your business exist? You can know now. You can look into your own future and see the possibilities. You can reinvent yourself and guide the way for your people to follow you up the path to enlightenment and success. You can become the best and greatest in your industry. You can influence more people by what you learn from these pages than you could have ever imagined. As we take the journey together, you will discover a brave new world that you can conquer. In this book you will see that reinvention is easy. Deciding to start it is the real test. Ready? Let's go!

Easy Action Step: What changes have you seen in your business, your customers, your industry and your geographical area in the last two years? Make a list of 20 changes that you have observed (I have found over 50, some you will see in Appendix B). How have these changes altered the way you function? What do they indicate that you need to start doing in reaction to them?

Chapter 2

THE WALL

Reinventing Your Direction

What Did You *Used* to Be?

If you ever have the occasion to socialize with a professional speaker, let me suggest that you ask what he or she used to do for a living. Every speaker I know left some sort of a career to begin speaking. One of two things probably happened: he either got tired of the job, or he got fired from it! And no, I'm not saying which one happened to me! Imagine your reaction if after paying four years of college tuition, your child returned home saying "I can't wait to graduate and move on to my career in professional speaking!" Not that being a professional speaker is a life of ease. The work is difficult and the travel can be a nightmare. Still many people go into the field when their previous job dried up. My point is this. Most speakers describe the sudden transition as being like hitting a Wall.

When I Hit The Wall

I *used* to be a Southern Baptist youth and Christian Education minister (I'm still a believer!). I spent over 23 years working in churches. It was gratifying and fun. I was priviledged to work in fairly large congregations and was told that I made a real difference in a lot of young peoples' lives.

And over time I worked in increasingly larger congregations. It was as if my life was on track to grow along with the churches.

Then I went to a church where everything was different. For the first few years we grew dramatically. But then with almost no warning, it seemed as if everything I and the other ministry staff did was met with opposition. Committees were at odds with the leadership. The church had grown for several years, but as the pastor neared his retirement his leadership skills began to take a backseat. Others moved into the void and people began to leave. The growth stopped and opposition began to arise. The momentum we had enjoyed for over 5 years came to a screeching halt. It was as if we hit a wall – BAM!

Sooner or later in life you are going to hit "The Wall." Not to discourage you, but you'll likely hit it more than once and at different places in your life. When you hit a wall, your momentum stops completely. You want to continue in the same direction, but "The Wall" is preventing you from moving forward. Many people have hit "The Wall" and it has stopped them completely. Walls are often unexpected, rarely welcomed and force us to stop and evaluate practically everything we thought was sure and secure. But keep in mind that hitting "The Wall" doesn't make you a failure.

Oh yes, hitting "The Wall" often makes you _feel_ like a failure. It certainly made me feel like a failure. If you're like me, a little voice hisses inside your head, "If you fall, you will never get up. You'll be a failure for life." And that little voice inside your head is telling you a lie. That's because failing and being a failure aren't the same. There is a huge distinction between failing at something and being a failure. Some of the most famous successes in life have come in the midst of failure. We learned in school that Thomas Edison was a brilliant American inventor, scientist and businessman who developed many devices that greatly influenced life around the world, including the phonograph, the motion picture camera, and a long-lasting, practical electric light bulb. Dubbed "The Wizard of Menlo Park" (now Edison, New Jersey) by a newspaper reporter, he was one of the first inventors to apply the principles of mass production and large teamwork to the process of invention, and therefore is often credited with the creation of the first industrial research laboratory. (Excerpted from Wikipedia) What is equally important to keep in mind is that:

Edison failed many, many more times than he succeeded.

A contemporary and friend of Edison was Henry Ford. Ford was the American founder of the Ford Motor Company and father of modern assembly lines used in mass production. Under Ford's leadership, the introduction of the Model T automobile revolutionized transportation, mass production and American industry. He was a prolific inventor and was awarded 161 U.S. patents. As owner of the Ford Motor Company he became one of the richest and best-known people in the world. (also excerpted from Wikipedia) Like Edison, Henry Ford was acquainted with failing at something. Ford was often heard to say:

"Failure is the opportunity to begin again more intelligently."

This healthy view of failure led these two men to success and collaboration. Both hit walls and failed – often - but neither man saw himself as a failure.

So why do you and I feel like failures when we hit "The Wall"? Why do we feel like a failure when we don't succeed every time? Because we don't understand the value of failing. There is value in success, but there is equal (and often greater) value in failing. The value in failing is that it removes from us our false beliefs regarding success. But we don't always see the successes that brought us where we are. Have you ever been to a prize drawing and the person next to you says, "I don't know why I bothered being here - I never win anything!"? Maybe you muttered these words yourself at some point. The truth is we have been advancing towards winning our whole lives. We simply chose not to notice the progressive victories. Instead of looking down on ourselves when we fall, we need to look up – at "The Wall". When you and I fall, we need to look with open eyes, minds and hearts to see what caused it.

Walls, Windows and Doors

When you hit a wall, you are stopped cold. The direction you thought you could go has been blocked. You were scooting right along and then BAM, you hit The Wall. The Wall is no respecter of position or prominence. Everyone hits it at some or many points in life. The question is; how are you going to respond when you hit The Wall? What is your reaction when you know what you have been doing or enjoying success in dries up?

Here are some tips for guidance when you hit The Wall in your life or career.

1. **When you hit The Wall, STOP**. Stop moving. Stop denying. Stop attempting greater efforts. Wasting your energy fighting The Wall simply wears you out even more. So just stop and know that you are not alone - The Wall stops everyone. Unfortunately, some people keep banging against it, trying to pound through it, all the while ignorant of the fact that they can't. Stop hitting The Wall. You are not a child's wind-up toy that, though having hit an immovable force, you must invariably and unsuccessfully persist. Unlike the wind-up toy, you are not pre-programmed and left on autopilot. Instead look around. Look at where you are. As author, speaker, and pastor John Maxwell says, "The next time life knocks you down, look around. Pick up something down there you can take back up with you." Find out why there is a wall in your path. What is causing The Wall to be in place?

2. The very presence of "The Wall" is forcing a change. Oprah Winfrey said, "Failure is really God's way of saying, 'Excuse me, but you are moving in the wrong direction.'" What is your wall forcing you to change? I meet people every day who are still trying to press forward and do or sell products and services that no one is buying. But they continue to defy wisdom. The Wall has told them they can't move forward, but they just keep ignoring it and pushing forward.

We can sense Walls every day and either accept them or reject them. Rejecting always puts off the inevitable. It costs us more in the long term to deny The Wall than it would to recognize and act on it. When was the last time you began to feel a cold coming on and denied it? Eventually you had to give in and just allow yourself to be sick.

3. **<u>When The Wall stops you, look around and up for a window</u>**. The Wall forces you to look at things differently. The Wall blocks your vision and gives you something new to look at. What is your new vision? What is the perspective you have now that you have hit The Wall? What can you see differently that you couldn't before The Wall changed your forward progress?

The death of Princess Diana in 1997 was tragic to many people. There were mourners in every corner of the globe. But the royal family didn't expect the magnitude of grief poured out by the British people. It changed their perspective of traditions they had for centuries held dear. They were forced to view this death as more than a private matter; it became more than something to be dealt with behind closed doors. Queen Elizabeth II had to see her role as a consoling individual, rather than the role of a withdrawn monarch. The Wall of Princess Di's death and the reaction of her subjects forcibly changed her perspective.

4. **<u>When you hit The Wall look for a door</u>**. Find a way to go past The Wall and move in a new direction. Every wall has a door. Even the Great Wall Of China must have a gate. The window tells you where to look; the door shows you where to go. What is the open door in your wall? And where does it lead? It may not be a door you would have chosen in the first place, but The Wall has forced you to take this new path. Don't ignore it. The path is opening for you. The Wall may have appeared through circumstances or you may have caused it yourself. It doesn't matter. There is a door in The Wall you might never have noticed had your wall not been there.

In November of 2009, Tiger Woods hit The Wall when his personal life became front page news. Matters he was personally responsible for had gone beyond his control. For a man who strictly guarded his private life, it was now VERY public. But in a concentrated effort, he looked to friends for guidance, sought help in counseling and rehabilitation and came out a strong contender in the 2010 Masters

Golf Tournament (tied for 4th Place). This is NO endorsement for what
he admitted he did to his wife, children, fans and sponsors. It is simply
an observation. The Wall forced him to seek a door and move forward
in a way he would have never moved previously. The Wall does that
every time. Tiger's wall was exposure; Tiger's door was ownership
and restitution.

On a more humorous note, I remember engaging the fellow seated
next to me on a recent flight from Michigan back home. We struck up a
conversation (something I frequently do when traveling) and he admitted
to being from Michigan, a state hit hard by the recent recession. When we
discussed the subject of walls, doors and windows, he adroitly observed
that you can't confuse the window with the door in The Wall. He noted
that losers look out the door of opportunity, but are scared to step out.
Instead they see the view and jump out the window! Don't confuse the
door of opportunity with the window of vision. It can prove fatal to you in
a very real or figurative sense.

Handling Defeat

Many famous people have hit The Wall and it has changed both their
lives and the lives of many others. Steve Jobs is known for his success
with the iPod, iPhone and Mac computers. But we forget that he hit The
Wall with the Mac 3 and the Newton. Would the Dalai Lama just be the
inconsequential leader of an insignificant country had the Chinese not
invaded Tibet? Abraham Lincoln is known for his leadership and winning
two terms as President in the midst of a country torn apart, but we forget
that he lost most elections he entered. Babe Ruth led the major leagues in
home runs for decades. He also led in strikeouts at bat.

Bernard Marcus was born to Jewish-Russian immigrant parents in
Newark, New Jersey in 1929. He grew up in a tenement and wanted to
become a doctor. He couldn't afford the tuition, so he worked his way
through Rutgers University and earned a pharmacy degree by working
for his father as a cabinet maker. Later, he worked at a drugstore as a
pharmacist but became more interested in the business and retailing part

of the business. He worked at a cosmetics company and various other retail jobs.

Thereafter, "Bernie" became president of O'Dell's, a manufacturing conglomerate, and vice president of hard goods merchandising for Vornado, a discount retail chain. Then he was tapped for the position of President and CEO of a chain of hardware stores called Handy Dan. As a middle-aged business man, Marcus had everything going for him.

But then he and fellow employee Arthur Blank hit "The Wall." On the same day both were fired from the corporation over a disagreement with their parent company's CEO. The angry boss threatened to destroy Bernie economically, professionally and personally. At age 49 he found himself without any severance package and no company stock. An investor friend exclaimed that he had been kicked in the rear by the golden horseshoe!

Most of us would've sat down and bemoaned our fate. Or we might wallow in self-pity and feelings of failure. After all, Bernie had no money to invest in any venture. But he possessed an enormous amount of creativity and the ability to make things happen. He dreamed of opening a hardware mega-store with extra low prices for the do-it-yourself customer. In his mind, the key would be superior customer service that excelled beyond any in the industry. He would train his employees to do something unheard of in the hardware business. When asked the location of an item, they would not point to where the item was; rather they would take the customers there personally. And they would stay there until the customer confirmed that this was the item they were seeking!

Funded by his investor friend and joined by his fellow firee, Arthur Blank, he bought into a chain of hardware stores that was already putting the dream into action. In the first year, though they lost $1 million out of the original $2 million investment, Bernie refused to quit. He stuck to his dream and opened his first Home Depot in Atlanta, Georgia.

Like all start up businesses, it was very difficult at first. He was so low on inventory that he learned to place empty containers on shelves behind full ones to make the stock look full. He also began bringing to

reality his earlier dream of superior customer services. He trained every
employee to know where everything in the store was located. Courtesy
and concern became the watchwords for employees and the acclamation
of customers. You didn't see employees point – they led. They didn't
direct, they conversed. Bernie laughingly threatened to bite off the finger
of any associate who pointed where something was located instead of
taking the customer there.

People eventually couldn't ignore the low prices and variety of top
name brands and as we know, the company went on to become the world's
largest home-improvement retailer with over 1500 stores nationwide and
locations in Puerto Rico, Canada and Chile. Both men became wealthy.
Arthur Blank went on to buy the Atlanta Falcons National League football
franchise. Bernard is worth over $3 million in Home Depot stock alone.

Bernie Marcus is also working to link the Israeli economy to his home
state. The country has the second-highest density of startups after Silicon
Valley, and the hardware mogul has helped persuade state officials to offer
the Israeli firms incentives to relocate in Georgia. "All the things they
want, we've got them," says Marcus, who notes that the state stands ready
to offer tech firms a variety of tax breaks.

Marcus is a local philanthropist in Atlanta. He and his wife, Billi
funded and founded The Marcus Institute, a nationally recognized center
of excellence for the provision of comprehensive services for children and
adolescents with developmental disabilities. In May 2005, Marcus was
awarded the "Others Award" by the Salvation Army, its' highest honor.
Marcus is currently chairman of the Marcus Foundation, whose focus
includes children, medical research, free enterprise, Jewish causes and
the greater community. He has also almost single-handedly funded and
launched the Georgia Aquarium, which opened its doors in 2005. Marcus
was inducted into the Junior Achievement U.S. Business Hall of Fame in
2006. Bernie says, "You cannot be stopped by failure. Handling defeat is
as important as handling failure."

Finding My Window

When I left church work, I knew that The Wall was preventing me from moving forward. It was a shock for me and my family, but a relief from the pressure we had experienced. I was scared. I had not done anything outside of religious work for many years, so I wasn't sure how to build a new life. And I was so used to being paid a steady salary and didn't want to have to work for each day's wages. Not surprisingly, I was scared of the unknown.

I once heard a pastor say that you should spend the first half of your life finding what you like to do and the second half getting people to pay you to do it. I knew what I liked to do. I knew what I was good at doing. And I knew that I wanted to do those things differently. I enjoyed seeing change in other people's lives. I knew I would be greatly satisfied with speaking to and training large groups. And there was My Wall. And in My Wall was this window of opportunity. So I embarked on a speaking career. I knew it wouldn't be easy.

A great friend of mine, Joe Bonura offered to help me get started. He opened the door for me to go through that allowed me to begin the transition and reinvent my career. He taught me how to get on the phone and make great calls to market my business – something I never would have had to do in the ministry. I was afraid to get on the phone and make cold calls to prospective clients, but Joe helped me see it in a new perspective. He said, "You aren't a telemarketer, you are a teleMASTER!" At the time I didn't understand the difference. What is the difference?

Telemasters are people who build a fulfilling, life-long career. I've known many telemarketers in my life. Most are doing the job because it pays them for making many, many phone calls – good or bad. I've known only a few telemasters. Joe said to me those many years ago that too few people are willing to put in the time and effort it takes over the long haul to build a career out of telephone sales. He is right.

In fact, in a study conducted by the National Retail Dry Goods Association it was revealed that unsuccessful first attempts lead almost half of all sales people to quit:

- 48 percent of all sales people make one call and stop

- 25 percent of all sales people make two calls and stop

- 15 percent of all sales people make three calls and stop

- 12 percent of all sales people keep calling and calling and calling…

And wouldn't you know that those 12 percent make 80 percent of all sales.

This made a difference in my life. By believing it enough to practice it, making the calls helped skyrocket my new career. I found myself on a self-propelled fast track. In a short time I was awarded the highest earned designation as a professional speaker, CSP (Certified Speaking Professional) by the National Speakers Association. This distinguished designation takes five years to earn and over 90% of all professional speakers haven't earned it. Through Joe's help, I earned it in my first five years!

The Wall had stopped me in one career, but looking out the window at what I liked to do opened a door in my life to a new direction and a new perspective. You can see a new perspective through the window in The Wall and find the door of opportunity for you as well. It just takes some looking around at where you are when The Wall stops you in your tracks.

The Corporate Wall

When a member of your team hits The Wall, it can reinvent your company and its culture. Reinvention often happens when people within organizations simply talk to one another. In fact, the Post-it Note was a result of internal collaboration between two employees of the same company who began talking to one another about a new adhesive and notes falling off a hymnal in his church choir loft.

Spencer Silver, an organic chemist with the 3M Company hit The Wall. He was working for 3M and experimenting with adhesives. One day he developed an adhesive that just didn't work very well. It wouldn't stick to any surface for a good length of time. All his time and energy had gone to waste...or had it? Spencer didn't give up. Instead of looking for ways to justify the new product, they looked for people who needed this specific adhesive product. He started talking with others in the organization. Working with Arthur Fry, a chemical engineer at 3M, he began to look for uses for a not-so-good adhesive.

Arthur had a difficult time with little bits of paper dropping off the hymnal he used in his church choir. They left notes using the very same adhesive for people throughout the company asking if anyone had suggestions for uses for his adhesive. Geoff Nicholson had a knack for marketing and BAM - Spencer Silver's wall became the catalyst for a new, innovative product and direction for 3M and the world of meetings and note-taking.

Spencer and his colleagues are credited with inventing the Post-It Note, the ubiquitous yellow sticky pad of paper found in almost every office today. Once derided in 3M's laboratories as an adhesive that could barely stick, the Post-it Note turned out to be one of the company's most popular products, helping to "cement" its position as an innovative company.

Geoff Nicolson, former top executive with 3M says, "That is the trait you should look for in your employees – people who are not afraid to make mistakes – if you want your company to go far in innovation." According to Nicholson, innovation and reinvention are about creating something that is new and of value to the world. He said in an address in early 2010 to SMU's Institute of Innovation and Entrepreneurship. If the company wants to grow, it needs to innovate and make improvements continuously. Innovation keeps products competitive and helps the company to survive. "If you don't continue to reinvent your products, your company will die," he said bluntly.

Although many people may think of 3M only for its grocery store offerings, like Scotch tape and Post-its, it is the company's tradition of innovation goes back 108 years to when the then-Minnesota Mining and Manufacturing Company (that's where the three 'M's come from) came up with products like sandpaper and masking tape. Today, 3M is a multinational corporation with operations in more than 60 countries. It owes much of its success to fostering a culture of reinvention. "We basically tell our technical people to spend 15 percent of their time working on whatever they want," said Nicholson. And the best part is: there is no need for management approval or supervision. This cultural attitude worked to its advantage when Spencer, Arthur and Geoff collaborated after hitting The Wall.

What Have You Done To Adapt

In my early speaking days, my topics focused on adapting to other's styles to manage, sell to and serve others. I used personality assessments that I brought with me from my church days. That is where I first learned about the DiSC® and Myers-Briggs personality profiles. They were a big seller for me at one time. Then I hit another wall in my speaking career. When the greatest drop in the stock market hit in 2008, I was instructing several groups in using the assessments to manage and coach their people better.

Suddenly no one wanted to take assessments. No one wanted to manage or work together better (my old motto). They wanted something fresh, new and on point regarding the struggles they were facing in the new economy of the coming decade. I had to adapt or my newfound speaking career faced extinction. When no one is buying what you are selling, you have to adapt to what they want to buy. If you are selling something obsolete, you must adjust and assimilate their needs into your inventory of products or services. For me it wasn't easy, but I knew I had to act or get swept away. Having adapted before under much more trying circumstances, I felt I could succeed.

I began to go to what I liked to do best. I sought my source of greatest joy in what I do. It lay in marketing and creativity. I enjoy helping people be more creative and market who they are and what they do. An executive coach told me, "Jim, you are the embodiment of reinvention, because you have reinvented yourself so many times over. You love to do it. You can make it easy for people who want to reinvent themselves." He was right. I was leading a marketing strategy conference and saw the "light bulbs" go on in people's minds. It was a kick to watch! That was the day I chose to no longer be a professional speaker. There are enough of them already. That was the day I chose to reinvent myself as a strategist…and not just any strategist. The world's one and only Reinvention Strategist.

Community Story – Pee Dee Tobacco Farmers

You've probably heard about how the farmers in lower Alabama hit The Wall when insects ruined their cotton crops in the early 1900s. At that same time, George Washington Carver was discovering over 100 different uses for the peanut. His findings came to the rescue of Southern US cotton farmers. An infestation of boll weevils changed cotton growers to peanut production and other industrial prosperity in the early 1900s. The citizens of Enterprise, Alabama even erected a monument to the insect. It stands today as a tribute to how something disastrous can be a "Herald of Prosperity" and a catalyst for change.

But have you heard about the tobacco farmers in North and South Carolina and the federal "buy out" of 2004? I work with a group of financial services providers in the Tobacco Road country of the Carolinas. Their economy hit The Wall when Phillip Morris and other tobacco companies were sued over tobacco products. The farmers who were the bank's customers were being forced out of businesses that had been their livelihood and that of their families for decades. But these people were indomitable. They reinvented what they raised and changed communities.

These people used to be tobacco farmers. They lived and worked the tobacco industry and profited from every aspect of it. They made a fortune in raising a crop that was in high demand for over two centuries. Hollywood glorified cigarettes, cigars and pipes for decades. Watch an old '60s television show and see who smokes. *The Andy Griffith Show, Laugh In, Bewitched, Perry Mason, The Danny Thomas Show* were either sponsored by or had characters who smoked. Even on the '70s hit show, *Barney Miller*, smoking was prevalent (while several characters smoked on screen, Jack Soo died of esophageal cancer during the run of the series.).

Then they hit The Wall. Times changed and their products were viewed differently. The deaths came...Yul Brynner, John Wayne, John Candy (heart attack and an avid smoker), Lucille Ball, Sammy Davis, Jr., anchorman Peter Jennings and many other box office and television idols lost their battles with lung cancer. Law suits followed and public opinion made a 180 degree turn and condemned "Big Tobacco." And unfortunately the family farmers in the Carolinas were at the heart of the controversy.

The Winston Cup NASCAR racing series, the Marlboro Man and Joe Camel had been ingenious advertising campaigns, but now they were being outlawed and scorned. NASCAR, a native sport to "Tobacco Road" in North Carolina changed its marketing and culture. Warnings were placed on cigarette packs that said, "Warning: The Surgeon General has determined that usage of this product causes cancer."

Not a great advertising gimmick and a disaster if you raise the lethal crop that is at the heart of it. But there is always a door in The Wall.

The Wall really made an impact in 2004 when the United States government changed the farmers' lives permanently. Known as "The Buy Out," the government ended a federal tobacco program by eliminating controls in a system that had been in place since the 1930s. In addition, the government also negotiated a federal tobacco buyout. They issued farmers compensation based on the amount of tobacco they were growing at the time. The farmers were faced with a decision of doors to choose. They had to either sell their farms or find something else to grow on their acres of land. Some took the "door" of early retirement. Tobacco farmers had hit their wall.

Then they saw an opportunity in a little-known crop that brings them great results and benefits. Many farmers made the transition to raising peanuts, like their counterparts in Alabama. But another crop that many adapted to was muscadines. This grape family fruit grows well in their fertile sandy soil. Muscadines were found to thrive in the same soil and climate conditions as tobacco – the southeastern United States. So a large number of farmers took the initiative to raise muscadines.

Muscadines? What good are muscadines? For that matter, what ARE muscadines? These little wineskins are members of the grape family.

According to eHow.com, "While muscadines are often used for wine-making, there are several other products created with the grapes. Jams and jellies, grape juice and even syrups are made from muscadines. In addition, muscadines are marketed as a delicious desert topping. Because the grapes yield less juice than other grapes, researchers have now found good use for the skin, pulp and seeds. These remnants of the grapes are now being used in fertilizers and livestock feed."

Muscadines are also a very healthy choice for you. eHow.com goes on to say, "In recent years, research funded by the USDA has realized the health benefits of muscadine grapes. Studies completed through Mississippi State University show that a puree created from the skins and pulp is very high in fiber--higher even than oat or rice bran."

Did you know that even their seeds are useful? They can be ground and used in making plastics! The Wall the farmers in the Carolinas faced could have ruined them financially, but they looked through a window of possibility and then walked through a door or opportunity to remain in the agricultural business through peanut and muscadine crops. Many of them now raise a more beneficial crop that can't be equaled in value. In essence, their Wall created the value that the southeastern farmers took advantage of. Just like the boll weevil changed the industry of cotton growers in Alabama 100 years previously, the change in attitude about smoking and the federal buy out created a new door for Tobacco Road.

So bring it home and ask yourself: Where have you hit The Wall? What has stopped your forward motion with a seemingly insurmountable obstacle? Having spoken with people from Maine to Central America, from Alaska to Nova Scotia, I know that everyone hits The Wall at some point in their business, community, and personal life and career. It isn't what you feel as much as what you choose that affects the way you react to The Wall. And how you choose reveals who you are.

We tend to live in the securely insulated world we've built in the attempt to resist change. And then along comes a wall. The Wall reveals what you are made of. It defines your character and the strength you have internally to reinvent yourself. When you hit The Wall, it seems as if your whole world has come to an end. The good news is: It has come to an end. Be glad. Welcome The Wall.

Running into The Wall means it is time to stop, look up at the cause of it, look for the window of opportunity and then reinvent yourself by going through the door in front of you. At some point everyone hits The Wall. We are fooling ourselves if we don't think we will hit it at some point. I know that on days I am feeling good, if something bad happens, it happened on that day because I was prepared for it. On a day I don't feel so well, I know that everything has always turned out good for me if I remained focused on what I truly liked and enjoyed doing.

And it hasn't just worked for me. I led a strategic planning session with a group of mortgage bankers and realtors in early 2010 who said they knew the housing bubble would burst. They knew the loans the United States government was allowing them to write were dangerous for the economy. Yet they continued because it was permissible and "everyone was doing it." They said, "We knew we should have been selling what people really needed, but the temptation and profits were too good to pass up the opportunities the loop holes and permissive policies were affording us."

When the bubble burst and the flood gates opened, they found themselves up against The Wall. They chose to seek out their customers and find out what their needs were in re-financing and new loans and that is what they started doing business in – successfully. The Wall afforded opportunities to go back to their buyers and mortgage holders and ask how they could help. What is The Wall forcing you to do that you know you should have been doing all along?

About two months ago I was flying to an engagement and happened to sit beside a friendly gentleman. As we introduced ourselves, he shook my hand and said, "I know I have heard of you. What do you do?" We talked about our businesses, families and lives. Still he looked confused.

He said, "I know I have heard of you. I can't remember where, but I know your name. Have you ever traveled anywhere?"

What a question! I started telling him that I strategize with groups and speak internationally. Cutting to the chase, I said, "I publish a professional development newsletter once a month. If you would like, I will be glad to send you a copy of this month's issue."

"That's it!" he exclaimed. "I sat next to you on a flight three years ago. You told me you were a speaker and told me about your newsletter. I still receive and enjoy it." Then he said something that both surprised me and gratified me. This acquaintance from three years previous said "I am so fascinated with the strategizing that you were telling me about just now, and it is so different. I didn't know you were the speaker I met three years ago. You are like a totally different person." It was a gratifying encounter that led me to this realization.

I used to be a professional speaker. But I hit The Wall. Speaking wasn't selling and becoming passé. Then I reinvented myself and became The Reinvention Strategist. The circle is complete – for now.

So it's time to ask the obvious: What is your wall? And what is next for you?

Easy Action Step: It's time to ask the obvious: How have the changes you observed and listed in Chapter 1 created a "Wall" in your business or personal life? What is next for you? What are you viewing different now that you see The Wall (that is to say, where is your window?)? Where is the door that The Wall provides for you to move forward?

Chapter 3

THE REINVENTION PROCESS

"Reinvention is simple; deciding to do it is the hardest part."
— Jim Mathis

Whenever possible, I enjoy a Sunday evening ritual. So every Sunday evening, my wife and I curl up together and watch one of our favorite television programs. As one of the best "feel-good" shows on broadcast or cable television, we're suckers for "Extreme Home Makeover." It's a show that has heart. On the other hand, my daughter has an eye for current fashion. It's not surprising that she controls the remote to watch "What Not to Wear". Everyone is thankful that both shows don't run simultaneously!

Both programs incorporate individual and family reinvention, don't they? And with the popularity of "makeover" shows these days, it's hard not to think about what it would be like to do a total makeover on yourself. Imagine being able to leave for a time of relaxation. You could glimpse from afar some of what was happening. And then you would return. Imagine the climactic moment of "moving the bus" in your life and the person you'd love to be and having the life you'd love to have would be right there!

The only problem with a show like Extreme Home Makeover is that someone else does all of the work for the recipient. Everyone shows up and reinvents their home while they are on a vacation, paid for and sponsored by the program's producers. Unlike their script, to replicate it in your own life, you can't get your friends, community and famous stars to do it for you.

You have to be the one to make the decision and accept the fact that you need to change everything yourself. Like "What Not to Wear," we often need an intervention from friends and family, but the final decision still lies with us. Are you going to stay the way you are, or are you going to make the decision to reinvent yourself today?

Reinvention Is Ongoing

Throughout my life I have reinvented myself many, many times. There was the transition from high school to college; then on to graduate school. There was my introduction to the world of work, building a career, finding a partner, commitment, buying a home, "you're going to be a daddy!", selling a home, transitioning to a new job, ending a relationship, and even the dreaded "parenting teenagers".

In addition to changing careers and retooling my skill set, there were numerous recessions and periods of prosperity. Through it all I endured the toughest times whenever I refused to face the changes by altering my behavior and/or beliefs. And while I believe that the process of reinvention is simple, it is the act of deciding - the moment of choosing - that is the hardest part.

Resisting Reinvention

I fought any and all changes growing up. I avoided the change in lifestyle when I ran into obstacles. I ignored the changes when I was comfortable with my situation and didn't feel like making changes in my life. I swerved from self-confrontation. After watching the same thing happen with countless others, I've come to think that most people are the same way. We resist change because we don't want to leave our comfort zone. And it only seems to grow more difficult as the further I go in life. And it isn't just symptomatic with the aging process. I see it in all ages and stages of people's lives. As I speak to groups and individual leaders about reinvention, this common theme emerges:

We inherently and often unconsciously resist change.

No one wants to jump in and totally overhaul their life. They want a quick fix to the current problems. They want a strategy to guide them on their journey. Almost everyone wants to know that there is a simple process. The good news is there is a process.

Equipped with a simple process or outline we can follow we are more prone to reinvent ourselves and take the risks involved. The process of reinventing yourself is **exciting**, at times **scary**, but ultimately **rewarding**. The exciting part is when you are energized by the possibilities for the future. The scary part is when you have to push through moments of self-doubt or disappointment. The reward is when you finally overcome your fears and feel the rejuvenating flow. Once you achieve this, you can begin to shake yourself out of your cocoon and fly off to explore the new world.

When you know what you want, though nothing even comes close to that feeling of contentment. As Ken Jacobsen, former corporate escapee puts it, "When you have the right calling card - to your soul - your world just lights up." Everything converges on your life purpose and mission. When you know where you are going the path becomes straight and simple. You see it everywhere you look. The world seems to make more sense than it did before you knew what you wanted. Why?

It's called convergence – the process of single mindedness. Your mind is looking for that same vehicle to reinforce your decision. Thus, you notice all the others just like yours. When you know where you are going you will be astonished at the events and words that guide you toward your goal.

There are many reasons why you'd be willing to embark on reinventing yourself. You might have lost a job. You might feel trapped in a vortex of dissatisfaction that comes from performing tasks that are not tapping into your greatest strengths. Maybe money or compensation is the issue. Perhaps you are sensing an inner restlessness that clamors to be addressed.

When To Reinvent

So how do you know when you need to reinvent yourself? What signals should we pay attention to which indicate a need for reinvention? One of the primary ways to know it's time to reinvent is when you hurt enough to want to do it. The "want-to" tells you that you are getting ready for the change. It reaches critical mass at the very instant in which this one thing occurs; it is when:

The pain of staying where you are is greater than
The pain of taking the risk and moving forward.

You may be facing an obstacle that seems insurmountable. You may be dissatisfied with your present situation. You may be at a stage in life where things seem out of control and reinvention is the only alternative you have to taking back control of your life and destiny. Now you are ready to begin the process of reinvention.

No matter what the reason, in most cases, there are 7 major stages that you visit and re-visit once you decide to reinvent yourself. So what do you do to reinvent yourself, your business or your personal life?

1. **A "Reinventive" Attitude** – Who is to blame for the recession?

    While strategizing with a group of bankers in Tennessee, I heard one of the leaders say, "I think the Democrats in Congress caused the banking crisis." Another disagreed and said it was caused by the permissive loan policies of the Republican administration of the last decade. Then someone started naming politicians who carried blame for cronyism and political favors. When the discussion was over, everyone was in the same place they were before.

    Quit pointing fingers at who is to blame. It doesn't matter WHO is to blame or HOW we got here. Change is inevitable and the recession just sped it up considerably. At some point, the "chickens were going to come home to roost," as my grandfather would say and someone was going to have to pay for the loans and credit crisis so many economists had warned us about. You can't say we weren't warned.

For years I heard Dave Ramsey, Clark Howard and many others talk about getting too deep in debt and warning us that there would be a price to pay for the mounting credit problems. We all saw it coming. But knowing that doesn't solve the problem.

"What are you going to do now that it has happened?" I asked the group of bankers. The room fell silent. It is easy to point fingers but at the end of the day, we are right back where we started from. Assessing blame won't get us out of the mess we are in. The time is ripe for cool heads who know what to do to move forward and show the way to everyone else.

You need a reinventive attitude that rises above the finger-pointing and blame game. You need an attitude that says no matter what situation I find myself in, I will succeed and look for a better way to do things. I am in stiff competition every day of my life…with myself. I get up every day and ask, "What can I do better today than I did yesterday?" Other questions come to mind: "Where am I not on the cutting edge? Where is there room for improvement? What am I doing with the resources, talents, skills and creativity that God has given me?"

How do you begin to have a reinventive attitude? I tell leaders to start looking at life as a challenge and every day as an opportunity to do better than yourself. If it means serving others better, then that is even better. If it means making the world a better place for your family, friends and community it is a worthy goal. You need to adopt a reinventive attitude that no matter what circumstances you find yourself in you will look for a way to overcome the problems and use the favorable times as encouragement to keep moving forward.

I encourage people to begin by making personal development a priority. Read books and blogs. Become a student and learn to ask questions. Be a listener, and tell less. Be a learner; not a know-it-all.

Most know-it-alls don't, in fact, know it all! In the reinvention process as with most successful pursuits in life you will learn that the highest performing people ask the most and best questions. This is true in sales, management, customer service and education. The best students make the best teachers. This process becomes much easier each time and allows you to stay in reinvention mode at all times.

2. **Vision to see what others can't see** – Who cares who moved your cheese?

When a crisis occurs you will see everyone scramble and look for ways to solve it immediately. Visionaries look around and say, "What can I learn from this experience?" Reinvention Strategists see the world of opportunities while those around them see a world of problems. Yes, it goes back to your attitude, but you can't see the vision with just an attitude change. You need to see life as a series of victories. I tell my daughter that you are either telling your victim story to everyone or your victory story. Victims run people away from themselves. Victors attract a crowd of admirers…and other victors.

In the movie, Patch Adams, Robin Williams' character runs into an older man who is a genius in a mental hospital for personal reasons. He continually asks other patients to look at his hand and tell him how many fingers they see. Each time they answer "4." Each time he rages that they are short-sighted and lack vision.

Finally one evening "Patch," Robin's character asks the man the meaning of the riddle. The older man likes him and shows him that when he focuses only on the hand in front of him, he can only see four fingers. But if he looks beyond the hand and sees across the room, his eyes show him eight fingers. "See the world anew. See beyond the problems. See what others choose not to see," he says.

Change leaders can see the big picture while losers only get a snapshot. Leaders are reflective. "Why did that work here, but not there?" Instead of saying, "Who moved my cheese?" leaders say, "What else is there to eat and why can't we make money selling it?" Don't get me wrong,

I loved reading *Who Moved My Cheese*; I just think that there should be a plan in place in case the cheese runs out and someone should start looking for it while everyone else is eating cheese. That way, when it gets moved, the leader isn't whining about who is to blame.

Do whatever is necessary to create widespread understanding and commitment to a shared vision of the future. Write about it, blog about it, tweet it, put it up on YouTube.com. Let everything you do convey your vision. Converge all of your efforts into one place – not several to confuse everyone. Send a clear, consistent message of what you want to do and where you are going. Plant your flag in the ground and claim your territory. This will help you commit to the vision, but will help others commit and understand it better. You are garnering support for your reinvention.

Usually you have a vague notion that you want to or must do something different. Perhaps you research ideas on the internet or you read books to try to zero in on a set of possibilities. This is a dreamer's stage and it is full of energy and possibilities. You don't need much motivation at this stage because it seems to drive itself. Often this stage is accompanied by taking a few steps in the direction of that dream. Get ready, because the self-doubt is about to begin.

Don't worry when you begin to act and others don't support your change. They don't understand. They are comfortable with you staying where you are or have been. Treat them as if they don't understand – not as if they are your enemies. Even Jesus told his disciples not to call down fire from heaven on those towns who rejected his message. He told them to simply shake the dust off their feet and move on.

I encourage people to make small steps in the direction of their new dream. I have them move in a way that others can see where they are going and be prepared. Even The Beatles released two singles that showed their new direction while they were working on *Sgt. Pepper's Lonely Hearts Club Band – Penny Lane* and *Strawberry Fields. Penny Lane* was different from anything the fans had heard. It wasn't a sweet, bouncy love song. It wasn't the cold lonely songs that had been on some more recent albums. But it was also another Number 1 hit single for the band. I did the same thing when I released *Reinvention 101* a year before this book.

What did we all learn? Let a little out while you are working on your reinvention. Give everyone a hint, or taste of what is to come. It is a great barometer for your success. If successful, you will know you are headed in the right direction. I help my clients with their Sgt. Pepper's projects by releasing a Penny Lane or two in advance.

3. **Are You Powerful Enough to Make Toughest Decision In Your Life?**

Deciding to act on your reinvention is the hardest part. Like writing a term paper in school, deciding to get started is the hardest stage. Please understand that I maintain that reinventing yourself is simple. The only hard part I have discovered is deciding to take action. The risk involved is frightening to most people. The resistance is strong. Leaders who reinvent themselves say that this stage is the toughest one to face. They know what they have to do, but are unwilling for one reason or another to make the change.

Perhaps it is pride – we thought we were right in the first place. Perhaps it is short-sightedness. I was told by a door manufacturer that he knew that he had employees who refused to change, but he wasn't willing to make them do as he said so he kept paying them to do what he didn't want them to do. Perhaps it is fear of the unknown – we don't know how circumstances will play out. But remember, you will decide to change when the pain of keeping the status quo is greater than the pain of making the transition to a better life.

In my own life I wasted too much time in denial and was afraid of taking the bold step forward. But when I finally overcame my fears and took the first step, the rewards were plentiful. I remember calling my wife while on the road and telling her that I wanted to fully commit to reinventing my personal life as well as my professional career. To that end I gave her permission, no, I gave her the authority to toss out everything in my wardrobe that she didn't like and thought was out of fashion. When I got home, my closet contents were decreased by almost 66%! But the clothes we bought were much better than what I wore before. I was now getting compliments on my image from people who were noticing the improvements.

Be intentional and deliberate. Be clear about what you are trying to achieve and test whether that is what you are getting. Most of all be confident in yourself. Recall the many times you have adapted and adjusted in life before now and how your strength brought you through. You are a winner, or you wouldn't be alive to tell about it today. An individual can get discouraged when going back and forth between dream and the reality checks it puts you through without realizing that it is actually a proving ground for resilience and stability in your new role.

I tell my clients that they will succeed when their determination exceeds their discomfort with the way things are. The more determination, the more success and the less the discomfort affects you. Does your determination outweigh your discomfort?

Which one is running your life?

4. **Reinventing your communication skills** – What are you saying to yourself? What message are others hearing?

After I went through the breakup of my first marriage, I took a course from a local college in self-talk. The teacher committed us all to write down positive attributes we saw in ourselves and repeat them every day to a mirror. I have found one of the hardest exercises for people to do is stand in front of a mirror and compliment themselves. I have a friend who says the best gift you can give yourself and others is a smile. Try it now. Go to the nearest mirror and look yourself in the eye and smile. Now pay a compliment. Do it without laughing or embarrassment.

Reinventing your communication skills also involves what you say to others. You may want to assess your ability to communicate. Take a DiSC® Personality Profile or Myers-Briggs Type Indicator assessment. Find out what your communication strengths are and where you need improvement. You might discover that the people you have the most difficulty with aren't actually difficult people. In every group there is someone who is the most difficult to deal with. If you don't know who it is in your group, perhaps it might be you!

Reinvention strategists are always on the lookout for how their words are read on both verbal and non-verbal levels. What is your body saying when you speak? What are your actions saying about what you believe in? When high-profile crimes are committed the police often utilize the services of body language specialists to observe the actions of the prime suspects. They know to look at all forms of communication when observing what the words are.

I have traveled in foreign countries where I didn't speak the language but was able to communicate and connect with people. I have also been in situations where I witnessed foreigners on American soil confused because no one spoke their language. I saw two gentlemen from China try to order breakfast at a casino hotel in Las Vegas, but no one spoke Chinese. You should have seen the wait staff attempt to explain orange juice to people who knew what it was, but didn't know the word for it.

Here are some suggestions I have for clients who want to reinvent communication:

- Reward people who disagree with you. Make a contest out of it!

- Get feedback to test whether what you think you communicated is what people actually heard. Again, make a game out of it.

- Acknowledge when you are wrong. Don't defend yourself. Just learn from your mistakes. Then move on!

- Don't forget that everything you do is scrutinized for meaning. Try to picture it from other people's (your customers, for instance) perspective.

- Spend at least 20% of your time in two-way communication with people at all levels of your organization -- and spend most of this time listening, not explaining. Losers talk, leaders listen!

5. **Reinventing your image** – How do others see you?

Image consultants make a fortune helping individual leaders reinvent their image. I know several people who speak on images and making a great first impression. I have a friend who sells fine-tailored men's suits. He is an authority on what is in style for the successful businessman. It is a worthwhile pursuit. In the past I have hired several image consultants over the years to help me reinvent the image I want most people to see in me.

I have found the best one to be my wife, Christine. She has very good taste – not just because she married me! She works for a corporation and interviews candidates for management positions every day. She knows what looks effective and what doesn't. Remember when I let her toss out the clothes she didn't like? She earned my trust with several suggestions she made in my hair style, my casual wear and my overall appearance. I started getting compliments and people noticed the positive changes.

Reinventing your image requires that you take a long look at yourself and how others perceive you. What do they say about you? Why do people buy from you? I ask this of meeting planners and executives everywhere I go. Why did you choose me over others who do the same thing? The answers surprise me often. Sometimes I am very flattered by their image of me. Sometimes they hired me because of my assistant's attitude, or my web site, or something I had no control over.

I had to let go of the idea that people were hiring me for my talent alone. They sometimes were hiring me without ever talking to me. I had to let go of the old image I had of myself. Akemi Gaines writes, "Before creating your NEW you, you need to let go of your OLD you. Physically taking care of your environment by cleaning and de-cluttering can stimulate letting go of your mental clutter that has been holding you in the old pattern. Now throwing away your old clothes… is easy. It takes physical work, but really, it's a no brainer work. The challenge is letting go of something that you once cherished."

Letting go of things that you cherish isn't easy, but it has to be done very often to reinvent yourself. Sometimes it can be difficult and fulfilling at the same time. There comes a time when you may need to let go of your friends, teachers, mentors, or even some of your family members who don't resonate with you any longer. What do you need to let go of?

To reinvent your image, I tell my clients to find out what people are attracted about to you. Ask those closest to you to be brutally honest and help you out. I asked my wife because she has a vested interest in my success and wants me to always look my best. (Yes, it is hard for a husband to do). Seek out people who are exposed to different environments or think differently than you do. See how your image plays to the people who you are trying to reach. I learned in church work that most "visitor activities" were designed for people who were already active in church. They weren't non-church friendly.

You might want to hire an image consultant, but seek out one who more than just money from you as their primary interest. Hire someone who wants to see you succeed. Finally take action; then listen to what they say as they observe you. Author Tom Peters says, "They watch your feet, not your lips."

6. **Reinventing your culture** – Why don't people follow you?

Do you know why you have supportive employees? Do you know why you have loyal customers? I asked Marti, my loyal assistant why she liked working for me. I was surprised. She didn't say what I thought she would say. It wasn't tied to the money (although that didn't detract from her loyalty). It wasn't the flexible working hours. It was because she saw me growing and releasing more responsibility to her to be more professional. She was being allowed to make more decisions. She wasn't following me for the reasons I thought. Why do your employees or staff follow you?

I asked my top clients why they hired me. What they liked about working with me. It wasn't the answer I expected. It wasn't what I thought they would say. They liked working with me because my office responded to them. They liked me because I was easy to work with. They liked me for the content I spoke on and the style I delivered it in. It was about the value we delivered. I learned a "value"-able lesson.

To reinvent your culture, you need to know what people like about you and your company. Maybe you deliver extraordinary service – better than your competitors and you need to know that. Usually when I ask why a person's company is better than their competitors, they say things like: "We have better people!" Really? Do you purposely go out and find employees that are better morally, physically, mentally and emotionally than your competitor? In most cases the answer is, "No." We just think our people are better because they work for us.

For example, we support a college or professional team almost blindly because it is in our culture – either we attended there (or a close relative did) or we live there. We think our college team or professional football team is better because they are playing with our uniforms on them… today. But when a player gets traded to a rival or out of our area, they become the enemy.

Your culture likes you for a specific reason. They are loyal to you for that reason. It may not be for the reason you assume. You need to know why. You need to know why they work for or buy from you. You need to know NOW. The longer you are ignorant of this, the more you will stumble aimlessly trying to target the wrong reason. You can't afford to wait that long.

I encourage companies to ask quality questions of their internal customers and their external customers. I encourage them to avoid rating scales (1-5, for instance) and ask deep questions that evoke emotions, stories and discussion that is supportive.

Some other suggestions I have to reinvent your culture within are:

- Begin your feedback with what you like about a new idea. Start positive.

- Create an environment where no idea is considered dumb. The "No Dummies" Rule.

- Require that 30% of all budget proposals include innovative products, processes, strategies, business models, or management approaches. How are you rewarding creativity and innovation in your budget? What gets funded gets done.

- Give the work back. Your job is to get the best that everyone has to give -- not come up with all the answers yourself.

- Ruthlessly eliminate fear from the workplace. Foster excitement and commitment.

7. **Reinventing your community** – It's easier to find a new audience than to find a new speech.

Everyone has customers. People who "buy" from them. Reinventing your community involves finding out why people like you and what they feel they receive from you. Nothing makes people take notes more when I am leading a presentation on reinvention than when I ask, "Who is buying from you? What do they buy and what do they wish you would do more of for them?" More of this is discussed in the chapter on Reinventing Your Customer Service, but have you ever asked YOUR customers, "Why DO you buy from me?"

Your culture defines your community. What is the experience like in doing business with you? Who is in your community? It is easier to find a new audience to appreciate your culture than it is to find a new message to deliver. This is a saying professional speaker's quote to each other. If one group isn't listening to what you say and you are too married to it, then find a new audience. Reinventing your community means finding an audience who accepts your message whole-heartedly. It means researching who you want to reach and targeting everything you do to that market.

IKEA is not intended for every homeowner. If you have ever shopped there, then you know it is smart, European designs for people on a tight budget (customers purchase, load and assemble their furniture with minimal assistance from employees) with tight space to put it in. Companies like Broyhill, Manone, Haverty's and Stickley aren't competing directly with IKEA. But even high-end companies feel led to attract a new audience.

Irion Co. furniture maker has a yearlong backlog for its flawless, handmade reproductions of Revolutionary War-era highboys, chests and tables, some of which sell for more than $100,000 each. Several years ago Irion, Co. reached out with a new line to target a new community and build a culture of excellence with a new audience. They sought to attract more customers for Irion's entire line, from $100,000 highboys to $3,000 beds.

The products were simpler but handcrafted to the same exacting standards as the fancy pieces. Irion started coming up with some original designs of its own. They were fashioned with the same quality but a different look. To avoid confusing or alienating existing clients, they decided to market their original designs under an entirely new brand. Management expert Eric Siegel observed, "Nobody wants an $80,000 Volkswagen," he notes, "but everybody wants a $30,000 BMW."

Is there a new community or audience you can attract with the value you deliver? What does the culture of your organization lend itself to?

Maybe not high-end furniture, but the idea that Irion took to heart was to deliver their value to a new audience by creating their own designs based on the quality of their reproduction craftsmanship.

There is a community that you haven't tapped into yet and they await your reinvented image and persona. They want to hear what you have to say directly to them. I ask clients who they could be reaching out to outside of their immediate community. Who hasn't heard your message yet? NOT people who don't want your message, but a community who you already have a message for but are unaware.

Singer Johnny Cash (The Man in Black) reinvented himself using an unusual, but easy method. His career as a singer was good, but he felt restless and stuck in the same rut.

Then he checked his messages.

Johnny started reading his mail. He noticed that he was receiving many letters from men in prison who were inspired by his music. Although he had never spent "hard time" in jail, he sang songs like *Folsom Prison Blues* that touched the hearts of those incarcerated. He performed a concert at California's Folsom Prison and recorded it live. The record producers warned against it, but Johnny felt it was his calling to perform and make a recording.

The result was an overwhelming success. The album was his biggest selling one to that point. He began performing in other penitentiaries and became known as an "outlaw" singer. His audience changed because he listened to what they wanted from him. He forged a new image that became his signature. His brand as an outlaw and "The Man in Black" is known and still popular today, years after his death.

I found it was easier to take my message of reinvention to different audiences. It began to snowball. Now I tell my clients to look at who is buying from them and find everyone who fits that demographic. Start by seeking out who you have attracted to your community of followers. What is in your mail, your voice messages or your inbox?

BUT THEN start looking for *who else* would be interested in the value that comes with the culture you have created. Who else would benefit from the quality of product and service that you (and only you) deliver? Remember: Anyone can beat you on price, but not on the value you deliver. Just learn from The Man in Black.

Moving Forward —
Leaders Convey Confidence And Generate Momentum.

Leaders empowered with a vision of their reinvention know how to go to all the right people and cast that vision. They go one-on-one and to groups looking for discontent with the status quo and use that to instill a desire for change. Losers prefer to maintain the status quo. "If it ain't broke, don't fix it." And "We've never tried that before," are their mottos. They fear the unknown and usually hope someone else will step up and take the reins. Losers don't want to go one-on-one for fear that they will be discovered as lacking the ability to lead. Nothing grows and everyone goes – away.

George Washington knew how to motivate his soldiers throughout the long conflict of the American Revolution. He carried the same vision when he was elected the first President of the United States. He visited every one of the new 13 states. He rode in style over the countryside, but as he would approach a town, he would get out, mount his horse and ride into town as a victorious leader. Wherever he went, he generated support and momentum as a successful looking leader. He was elected to a second term without much opposition.

Abraham Lincoln motivated everyone he met during his presidency. He personally went out in the field to coach new generals. He would venture to the Union Station in Washington, DC to greet and say "farewell" to the soldiers being shipped out to the battlefield. The result was the undying support of each and every soldier who felt personally motivated by the President of the United States.

General (and future American President) Dwight Eisenhower went to meet with a group of airborne paratroopers before they left on their D-Day mission to invade France – hours before they were to depart. He knew most of them would not be alive in a few days, but wanted to encourage them and keep them motivated. They felt close to him and wanted to support the cause even more because their commander had personally taken the time to visit them.

Now let's look at you and your momentum. The groundwork you have laid in the reinvention process has paid off. You sense momentum and your confidence builds as a result. You will be on the right track when there is no longer an internal resistance you have to overcome every time you set out to achieve your goals. Certainly there will be more reality checks and occasionally you might even start to dream of something altogether new again. Bravo! Your journey of reinvention is on the right track.

Assessing Your Momentum Generation Abilities

I have prepared several questions that will give you insight as to how you are generating momentum for your personal and professional reinvention:

1. Are you self-motivated and a self-starter?

2. Do you sense urgency and intensity among your people?

3. Have you identified any problems that may be blocking your momentum?

4. Have you written a plan to solve the momentum blocking problems?

5. Are you investing time into the lives of key momentum supporters within your organization?

6. If your organization is already experiencing momentum, do you know what is driving it and why?

Easy Action Step: Find two organizations in your immediate area that are experiencing great momentum. Interview the president or chief executive of both. Choose one in your field of work and one that is outside to get a difference perspective. Also set up an interview with a crack support staff member—they will often offer different but helpful insights.

Chapter 4

REINVENTING YOURSELF

"Still crazy after all these years!"

— Paul Simon

In 1986, recovering from the breakup of his celebrity marriage to actress Carrie Fisher, Grammy Award winning musician Paul Simon was listening to a recording in his car of the South African group Boyoyo Boys instrumental "Gumboots". Inspired by the unusual sound, he wrote lyrics to sing over a re-recording of the music, which became the first song of his greatest musical project, *Graceland*, an eclectic mixture of musical styles including pop, a cappella, isicathamiya, rock and mbaqanga. Much of the album was recorded in South Africa and featured many South African musicians and groups, particularly Ladysmith Black Mambazo.

Warner Brothers had serious doubts about releasing an album of this category, but when it did, *Graceland* was praised by critics and the public and became Simon's most successful album. The singles "You Can Call Me Al," "Graceland", "The Boy in the Bubble" and "Diamonds on the Sole of Her Shoes" became standards and were highly praised.

Simon, whose career had been struggling for the previous 5 years reinvented himself at age 45, and was back in the forefront of popular music. He went on to receive the Grammy Award for Album of the Year for *Graceland*, and embarked on the successful "Graceland Tour".

Six Skills Self-Reinventors Share

What do people who reinvent themselves have in common? What makes visionary entrepreneurs such as Apple's Steve Jobs, Amazon's Jeff Bezos, EBay's Pierre Omidyar tick? What do they do that you can replicate in your own life and business? Are they born innovators with creative abilities beyond our comprehension, or do they know particular skills that they employ to re-purpose themselves and their organizations?

As I have observed innovators and practiced the art of reinventing myself, I have identified six skills that all creative innovators have in common. They aren't technical. You don't have to be highly educated or talented to use these skills. You only have to be open to the possibilities around you and seize the opportunities the universe and God put before you. Here is what it takes to become a "self re-inventor."

Skill One: Observe Details

The first skill is the ability to closely **observe details**, particularly those of other people's behavior. For you it might mean having to reposition your focus, of becoming alert and aware of folks around you. Certainly, you'll have to sit and watch. My wife and I enjoy a television show on the FOX Network called *Lie to Me*. The show centers on a body language specialist who helps solve crimes by observing the subtle movements, gestures and expressions of people who are under suspicion. He calls them "tells." You and I call them clues. The clues you observe will give you an advantage over those who talk and don't observe.

You can learn a lot from the things you observe around you. I learned, through my own observations that there are patterns to people's buying habits. There are patterns in history to recessions and economic crises. Observing the patterns in behavior helped me determine what my clients were buying. Observing the shifts in the meetings industry gave me an advantage over everyone who spent more time talking about themselves and what they could do.

Top sales people know that you sell your benefits to prospects, not your features. Keen observation will help you find out the needs of your customers and sell them on the benefits you (and only you) can bring. Focus on what you observe in others and what they want and you will know what benefits they will buy. Focus on your own features and you will fail.

Skill Two: Leaders First Listen

Before they talk, leaders use their **listening** skills. In most conversations, people will tell stories about themselves. Self re-inventors listen. Mark Twain once quipped that a wise man closes his mouth while the fool opens his and reveals to all in earshot his foolishness. Newt Gingrich wrote a great series on the "what if" scenarios on Gettysburg. What would the outcome have been at this turning point battle during the American Civil War had Robert E. Lee listened to his most trusted advisor, General Longstreet? Longstreet advocated a flanking move, rather than a direct ill-fated attack on Cemetery Ridge. How would the war have come out different?

Market leaders know that they must constantly hear new ideas from people who have never had an opportunity to share them with anyone. Your greatest skill in leadership is the ability to initially keep your mouth closed and your ears open to listen for trends, ideas and opinions. Talk more and others will quit talking to you. Listen more than you talk and you will learn more.

A companywide culture of creativity starts in the C-suite (the top offices where the CEO, COO, CFO and other chair persons work and reside), so every leader should take a hard look at whether they're doing enough to foster reinvention in their own life. If you aren't reinventing yourself it is doubtful you can reinvent your organization. You are responsible for starting the reinvention process within you before bringing it to the organization. You as a leader have to be open to changing your fundamental processes, systems and beliefs before your people will buy in. People resist doing what you follow, but surge forward to follow what you do!

History proves this out. President Abraham Lincoln made his cabinet up from his political opponents. Lincoln purposed to listen to divergent opinions before he made a final decision, and used his cabinet effectively to that end.

Likewise, President John F. Kennedy recognized that he lacked expertise in many areas of government and science. With that in mind, he surrounded himself with advisors who were smarter in those areas so that he would get the best advice when he needed it. Great market leaders listen to other people's ideas. They seek out opposing viewpoints to test their own logic. Leaders are willing to hear divergent opinions from others. In this way leaders avoid falling into an age old trap. Losers attract "yes men" who will bolster their opinions.

Skill Three: Ask the Right Questions

The third skill is **questioning** - an ability to ask "what if", "why", and "why not" questions that challenge the status quo and open up the bigger picture. Reinvention leaders constantly question the status quo. They ask questions like, "Why does that work in this place?" If you want to get ahead in the market, you need to go to your most loyal customers and ask them why they buy from or do business with you. It might surprise you.

At the end of this book you'll find an appendix containing the evaluation questions I use as a Certified Speaking Professional. In addition, I've included explanations of how I use them effectively to uncover needs and stay in touch with the ongoing interests of my audience.

Skill Four: Risk & Experiment

The fourth skill is the ability to **experiment** - the people we studied are always trying on new experiences and exploring new worlds. You have to have the courage to take risks, even with the full knowledge that you might fail. But know that any momentary failure will bring you closer to ultimate victory. More people are hired because they are willing to take risks. Conversely many people lose their jobs because they refuse to take risks for the organization. It is risky to go against company policy to satisfy a customer, but the employees who learn to put customer loyalty above the policy manual are often the most rewarded.

Frank Lloyd Wright constantly experimented with ideas that ultimately failed. He proclaimed "How else can you succeed unless you try something new and learn from it?" More of his designs were built than his two top architectural rivals combined. He pushed his apprentices to take risks and learn from their mistakes. When they would write him from overseas job sites about difficulties they faced saying, "How do you solve X problem?" he would wait several weeks then write them back with the reply, "How do YOU solve X problem?" Only through repeated trial and error do you learn and grow. With failure comes growth, but only if you are open to learning from your failures.

Skill Five: Associating Unrelated Areas

Professor Jeff Dyer of Brigham Young University calls the next skill "**associating**." He says, "It's a cognitive skill that allows creative people to make connections across seemingly unrelated questions, problems, or ideas." It is the ability to take an idea that is not associated with one industry or environment and bring it to another. Associating is the skill that Dave Thomas, Founder of the Wendy's Hamburger chain used in bringing the drive-up window from the banking industry to the fast food world. The story goes that he got resistance at first, because drive-up windows were rare in food service. But Wendy's was the first nationwide restaurant chain to install a drive-up lane. An idea that was transferred from another industry.

Associating is what Ray Charles used to combine his love for gospel music with rhythm and produce his special brand of blues and boogie music. The ability to see the transfer properties is one that only comes from careful observation of the world around you. The transformations they produced started when both men began to observe what was going on around them, listened to people's needs, asked the right questions (What if...?) and took a risk on something new and different. What is going on outside of your industry that is a hit and can be transferred into your services or company?

Skill Six: Build A Network

And finally, self-reinventors are excellent at **networking** with smart people who have little in common with them, but from whom they can learn. Who do you network with? There is an old saying that goes, 'If you want to fly with eagles, it doesn't pay to hang around with turkeys.' Did you know that most of the people close to you make within 20% of your income? If you want to increase your income, start building relationships with people above your level.

When I reinvented my presentations in the spring of 2009, I was advised by several friends to seek out speakers who were above my proficiency level. They encouraged me to invite these people to hear me in person and critique me. Now I have to admit, that wasn't easy for me. It was hard to ask someone better than me to come and hack my speech and methods apart. But I did just that. None of the critics were negative. Each was honored to be asked and gave me some of the best feedback I had ever received. How well do you take constructive criticism? Could you go out and ask others whom you admire to hack your ideas and methods to pieces? Are you willing to take the risk?

Back to the Future

Well if it is that simple, then why aren't more market leaders reinventing themselves? I believe it goes back to our growing up experiences. If you look at 4 and 5 year olds, they are constantly asking questions and wondering how things work. But by the time they are 7 years old they stop asking questions because they quickly learn that teachers value the right answers more than provocative questions. It seems to be true that we are raising a generation of automatons where conformity and group thinking is more valued than individual expression.

High school students rarely show inquisitiveness. My daughter is often afraid to raise her hand in class for fear of the teacher rejecting her more creative ideas. And by the time they're grown up and are in corporate settings, they have already had the curiosity drummed out of them. 80% of executives spend less than 20% of their time on discovering new ideas. Unless, of course, they work for a company like Google. Conversely, the 20% of executives who spend their time in creative thought processes are the ones who come up with the great ideas.

In my own experience, I was very lucky to have been raised in an atmosphere where inquisitiveness was encouraged. Many times in my life I was sustained by people who cared about experimentation and exploration. Sometimes these people were relatives, but often times they were teachers or other influential adults. I attended a college preparatory school, where I learned to follow my curiosity. In that environment, I was challenged to think for myself and reason through ideas. That climate carried on into college where I exercised creativity both in the classroom and in extra-curricular activities.

I came out of the church environment where I had been employed for over 20 years in 2003 as a major proponent of team work. "Teamwork makes the dream work" was my mantra. I taught this rather successfully for over 6 years to the various groups I presented to and consulted with. As I mentioned earlier, at the start of 2009, as the economy seemed to be at its worst (or most different), I realized that no one was buying team building. I began to ask my clients what they were looking for in their businesses. I had authored my first book, *Reaching Beyond Excellence*. Suddenly I realized that nobody wanted to be excellent. They wanted to survive; to endure; to learn resilience techniques to weather any economic storm.

I experimented with several ideas. Friends and associates encouraged me to move out in different directions. One wanted me to join her in selling construction proposal forms to the contractors and construction groups I spoke to. It just didn't seem to fit. I networked with various individuals I looked up to. Their advice was to go back to my best customers and ask them why they hired me in the first place and what I could do for them that I wasn't already doing. They also advised that I look within to see what gave me the greatest personal return. What did I enjoy speaking on? Who did I enjoy speaking to? Jean, a friend suggested that I ruthlessly eliminate anything that was a distraction – be it a client or concept that I had been wedded to.

I remembered my days working in the church. What had I learned from the experience? I spent most of my time trying to get people to show up. However in the waning days of my religious-based employment I began to notice that most churches tried to reach people who walked, talked, looked and acted just like them. They said they were targeting "lost" people but no one who had never attended a church would feel comfortable with all of the traditions and hoops one had to jump through to fit in. This annoyed me so much that it led to my eventual departure from the ministry. BUT I took the marketing lessons I had learned about reaching people's wants and needs with me. That kept going through my mind during January and February of 2009.

One day, while driving to a speaking engagement in Nashville, I had an epiphany. Listening to recordings of successful business individuals, I began to see a pattern develop. I observed several traits successful businesses had in common who had reinvented themselves. To my surprise, most of the ideas weren't that technical or deep. They were basic concepts that anyone could use to improve their marketing and management styles. They matched perfectly with what I had brought with me from working in the church and marketing there.

I experimented with several concepts, calling them "Indisputable Truths About Business", sort of a "vanilla" title in my opinion. As I worked these ideas, the ones you are reading about in this book, into my presentations, I received very positive feedback. Beginning in April, clients began to reach out to me in greater numbers than I had ever experienced in my speaking and consulting career. I am involved in a mastermind group on a regular basis that challenges me to think beyond my boundaries. They pushed me to look at the possibility that I was not a team building coach but The Reinvention Strategist. I could do for others what I had done so many times in my own life successfully. I owe a lot to those who encouraged me and supported me through the many changes my life has taken. It brought me to where I am today.

What is in your past? When were the times you changed or adapted to an environment that was different than what you were used to? When have you gone in a new direction? Are there episodes in your past that point to ways you can benefit today? My executive coach (yes, I employ one) believes strongly in looking into your childhood to see where you can be most effective as an adult. She challenges us, her clients to dig deep and remember people or characters we admired when we were 4 and 5 years old – you know, back when we were asking questions and imagining possibilities that would change the world. Back before we were beat down by society and negative expectations. Who did you admire when you were very young? What traits did they have that you employ today in your life and career? Was it a relative, a hero, a cartoon character or an influential adult?

The answers you seek can be found by delving into the abilities you bring to the table. I didn't realize until I attended a class reunion, that I am using skills now that I first exhibited in high school. I ran successfully for student government and used some of the tactics I employ now to get elected. I called people on the phone to find out what they wanted in a successful candidate and their student government. "What can we do for you?" I would ask. I then took their advice and ran on what they said they wanted from their government. I had to prepare a speech to deliver at a student body assembly.

To do this, I studied famous leaders to see what they employed to motivate their audiences – techniques like repetition of a single catch phrase, brevity of words and building to a crescendo. I applied it to my preparations and delivered a resounding speech before the student body the day before the election. The result was a landslide victory on Election Day. These same skills are what I use today to market and build my business. I didn't realize I was writing my resume as a young man in high school. What is in your past that you can bring forward into your future to reinvent yourself? What do you need to encourage in young people around you as they develop their future now?

Finally, get going. Tough times demand leadership. Courageous organizations who are aggressive when others are scared are the ones that will excel when things get better. As a leader you have to make decisions. No one ever cut their way to success. Leading companies ALWAYS invest in their people regardless of the environment. It's easy to say people are your greatest resource. It's an entirely different thing to act on that. Look at organizations like Abbott, Oracle, Nationwide, Cardinal Health, Proctor and Gamble, Heinz, Bain Capital, and others. What do they have in common? They're all leaders in their industries. Why are they leaders? They lead because they make smart investments and take risk even during challenging times.

Business blogger Mike Figliuolo says, "Taking risks requires intestinal fortitude. On the back end, however, those bets pay off for leaders. While everyone else is emerging from hunkering down and beginning to figure out what initiatives to pursue, these leaders have been ACTING for months. They're way ahead in the race. They make it hard to catch up to them."

Holding On Is Holding You Back

Reinventing simply for the sake of change isn't a valid reason to reinvent yourself. I realized several months ago that for my organization to grow, I had to grow and let go of some of it. I have the best assistant in the business. Marti keeps the office and my schedule running like a well-oiled machine. But I had failed to notice that she was continually bringing every problem to me for advice and review. One day when I already had too much to deal with around me I said, "Marti, you have always known the right thing to do. You are creative and brilliant. Most importantly, you are trustworthy. That is what I like about you most." She smiled and I went on. "You recently got a raise because you have raised our business level this past year. With additional pay should come additional authority.

I don't care how you handle these day-to-day problems. Just handle them in the way you normally do and we will be just fine."

"Okay," she said, "But that is totally against the way you manage, you know." She was right and that hit me like a ton of bricks. We were being limited by my ability to let go of what I couldn't or shouldn't handle and allow her to do so. John Maxwell says you have to give up to go up, and grow up. I had to give up being a control freak and allow her to handle the problems in the reliable way she had for years. Marti has proven herself to always have our client's best interest at heart. Her three rules have always been: 1. Keep the clients happy; 2. Make us money; and 3. Make everyone look great. She loves the new responsibilities and freedom of not having to run everything by me.

Your employees are reading this and either salivating or enraging. Sorry, but that is an indisputable truth…and you already know it.

It is hard to not know and be able to control everything, but I weigh that against knowing too much and having to give permission to please someone. Most leaders are limited by their abilities to let go of the reins and hand them to reliable staff. Most staff members and employees are frustrated with leaders whose need to control makes them feel as though they don't trust them to do the job well. To reinvent myself, I had to let loose of the reins, choose to trust Marti and after handing them over, allow her the freedom to exercise their talents.

You should know that whatever you're holding on to not only holds you back, **it also holds others back**. Some of my best "Daddy" memories are when my little girl would run up, throw herself into my arms and hug my neck. If you're a dad like me you miss the days when your children were younger. They grow up so fast. I once joked with my daughter that I was going to hold a board over her head to prevent her from growing up. She would laugh and say, "Don't, daddy, let me grow up!" The board represented the way I had become comfortable with her as a child. Of course it was silly, but I had to allow her to grow, make mistakes and find her own answers. It involved trusting that I had taught her the right things to equip her for the life she would lead on her own one day.

What you are holding on to will hold you back. It holds you back from growing. I worked with several pastors throughout my ministry career. They all wanted to grow their churches, but couldn't beyond a certain level. The reason became clear after observing this in several different locations and scenarios. Each was limited by their ability to lead beyond a certain level. It was different for different leaders. But they all had a level or "lid" that kept them from growing any more. Each pastor would grow the church for the first few years, but then when it got too big for them to manage in the style they used to grow it, something would always happen that would either bring attendance down or keep it where it was.

Marshall Goldsmith wrote an entire book based on this principle: _What Got You Here Won't Get You There_. It is based on the principles I observed working in the church. The growth strategies that would get attendance to around 500 members each week couldn't be used to increase attendance to 750. At that size, each pastor would be forced to give up some control and authority to those supporting them. But most weren't willing to do this. They resisted giving up the authority or permission to others. So problems would develop and the attendance would drop off, or maintain the same level.

Self re-inventors know that to grow you have to let go, or give up. You can't go up until you give up. You are holding a board on the top of your leaders preventing them from growing up. You are keeping them in the dark, outside the loop and away from your private leadership space. If you want to reinvent the organization, you have to reinvent yourself by letting loose the information, authority and permission everyone has to seek from you continually to receive.

What are you holding on to that is holding you back? Your level of trust and security may be the impediment that is keeping your own organization from growth. In fact it probably is. The company can't grow until you do. Either give up or let go of the power and authority you are holding on to. It is stifling your followers and the structure of your organization. Once you empower the people around you to take action, you will release their creativity and intuition.

During a recent strategizing session with community bankers, an attendee was inspired to go home and ask his frontline tellers and loan officers what they were hearing the customers say and ask for the bank to do for them. He knew his employees already knew the answers from years of working directly with their customers. The results will be a stronger organization...and more free time for you to be more creative and innovative on your own.

Google is a great picture of empowerment. Part of Google's success worldwide has included empowering their employees to take action on their ideas. Steve Myers writes in his cyber-journal, "Many products and product improvements at Google start with one person having an idea, sketching it out, showing a prototype to others, getting feedback, and soliciting support from others." Notice that getting permission, or running it by one's supervisor is absent from the natural flow at Google.

"Any engineer on our team is empowered to try something they feel strongly about," Todd Jackson, a product manager for Gmail and Google Buzz said. Myers writes, "One example of this is the *undo send* feature. For several years, people at Google debated whether they could or should enable users to pull back an e-mail they sent. Then an engineer in Japan -- who didn't even work on Gmail -- decided he wanted this feature and built it." At that point, "we didn't have to argue about whether it would work," Jackson said.

Act now. This applies whether you're a Fortune 500 conglomerate or an entrepreneur. Leaders in the race never slow down. They can be cautious as they navigate tricky patches but they never stop running. They make it hard for the competition to catch them and they look to extend their lead when their competitors slow down. In short, you have the power to eliminate fear and uncertainty. Let the reins loose. Take a risk. Build and extend your lead by focusing on the long term.

Chapter 5

REINVENTING YOUR THOUGHTS

10 Qualities That Reinvention Strategists Possess

"It's really not about what happens to you in life;
it's about how you deal with it."

— David Neeleman, founder of Jet Blue Airlines

The one question that I am asked more often in conferences is: How can a person be creative?

Of employers seeking creativity, 63 percent prefer creative employees over those who are technically skilled, and employers who are concerned with hiring creative people use job interviews as their primary tool for assessing creativity. In these interviews, employers say they evaluate the candidate's ability to look spontaneously beyond the specifics of a question (78 percent); responses to hypothetical scenarios (70 percent); elaboration on extracurricular activities or volunteer work (40 percent); and appearance (27 percent).

I like to think of myself as a creative person. In the early days of my speaking career I came up with a presentation called: "The Seven Dwarfs of Change." It was a speech about coping with Change and Transition. I noticed that in the opening exercise there were seven reactions to change and I wondered how I could teach this so it would stick and people would remember it. A friend of mine uses the characters in the Wizard of Oz to drive her points home, so I searched my past for something that came in sevens that would help with the reactions to change.

Bang! It hit me: The familiar story of Snow White and The Seven Dwarfs. The Seven Dwarfs were in a stable environment until this pretty young girl came to live with them. Their world was turned upside down and they reacted according to their character names. That's what being creative is to me: Looking for ways to make different ideas work better together. For my first few years, this was one of my most popular presentations.

That worked for me "once-upon-a-time", but how can you TODAY be more creative? Have you ever noticed that creative people seem to have fun in life? Have you ever noticed how they seem to be indispensable to the executives? What steps can you take to get your creative juices flowing? Here are ten suggestions to get your creativity in gear.

1. **Network with creative people.** I get my best ideas at conferences and seminars where great speakers and idea people tell me what they are doing and how they came up with it. I love going to our National Speaker's association conventions, conferences and meetings. Some of my best ideas come from hanging around these people who are the most creative people I know. When I travel, I post a notice on a web site called "Trip It" to see who is in the area that I can meet, have lunch and network with. We share ideas and challenge each other to go one step further.

   I belong to several organizations that involve entrepreneurs and creative people. Most are inexpensive and the ideas flow freely. I am in a mastermind group that meets regularly. We share ideas and bring roadblocks we are facing to the table for each other to solve. It helps me solve my own problems by helping others solve theirs.

   Several months ago a friend, Rob met with me for a day-long retreat. We worked on each other's business strategies. Rob suggested that I find someone who was above and beyond me in business to critique my presentations and business practices. It was a great suggestion.

Everyone likes helping someone else. I met with three other speakers who are above my income and business level. Each had great suggestions and was honored to be of help. Have you ever noticed how easy it is to come up with solutions for others and how difficult it is to come up with your own? Networking and associating with other creative people is the best solution.

2. **Look for & do the obvious.** There are times when an idea just comes to you through observation of the world around you. Back in 2001, Komatsu, the world's largest construction equipment maker after Caterpillar, began looking for ways to edge out the competition. Komatsu knew it couldn't fight Caterpillar on all fronts. So the company's strategy was to defend its turf in Asia, where its share was larger.

To distinguish itself and avoid a price war with rivals, Komatsu began playing up the high-tech, money-saving features of its construction machinery. It was the first in the industry to develop diesel-electric hybrid excavators that save on fuel by reusing energy captured when the brake is applied to stop the machine's swiveling arm. Komatsu was also the first to commercialize a fleet of giant, wirelessly controlled, unmanned dump trucks, bulldozers, and shovels that can be monitored remotely and help mining companies trim labor costs.

Their leadership is very optimistic about the future. One reason for the optimism: China. Thanks to Beijing's $585 billion stimulus spending, China is enjoying a building recovery. In the latest quarter, China was Komatsu's biggest market, accounting for 20% of global revenues and surpassing Japan in sales for the first time. In recent years, Komatsu's focus has been on what it calls "Greater Asia"—Asia, Japan, Russia, and the Middle East. Those markets, plus Africa, currently account for nearly two-thirds of the company's revenues.

Similar to the Dwarfs presentation and seminar, when I developed my speech on <u>Dealing With Storms In Life</u>, I tried to find a medium in which to deliver it so people would be interested from the outset. Growing up I remembered that the most famous people involved in a storm in my childhood were the castaways on Gilligan's Island. Just about everyone knows who they were because the theme song told about each one of them. This became my introduction to a speech I present on how to survive terrible events in life (Trying to Reason with Hurricane Season). There's the story of a chicken farmer who continually had to move his chickens to higher ground in the rainy season because of flooding. He got tired of doing this continually, but kept on in desperation. Finally his wife said, "Why don't you switch to raising ducks?"

3. **Stay in search mode.** Look for many options continually. Steelcase's CEO, Jim Hackett and A.G. Lafley of Procter & Gamble are among a growing number of enlightened business leaders who understand that a steady flow of innovative products rests upon an underlying culture of innovation. They stay in search mode. While they are excited by the challenge of designing new products, they are even more excited by the challenge of designing the organization itself.

"All true innovators have some mix of four key traits," write Rowan Gibson and Terry Waghorn. "Among them: ability to spot trends before they're obvious to everyone else and an ability to intuit hidden potential in existing competencies."

Since Hackett became CEO, Steelcase has come to look like a very different company from the one that offered the world the first fireproof wastebasket back in 1914. Where technology and manufacturing capability once drove most of its new-product development, the innovation process at Steelcase now works outward from the perspective of human-centered design thinking. This new approach is evidenced by a unit that operates as a kind of internal think tank who conduct observations in the field to gain insights into the problems of Steelcase's actual and potential clients.

The most innovative thinkers are inquisitive. They continually search for solutions and creative methods of doing things differently. The problem is, not enough leaders are willing to take the risk. There are probably far more discovery driven people in companies than anyone realizes. Studies show that 15% of executives are deeply innovative. In other words they've invented a new product or started an innovative venture. But even the most creative people are often careful about asking questions for fear of looking stupid, or because they know the organization won't value it.

Albert Einstein has been credited with saying, "Doing the same thing over and over, expecting different results is the definition of crazy." Emile Chartier, the Philosopher said "Nothing is more dangerous than an idea when it's the only one you have." Always keep your eyes open for new ideas and options to age old routines. Robert Kreigel and Louis Patler wrote a great book on this called, "If It Ain't Broke, Break It!" Remember that most good things come to an end. People who generate alternatives will have something to fall back on when the present solution is no longer effective. Stay involved in the creative process. That leads us to...

4. **Look for many solutions—not the fault.** Great creative leaders are known for finding solutions when others would find fault in the same situations. They know how to make failure their best friend. Jen-Hsun Huang, President and CEO of Nvidia, a maker of graphics chips is well acquainted with the process of finding solutions. He spent years in his childhood playing computer games...and losing them. Then he waited tables at Denny's during his college years. It all prepared him to look on adversity as an opportunity.

Today Huang says, "If we think something is really worthwhile and we have a great idea, and it's never been done before but we believe in it, it's O.K. to take a chance. It's O.K. to try, and if it doesn't work, learn from it, adjust and keep failing forward. And if you just fail forward all the time — learn, fail, learn, fail, learn, fail — but every single time you're making it better and better, before you know it you're a great company."

Jet Blue founder, David Neeleman has lead four airlines, two that he founded. He made enough money when he sold Morris Air to Southwest that he really didn't need to ever work again. That wasn't for him, however. When he got fired from Southwest and nudged out of Jet Blue, it would have been easy for him to give up. Sure, he had his cry, but he kept going. He left Jet Blue a year after being relieved of his CEO position and started another (his fourth) airline, Azul. What makes him different is his philosophy of life: "It's really not about what happens to you in life; it's about how you deal with it."

We are constantly surrounded by fault finders and "fruit inspectors." The creative person who not only can see what's wrong but provides a solution will get rewarded with more authority and better responsibilities. Henry Ford said, "Don't find fault...find a remedy." Charles Kettering former CEO of General Motors always told people to leave their slide rules (remember what a slide rule is, kids?) behind when attending meetings, because participants would take them out and use them to compute fault with new ideas. Try this rule in your next meeting: No one is allowed to discuss a problem unless he/she can provide some workable solution.

5. **Be unreasonable.** Reasonable ideas can kill a company or a market vision. Henry Ford's lack of reasonability was instrumental in the development of the V-8 engine. He wanted to put more pistons under the hood without extending the length of the motor and the length of the automobile. He required his Research and Development team to come up with a motor that fit these qualifications. Continually they would come back to him with excuses for why it couldn't be done. Ford was unwavering in his determination, though. He demanded that they go back to the drawing board and come up with the design. After multiple disputes with an unreasonable CEO, the team came up with the V-8 motor that allowed multiple cylinders to be squeezed into a small space.

Go for the unreasoned response to problems and difficulties. Think differently. Creative people don't waste time calculating. They think ahead, regardless of the consequences. Jim Stovall is a man who became blind by age 19. Rather than sitting around feeling sorry for himself, he invested everything he had in developing a network for blind people to hear not only the dialogue but a narrative track describing the action taking place in movies. No network official would give him an opportunity. Everyone told him it wouldn't work and was a useless idea. Today, he is the CEO of the Narrative Television Network. Life is full of people who will refine, or shoot down your ideas, let them do it. You just spend your time thinking outside of the box. And if that doesn't work for you, build your own box.

6. **Always be thinking.** "Managers are quite fickle," says Stuart Crainer. "They're looking for the next big idea all the time." Creative leaders are constantly scanning the horizon for ideas and inspiration. They have the ability to make connections across seemingly unrelated questions, problems, or ideas. They also are able to come up with ideas and ways to deliver them or market them to consumers. History records that Cyrus McCormick is not only credited with inventing the reaper, but he came up with the installment plan to help farmers pay for the machine.

To be more creative, practice mental calisthenics. Dr. Win Wenger says, "Make time for regular frequent practice of creative processes yourself, and support regular practice of such processes by your staff. The methods only serve you well if you practice and use them consistently and often. Even in the core of the creativity movement, it is too easy for people to settle for one or two successful answers and then coast, missing even more significant opportunities."

Develop a system to file your ideas so when the BIG one comes you can make it mesh with several others. If you don't file well, this is a great way to get a system started. Read voraciously and clip articles. Start placing clippings in file folders to use later. Copy articles from blogs and online newsletters to use for inspiration and quotations when the time comes to write your thoughts down. I use a service sent out from Smartbrief.com. They send out daily updates and articles from sources around the business world in both publications, like the Harvard Business Review and blogs on futurist thinking and innovative leaders.

7. **Get out of the Cookie Cutter mold.** Speaking of cookies, have you ever heard of Hydrox? It was an inventive cookie developed years ago. It consisted of two chocolate cookies sandwiching a creamy, white center. You know it as the Oreo. Most cookies are sold because of their brand name identity or their ingredients. But the name "Hydrox" (taken from the chemicals of hydrogen and oxygen used to make the creamy center) prevented the public from embracing the snack.

    Then the developers of the Oreo decide to sell the experience of eating the cookie instead of the cookie itself. They talked about twisting off the top layer, licking the center until it was gone, and then eating the two chocolate halves. They ran a campaign with the jingle: "Oh, a kid'll eat the middle of an Oreo first, and save the chocolate cookie outside for last." The cookie became a hit because of the experience of eating it.

    Find ways to do things differently. Dare to be different. Don't bother with the criticism you will receive. Albert Einstein said, "Great spirits have always encountered violent opposition from mediocre minds." The reason things haven't changed in your organization lately might be that no one wants to challenge the norm. Learn to see what others refuse to see. Rent the movie "Patch Adams," starring Robin Williams. It's the true story of a med school student Hunter Adams, who challenges the norm and does medicine in creative ways. He is advised by a friend to see the world anew each day. He is criticized and almost forced out of school but he persists with his dream of practicing medicine for the common person. You can, too!

8. **See problems as opportunities.** Working with a trucking company manager, I was told that he didn't believe in opportunities. He said, "When you have a truck broken down on the side of the road in a snow storm, that's not an opportunity, that's a problem!" How sad. He didn't realize that truckers talk to other truckers. They watch each other's backs. His truck broken down is an opportunity to demonstrate how he takes care of his employees. It is an opportunity to help someone and increase organizational loyalty and set up a system for taking care

of breakdowns. He retired early several years later when the problems began to outweigh the opportunities he could see every day in the trucking company. How sad.

`John Maxwell says, "When we see problems as problems, we want to be controlling. But when we see problems as opportunities we want to be creative." There is a famous story about a shoe company that sent a salesman to a South Seas island. He wrote the company back: "This place is a nightmare! Everyone is used to being barefooted and nobody wears shoes here. Send me home!" They recalled him and sent a second salesperson. This one wrote the company: "This place is paradise! Everyone here is a potential customer. Send more shoes!" Which side are you on?

9. **Challenge rules and assumptions.** What could your organization do that just isn't done in your industry? Southwest Airlines continues to be the industry leader (and only profit maker) by challenging perceptions. They can turn a plane around on a layover in 20 minutes. They have no checked luggage fees. As a result they always come out at the top of customer service rating polls. They are more on-time than most of their competitors. They make flying fun and as a result, their customers keep coming back for more.

This is very difficult for personality/behavior types that always have to play (abide - their word) by the rules. Thomas Edison hated playing by the rules. One of his famous quotes about his workshop in Menlo Park, NJ was: "There ain't no rules around here. We're trying to accomplish something." Often the very rules of an organization are the same ones that keep it from growing and being creative.

One of the most frequent complaints I hear during strategy sessions with executives is that their people don't use creative ways to cross-sell, or extend themselves with customers. Then I find out that the workers are afraid to step out of the rules (or don't know them well enough to be empowered to act) in trying out ideas. What rules do you have in place that stifles your employees' creativity? What rewards or incentives can you put in place to turn them around? Give bonuses to people who extend themselves beyond the rules and make your company/organization a winner. Recognize them publicly so that everyone will get the idea that this behavior is what gets rewarded.

10.   **Have fun!** It's okay to enjoy your work and your life. In a recent survey it was revealed that an adult of 40 is about 2% as creative as a child of 5 years of age. By age 40, 98% of the creativity has been squeezed out of us. Theodore Geisel (aka, Dr. Seuss) said, "Adults are obsolete children." A chart I saw one time said that ages 1-7 are filled with asking "Why?" Ages 7-17 are filled with asking the question, "Why not?" Ages 17-70 are filled with the statement, "Because!" Be a kid again and ask, "Why not?"

Creative people are fun to be around. They see the world in different ways and have an infectious humor about them. In "Patch Adams," the character Robin Williams plays (based on a true story) is a medical student who seeks to get closer to his patients. He puts on rubber noses to amuse children, dresses up as an angel for a terminal adult and throws parties for his less-humorous friends in med school. SPOILER ALERT: He stays in trouble with an administration that wants to keep the medical profession aloof and austere around patients. But his character resists and is awarded his degree in the end.

Creativity can be the quality that makes you shine. It can turn your "bland" days into "blast-off" days. It all depends on your attitude towards circumstances and finding solutions. You can make the choice to be creative, swimming upstream, or just go with the flow.

Which way are you going?

Easy Action Step: What is stifling your own creativity? What are you doing in your organization that punishes people for being creative risk takers? List ways people are discouraged from creativity around you? What can you do to encourage creative thinking in your people tomorrow? How can you change your daily routine to allow yourself to be more creative and empower those around you to contribute?

Chapter 6

REINVENTING YOUR THOUGHTS

Getting Rid of and Over Bad Habits

"Bad habits make us miss the mark on a habitual basis."

I Know a Secret

In my opinion, you need to reinvent your business constantly. If you are NOT continually evaluating your results, you aren't in touch with your business. I constantly question my habits and my systems for generating income. I believe that if you don't reinvent yourself at least every two years in this fast-paced market and business environment, you will be OUT of business. But the desire to reinvent comes with complications, fear and trepidation. Sometimes we just don't want to take the risk involved to reinvent ourselves. There is a fear of what we will lose in the process.

A friend once advised me to move forward under the assumption that I would succeed. "Act as if you cannot fail," he said. I find this to be one of the most useful suggestions I ever received. The fear of failure holds most people back from taking a chance and making changes. If we knew we couldn't fail, we would seem invincible.

I was waiting on a client in the lobby of a large hotel. Seated near me was a woman dressed like she was interviewing for a job. She seemed anxious. I asked what she was doing at the hotel and she confirmed that she had an important interview. When she heard I had experience in motivating people she asked if I had any encouraging suggestions for her. I passed along to her what my friend had given me: the encouragement to act in the interview as if she couldn't fail. She should walk in with such an air of confidence that everyone in the room would experience an "electric" moment.

"To do this," I said, "just before you go into the interview room, say these words out aloud to yourself: 'I know a secret.'" She smiled and the expression on her face reflected that she was confident. I said, "That is the look you want to convey to your future boss." She took that suggestion to heart and subsequently got the job. She was later told that during her interview she had looked and acted the part of a successful person who they wanted on their team.

How about you? What would your business look like in two years if you didn't fail at anything you did? How much money would you be making? Would you be dominating your market? If you answered, "Yes" then you know what the greatest obstacle in growing your business is – your lack of belief in yourself. Your fear or avoidance of failure is limiting your success. You are your own worst hindrance. Whether it is your fears, your sense of inadequacy, your failure to commit, or your relentless clinging to bad business habits... If you could get out of your own way, you would be overwhelmingly successful. So what is stopping you?

Bad Habits

"If I cannot change when the circumstances demand it, how can I expect others to?"

—Nelson Mandela

We fail when we adopt harmful habits and incorporate non-productive practices hindering us from success. Sometimes we become our own worst enemies. We begin by believing we cannot succeed; we then must prove it by acting it out in our daily routines. If we could really see what we were doing in "big picture" perspective, we wouldn't do it. Unfortunately, too often we are distracted by outside events and circumstances and can't see the big picture.

The movie *Invictus* is a look into South African history at their pivotal moment in time when Nelson Mandela was striving to unify a country deeply divided along racial lines. With apartheid just ended, he discovered one critical element to the process in the national pastime of World Cup Rugby, and challenged his predominantly Afrikaner team to go from mediocrity to excellence. Surprising the world, they made it to the 1994 championship game against their heavily favored rivals, the "All Blacks" of New Zealand.

Sharing the stadium's executive suite with the leader of New Zealand, Mandela leaned over during pre-game and offered to place a wager, to which then Governor General Michael Hardie Boys responded: "If you win, we'll give you all our sheep. If we win, you give us all your gold." Suddenly he saw the big picture – what was important to him was winning the World Cup. What was important to New Zealand was the gold South Africa possessed. They settled for a case of wine. You have to see the big picture to gain the proper perspective on everything.

It has been my privilege to build a career out of helping leaders see their big picture - the actions, items, priorities and general things in their lives and work that they could never have seen on their own. I begin by holding up a mirror and asking my clients what they see. Many times they are surprised to see what everyone around them has seen and have been trying to tell them for years.

While many of the bad habits they have adopted are individual problems, I've noticed a commonality in some of their habits that seem to infect on a wider scale. Even the successful executives that I talk with and the organizations they lead are guilty of falling into the same traps. After several years I began to compile a list of these habits that I noticed everyone seems to have problems with in their lives.

Here are the "Top Ten Bad Business Habits You Need To Let Go Of" (with a Bonus) that prevent us from being successful and dominating our markets. They aren't secrets. Most of these habits are obvious. The problem is that we are afraid to face them and let them go. So what are the Top Ten bad habits we practice regularly that inhibit our growth?

1. **Blaming the economy.**

> *"There are no money problems; there are only idea problems."*
>
> —Ford Saeks

I was speaking in Canada in early 2008 and stopped in to see a client in Toronto. I noticed in reading the *Globe and Mail* (Canada's nationwide newspaper) that the Canadian economy was doing much better than the American economy at that time. I asked my friend if Canada was experiencing the same recession fears we were. She said, "No. Our press isn't trying to convince us that our economy is bad." Hmmm.

As I said in the chapter on The New World of Work, I believe that most economies are driven by fiction, rather than fact. We have assigned human emotions to the rises and falls in the market and too often, fear and frenzy rules the day's trading. Fear drives more economic decisions than truth does. Fear of our own inabilities. Fear of failure. The successful people I network and socialize with choose not to participate in talk of fear and recession. They participate in the recession by using it to their advantage and they don't allow the negative talk to falsely influence them and their decisions.

You can't allow yourself to be motivated by your fears. If you live in fear, fearful things will happen to you. Sow the seeds of fear and you will reap a harvest of failure. I am having the best year ever in my business because I believe that if you work hard there is always enough money circulating and you will receive an ample amount of it. Senior leadership that won't spend money on improving customer service and educating their people will pay dearly when the present "crisis" is over and they find themselves without customers, employees…and a job.

It's time for you to get over it, too.

It's not about the economy. It's about your attitude.
It's about your fear. Get over it!

2. <u>**One-time motivational meetings or training**</u>.

"Training is a life-long process. You are constantly learning."

Successful sales are the result of a process, not an event. Customer Service is a process, not an event. Managing people is a process, not an event. So who came up with the idea that a one time event would turn these processes around? The only event that can change a culture is apocalypse. The only event that can change a climate is cataclysmic. Both are destructive in nature. To change the culture and climate of your business positively requires retraining and reinvention over time.

I am constantly contacted by business leaders and meeting planners to come in and do a keynote presentation for their corporation or organization. Before accepting the invitation, I always ask "What is the purpose of the meeting?" Invariably the response comes back, "We want our people motivated to work better, make better sales, and treat the customers with respect." And when I reply by asking, "Do you think a one or two hour presentation is going to do that?" their answer is often "Uhh. Yes, we think so..."

There is no magic pill you can take for your employees. Look, if it took several years to get this way, what makes you think it can be cured in one quick-fix? Wouldn't you agree that it will require a process to cure a process? Yet year after year, we have a big annual corporate meeting where we bring everyone in at great expense to hear a few motivational speakers (yes, I know I used to be one) and everyone leaves the meeting pumped up. Two weeks later nothing has changed except the degree of apathy. The resistance to change has increased while productivity has decreased to new, lower levels. The motivational meeting now looks more like the "flavor of the month" and likewise everyone can go back to being "plain ole vanilla" in their work habits.

Thus we experience another year, and reinforce another "rah-rah" meeting with little to no results. The reactions range from "Oh, that guy we had last year was great" to "Everyone laughed and we had a great time." OR worse: "He was a sports hero and got everyone pumped up about the Dodgers." But what really changed? Nothing. Why not hire one person to come in and work with our employees and leadership over a period of time and get real results? "Oh, that costs too much!" So let's have another meeting with a bigger name, or a sports figure to inspire our people to hit a home run, go the distance and carry the ball all the way! Are you as frustrated reading this as I am writing it?

It isn't about a one-time annual feel-good fix. It's extinct. Get over it!

3. <u>Negotiating Away the Non-Negotiables.</u>

*"If you just agree to sell your boat in order to buy a trailer,
you might be a bad negotiator!"*

—Mike Pfeiffer

Too many people make bad trades for useless results. As an Atlanta Braves fan for many years, I watched my team make trades for players who wound up costing us wins, while the people we got rid of became stars for other teams. We secured pitchers that gave up decisive runs, outfielders who dropped the ball and hitters who struck out continually. I imagined fans in the cities these terrible players came from were quietly saying, "We told you so." Yet our cast-offs were making the All-Star team and entering the Hall of Fame. What dumb trades!

I see people in business do the same thing daily. They trade away the important items for unimportant ones. Sales people will spend (waste) an hour on a lunch meeting for the social convenience when they could have invested the hour in selling on the phone. We travel hours for meetings when an email or a phone call would have gotten the same results…and allowed more time to make more sales. Managers will call meetings to get information they could have received from a report or a quick memo. We spend an eternity, it seems, to get out a proposal for a client that we know we won't secure, but cancel important tasks to get the no-return tasks done.

When I first started cold-calling, I was rudely hung up on by a woman in the third week of calling. I picked the phone back up with the intention of calling her back and chewing her out, or correcting her misguided advice to me as she slammed down the phone. Then it occurred to me that it wouldn't have done any good. She wasn't going to buy from me, if I won the argument. She wasn't going to buy from me at all. I hesitated and thought: "Jim, you could spend the time making three more calls to people who won't be rude to you, instead of trying to convince someone who already is rude." I made the three calls and got one client for my efforts.

What are you negotiating away to satisfy your convenience? Businesses trade customer service away for employee convenience. Have you ever heard this while on hold? "Your call is important to us. Please stay on the line." Or have you flown an airline lately that made you go to a kiosk because their customer service staff doesn't like to greet and assist customers? The company has bartered away good service to save money or employee efforts.

One of the first signs that your business is in trouble is negotiating away the work to enjoy the pleasure. Do personal calls interrupt your daily work or important meetings? Do you allow email interruptions to discourage you from completing important tasks? Do you trade away an hour of good work for a task that leads nowhere?

Leaders who reinvent themselves know what is making them money and what is costing them more than it is producing. Whether it is inventory, storage space, out of date software, non-productive habits or just beliefs in failed systems, they know what to negotiate out of their lives. Too often, we barter away a non-negotiable to our success for a second-rate objective. How have you traded away the critical actions that would lead to your success in order to maintain a level of personal or professional comfort?

It isn't about you when the sale, the deal,
the customer is on the line. Get over it!

4. **<u>Out of touch with your employees</u>.**

"You've got to circulate to percolate."
—Cavett Robert

The early 1980s produced several books by Tom Peters on excellence in business. In "A Passion for Excellence" he introduced the concept of MBWA - Management By Wandering Around. While Peters applied the humorous moniker, the technique had already been well proven as a way to stay in touch with your key people. Leaders who manage others by wandering around the factory, the showroom, the customer field, or the office stay in touch much better than those who lead from a distance.

Military history is replete with generals who spent time alongside their troops, thereby inspiring the greatest commitment and support. The soldiers not only exhibited greater loyalty to their leader, they also held together as a unit better in the face of combat. Have you seen the films of Field Marshal Bernard Montgomery (known to his troops as "Monty") brandishing an umbrella, smiling and cheerfully waving to the British soldiers under his command in North Africa? He drove the Nazi General Erwin Rommel off of the continent. His men were inspired by his presence. They fought for him and won.

In the "trenches" of business the leader must be willing to spend time with their people to understand them and motivate their success. You can't distance yourself from your people and expect it not to influence their actions and their attitudes. I heard Bill Hybels, Senior Pastor of the large Willow Creek Church in Chicago aptly state: "The speed of the leader determines the speed of the team."

I worked with a CEO whose daily routine began by coming in a back, secret door to his office and only coming out to get coffee. He feared dialogue with his staff and employees because he didn't feel comfortable with them. He called me because he wanted customer service training for his "cold" staff. They weren't being friendly to his customers. His cold style was being passed along to his team. The speed of this leader was determining the speed of his team. It is safe to say that most customer service problems aren't the fault of employees; they are rather the fault of poorly trained management.

It isn't about distancing yourself from your people. Get over it!

Which leads to the next bad habit...

5. **Out of touch with customers.**

> *"If we concentrate on our top customers and meet their needs, we can survive in any economy."*

A good leader knows what their customer wants and satisfies it. The greatest way I can think of to know what your customers want is to ask yourself, "What are they complaining to me about?" **Their complaints are a gold mine of profits for you.** In fact, you need to know the #1 complaint of your top customers. Maybe you already do.

Perhaps it is keeping you up at night. Maybe it just won't go away, no matter how much you ignore it. If that is so, then solve it for them! When you do two things will happen. First, you will begin to dominate your market. Your customers will turn to you to have this need met – and they will tell others about you. This will make you the only one meeting that need. Everyone will turn to you for the resolution when they have this problem or complaint. And you will sleep more. Start viewing your complaining customers as your greatest source of feedback. They are the lifeline of your business.

It was reported in June, 2010 that Chevrolet Motors corporate office sent a memo to their dealerships telling them to refrain from using the word "Chevy," instead of the formal name of Chevrolet. They cited that traditional branding has succeeded in several successful companies, and they used Coca-Cola as an example in the memo (Has anyone ever heard it called a "Coke"?). Why not go with a nick-name that your customers like and are comfortable with? If the customer wants to buy a Chevy is it *that* important to correct them and call it a Chevrolet, or just sell them the car they want? If your customers want something from you that is reasonable and will make more money for you, why wouldn't you want to satisfy them? I talk to leaders every week who refuse to offer services to their customers that they COULD offer, but they choose not to. It's against their "policy."

Have you ever been the recipient of poor service, but because you insisted, told a good sob story or asked to speak with a supervisor, they cut you a deal? They "bent the rules for you this time." Really? They could have served you better in the first place, but told you they couldn't. They just chose NOT to.

My advice is to shop your business. Find out what the customer experience is like. Are your people adhering to policy, or customer needs? When you find out what their experience is like, find out why. Then do something about it.

There should be a law! Every computer company CEO should try to get his laptop repaired by anonymously calling his/her own service department. Every airline executive ought to be a regular passenger on one of their flights to see what their "Joe Passenger" goes through. Every bank executive should call in to their customer service line to see how promptly the call is answered and correctly routed. Test your firm to see how the service *really* is. Every general practitioner should be a patient in their own practice. Imagine the possibilities if senior executives really knew what the average customer had to put up with to get served by their business.

Elsewhere in this book you'll find a section about a creative television show called "Undercover Boss", where CEOs disguise their true identities and go to work for their organizations to find out what their workers think and feel. Unfortunately, they don't get enough taste of what their customers feel. Still, the results surprise everyone – except the employees and customers who knew the "up-close" truth all along.

It isn't about insulating you from your customers. Get over it!

6. **Cutting your throat by cutting employee training.**

> *"Train everyone lavishly. You can't overspend on training."*
>
> —Tom Peters

Having experienced the good, the bad and the ugly in the workplace, I have decided that nothing costs a business more than ignorance. Untrained, ignorant employees are a crutch that won't support your goals or profitability. Nothing causes greater upset than dealing with an untrained worker who doesn't want to improve. As Ron White, the comedian says, "You can't fix stupid." I know that sounds harsh, but let me ask you this: How much is ignorance costing your business? Does it equate to 2% of your profitability? 5%? 10%? Whatever it is costing, the question presents itself: Why aren't you fixing it?

The better your training program, the better your response to customer needs. But the first budget line-item that gets cut by short-sighted CEOs is training. When the economy changes direction, instead of changing their employees and sales staff direction, they circle the wagons and try to do more of the same thing.

Doing something that is worthless MORE won't make it better.

Dancing With The Stars pairs a celebrity with a professional dancer. It is amazing to watch as the professionals sense the shortcomings of their partner and adjust their body movements to anticipate and flow with them. They additionally intensely train their celebrity to handle certain steps with a new level of excellence.

In short, the professional adapts their actions in order to keep in step with and influence the steps of the novice. And this is considered to be normal and expected of them by the judges and the audience. In order to win, they adapt and teach. There is seriously wrong thinking within the organization that believes that doing more of the same will produce different results. It just doesn't make sense. And it simply doesn't happen.

I led training for a bank that wanted a new direction for its management team. They had everything planned to take their leaders into a new future. Then their revenues dipped. So of course, they cut the training program. Two years later they contacted me again. Now they were desperate. I knew that had we implemented the plan we designed earlier they would have avoided the terrible two years. But they had to learn the lesson on their own. And they knew to never do this again.

> ### It isn't about cutting your people's future
> ### out of the budget. Get over it!

7. ### Keeping bad employees.

"Bad employees are made when you pay them for being bad."

In a strategizing session with an association of medical companies in New York many attendees told me that the most costly expense to their businesses was "dead wood." These are people who are being paid and don't produce results. As I travel around the globe this is the dirty secret that most leaders share with me. They are paying people who are NOT producing. They are paying people for their bad habits, so of course the habits continue. But you must also stop and remember: These people are not your problem. If you are paying people who are running off your customers or not working like you want them to; they aren't the problem. You are the problem.

Ouch, that hurt, didn't it? The same is true in parenting. If you reward your children for bad behavior the same amount you reward for good behavior, what is their incentive? I used to take my daughter to get ice cream when she got a good grade in subjects she struggled in. A bad grade and ice cream wouldn't have produced good grades. She was motivated because what gets rewarded gets done.

Disclaimer: This is not legal advice. Don't go out and fire people because you read between the lines. This is business advice on how to cultivate the best performance from your existing employees – and hopefully turn things around for the better.

Having said that, one of the biggest mistakes employers make is hiring too fast. You have problems because you hired them into the organization in the first place. We don't check into people enough to find out if they are competent and can be trusted with authority to do the responsibilities you want to dump on them. And that is what it should be all about – authority and trust. If someone isn't producing results you require, they need to be freed up to find a position where they can be trusted to take on authority – not here.

A radio station owner in Nebraska called me to strategize with him to turn a sales manager around. She was sitting in front of her computer and not out making sales. After asking him some easy questions about the hiring process he used to secure this person in their job, he said that he had hired her to work on a fixed salary alone. She was making the same thing whether she made sales or not! Is it any wonder she wasn't motivated to go out and make sales calls, or teach the staff to do the same thing?

The average workplace has a slate of workers that don't produce. The top ten to twenty percent are usually producing most if not all of the results. This is called the "Paretto Principle" – named for an Italian economist in the late 1800s. They aren't necessarily coming in early or staying late. They are simply getting the job done better than the other eighty percent. The bad news is that you are paying everyone to produce the results that the few are accomplishing.

Yes, I know. That person is knocking themselves out night and day. You just can't bring yourself to let them go. Meanwhile your high achievers are getting tired of being held back and will, eventually, find another place to work. They will find someone who appreciates their performance and trusts them with authority and leave you. So why not keep them and get rid of the poor performers that aren't contributing to the bottom line?

If you judge people based on the results they are producing and how much they can be trusted, it will amaze you who is really doing their job and who isn't. I know a speaker who brags about how hard she works every day and every week. Yet she only has about one client per month. On the surface she looks busy and productive, but at the end of the day (or month in this case) very little results from her efforts. Start looking at the results and see who is really at the top and who isn't. There is a big difference in talking a big game and winning it.

It isn't about keeping the dead wood in place. Get over it!

8. **Putting off critical tasks and decisions.**

> *"A good idea implemented today is better than*
> *a perfect idea implemented tomorrow"*
> —General George S. Patton

Procrastination is one of your worst enemies. You can come up with a myriad of great ideas. You can be so motivated to get the task done. You can be creative beyond anyone else. But putting it off will kill the whole program. Most of the time we let other, less important matters get in the way. Then after a while we realize that nothing got done.

I have an acquaintance who plans some of the greatest ideas for her business. She plans a newsletter, public seminars, top CEO conferences, book manuscripts and many more great ideas. She has a "To Do" list that is very, very long. Yet none of these great ideas will ever happen. Why? She procrastinates. She spends most of her time planning and talking about what she is going to do…later. But later never comes. That's right:

Later Never Comes

Time management is the Number 1 subject most people want coaching on. Procrastination is costing millions of dollars, euros and yen each year. One popular style has taught that we should take all our jumble of tasks and write them down, then go back thru to prioritize them. Then follow through on the top ones as far as we can get down the list. If you've never organized your life before, I suppose this is someplace to start. But surprisingly most people lack the ability to prioritize tasks in their personal life or in their business world. Never put off until tomorrow what needs to be done *right now*.

It isn't about making another list. Do it now…and get over it.

9. **Leading everyone the same way.**

> *"The millennial generation has no loyalty to an*
> *organization that doesn't value their contributions."*

Times are different. People are different. They have different talents, different communication styles, different motivations, different speeds of work and thinking, different needs and different goals. You can't assume that someone is similar to the other people in your organization (and especially you!). If you have been trying to motivate everyone the same way or force them to adjust to your style and you...how has that been working for you? Let me guess; not so good.

History teaches us that the best leaders led their people according to their talents, personality skills and developmental level. Even in the Bible, Jesus had 70 followers, but 12 disciples and an inner circle of three men (Peter, James and John) with whom he spent more time in detail. John even says that Jesus loved him the most, but selected Peter to lead the group.

George Washington had generals he relied on, even when they failed. He treated some favorably and they produced for him. Others, who were incompetent were let go. Benjamin Lincoln lost Charleston, South Carolina to the British. He eventually accepted the sword of surrender at Yorktown on Washington's behalf. Yet Charles Lee, an accomplished military tactician, ordered retreat at Monmouth, New Jersey, refusing to obey orders. Washington relieved him on the battlefield and personally rallied the soldiers to victory.

The days when the boss made everyone dance to his tune singularly are gone. Say good bye to them. They aren't coming back. People can and will find another job that pays them just as well with less hassle. How long an employee stays at a company and how productive he/she is there, is determined by their relationship with their immediate supervisor. It was reported in a recent Gallup Poll that the Number One reason people quit their jobs is dissatisfaction with their supervisors - not their paychecks.

If you can't learn to manage people according to their talents, skills, personality styles and performance, it isn't their fault that they bicker, gossip and argue. Nothing destroys staff morale like treating everyone as equal producers when even they know that not everyone produces.

Resentment is growing and you refuse to recognize the differences in productivity. Your denial is killing your unity.

It isn't about treating everyone "fair." Get over it!

10. **Meetings...with no point, purpose or goal.**

*"Regular meetings usually produce nothing more
than bored staff and tired managers."*

Work is difficult enough. Everyone has a job to do and on top of that we often stack meetings just to have them. It makes the staff unified, right? Wrong. It makes your people frustrated and bored. The first problem is that meetings are held on a regular basis. The weekly staff or sales meeting has to be held on the same day at the same time. So even if there isn't a need, an agenda has to be created. Petty problems are discussed. Sales goals are evaluated with little or no change. Contests are announced and no one cares because the same people win them every time. Does this scenario sound familiar?

Meanwhile, the high achievers are spinning their wheels and waiting to get back to work. They are anxious to get to doing what they do best. They want to do what they are paid to do. Make your business successful. Are they out making calls? Are they supervising their teams? Are they thinking up new ideas? No. They are sitting in a useless meeting...hearing how everyone *else* is doing...or being told they need to be motivated more...by supervisors who have no clue what they are actually doing on the job.

I was coaching an office products company on what they needed to let go of to move ahead in business. One of the sales representatives finally broached the subject of eliminating the weekly sales meetings. The CEO was there. He thought the meetings got everyone motivated. The ones already motivated told him, "No." They said that they could spend the morning making sales calls on some of their top customers instead of showing up to turn in a report and hear the same message every week. His unmotivated people didn't care for the meetings either (and who is surprised by that?). He decided to eliminate the meetings on the condition that the sales reps give him accurate updates on their progress. The meetings were gone and everyone was happy.

A post-mortem on most meetings would indicate that they could be better handled in a short memo. How do I know this? I spent 23 years attending weekly meetings that produced nothing for various organizations. My best ideas were great. But they were shot down by people who didn't want to be outpaced. I also worked in a sales environment and was the top producer. The biggest waste of my weekly time was the weekly (weakly?) sales meeting. The sales manager knew it, the sales staff knew it. But there we sat week after week hearing the same message with little or no incentive thrown in. The hard workers left angry and the slackers just left to go back to not producing. No one left more motivated.

It isn't about holding meetings to symbolize unity. It isn't about going through the motions. It isn't about making you feel important and in control.

A meeting without an accomplished result
is a waste of time. Get over it!

Bonus: Uneducated boards or committees.

"The person who knows HOW will always have a job.
The person who knows WHY will always be his boss."

—Diane Ravitch

I spent years leading non-profit organizations which had very supportive, though untrained boards. You can't run a multi-faceted company with a group of people whose primary qualification is that they won a popularity contest. Election to a board does not mean you can run a business that is not related to the field you are successful in. The same is true in the public sector as well. Untrained, uneducated leadership inspires no one. You can't lead on popularity alone.

Yet banks, credit unions, hospitals, churches, fire departments, non-profit associations and many, many more organizations are set up to be run by untrained board members who question the authority of the trained executives they are paying to operate the day-to-day operations. I hear CEOs and presidents complain that they can't get the funds to do what they know needs to be done because the board is afraid to spend money.

Don't misunderstand me. I believe that boards are important to managing certain organizations. They keep unscrupulous employees in check. But if you answer to a board of directors or to a committee, you need to spend a lot of your time educating them in what you need to do your job the best way you can. That is a shame because you should be spending your time operating the business

A friend told his board one evening to let him do the job they hired him to do and fire him if he didn't produce outstanding results. They were skeptical at first. But he pressed them that they had hired him for such times as these. The group began to see his logic. He delivered the ultimatum that he would succeed or they could let him go as a result. They gave him the freedom and he came through for them. If you can't get permission to do your job, then you haven't done a good job educating your board that you are competent.

It isn't about getting permission from the board to do your job. Get over it.

Take a long, hard look at your leadership style. Is it falling victim to these habits? Is it moving forward? What can you do to catch these habits before they get bigger?

Say it with me... *"I'm over it!"* Rid yourself of every habit that is costing you more money than it is bringing in. Don't put it off. Start today. Let this be the new beginning of your successful future.

Easy Action Step: What is costing you more in money, time or resources that it is bringing back in for you? How do the changes you listed earlier reflect the changes you need to make in your thinking? Rethink all of your habits, hiring, spending, policies, practices and inventory. What do you need to "get over?"

Chapter 7

FINDING YOUR VALUE
Discovering What Makes You Unique

"Real experts are constantly looking for patterns and best practices."
—Brendon Burchard

"Everybody's working for the weekend." A 1980s rock group named Loverboy made this phrase famous. It struck a note with people who only wanted to get the job done and go home. Today is no different. Many people are working for the weekend, holding on for a paycheck and aspiring to nothing more. I call on businesses every day of the week and it seems like 50% of the workforce is out on Friday – the leadership in particular. Experts in the mass electronic mailing industry recommend never sending bulk e-mails out on a Friday because so many "leaders" take the day off and won't read the contents until Monday (when it will be deleted with all the other weekend spam).

Losers can't wait for the weekend. They are myopic – lacking the ability to see beyond Friday at 5PM (or Noon, or even Thursday). Is it any wonder employees are short-sighted when their leadership has a tee time on the golf course just after lunch?

Market leaders are different, though. They constantly scan the horizon for what is coming in the next year or decade. They aren't affected by a downturn the in economy. They don't listen to the negatively biased media when it says, "This is the worst economic downturn since the

Great Depression." They know that the market always recovers and rebounds at a higher rate. They are aware of the average length of decline in economic forecasts.

Leaders are prepared. They plan ahead and are ready to seize the opportunity when the climate is more attractive for growth. Clark Howard, a well-known syndicated Consumer Watchdog living in Atlanta, Georgia says the best time start a business is when the market is down. A recession is when everything is cheaper to buy: office space, equipment, labor, etc. Howard looks beyond the next few days, and as a result is a market leader in his industry – consumer protection.

Market leaders instinctively grasp the importance of a current value proposition. They also know how to spot value in consumer purchasing preferences as well. Losers are continuously foisting unwanted product to consumers using "special deals" on a never-ending basis. Let me illustrate this fact. I was having lunch with a friend who is in the training and consulting business. She was telling me about her service to top executives. She helps business leaders in three specific areas: improve their image, create impact for first impressions with clients and update their personal grooming. When I inquired as to what her greatest obstacle yet encountered was, she immediately replied, "Trying to educate business leaders about the need and value of what I do. If I can convince the senior executive of my value, then he or she will want my services to improve their sales team and entire staff. "

I understand where she is coming from. I used to do this, too. I spent hours on the phone and in emails pushing what I was selling – teamwork seminars, personality assessments, time management workshops, etc. Yuck! All the while I was guilty of thinking that I was smarter than the prospects who just didn't get it. I came to the realization that customer values to dictate the market. Customers know what they want and don't want to buy. I published this on my blog, on my Face Book page, on my Twitter account and in my monthly newsletter sent to clients and friends.

Cheap advertisers want us to think this way so they can push any piece of trash on us. Many people are suckered in by their tactics, too, but overall consumers remain very smart. Customers DO know what they want, and they vote with their pocket books. Every time they open them up, they cast a vote for the products they like and a vote against the products they dislike. They know the real from the fake. They know what they want and show it in purchasing studies and on company profit statements.

For instance, people voted with their wallets in the late 1980s, indicating that they liked CDs over cassette tapes so that by 2006, Detroit and Japan ceased offering cassette players in automobiles. We study car sales and see that consumers preferred the Chevy Tahoe to the Pontiac Aztec (which looked like an SUV that had been dropped on top of an ugly sedan). Consumers have always preferred vanilla ice cream though, over chocolate. But musically they wanted Michael Jackson over Vanilla Ice. Recently they voted for electronic superstore Best Buy over its chief competitor Circuit City.

Riding the Wave

For over a century advertisers have tried to coerce consumers into buying their products and services, whether consumers wanted them or not. Slogans like "30 minutes or it's free!" and "40 percent off!" and "But wait, there's more!" have become red flags to shoppers. Chopping the price is the basest form of advertising gimmick, but it doesn't determine the market leader. Notice how many people flocked to buy the latest version of the iPhone when it first came out and when it was at its highest price? They weren't willing to wait for the price to go down. Why? Because price wasn't the main consideration. The deciding factor was the value to get the latest and greatest gadget NOW. When you start differentiating on price alone, you are already on the ropes and losing.

Focusing on your price or product is NOT the way to get people raving about you. Rather, focusing on what your customers want IS the way. The public gets buzzed about you when you provide what they recognize that they're already wanting and can't live without. When your product resonates with your marketplace, consumers find something worth getting excited about and immediately share it through word of mouth and social media. Almost overnight your logo, product or service will become a movement or a wave. Values really are like waves that you surf in the ocean.

I learned to surf several years ago while on vacation in Hawaii. It took more than one attempt – in fact it took a LOT of attempts (no, I won't provide a number as I finally lost count!). You have to paddle hard while lying on top of the board to get enough momentum, but once on top of a wave, there's nothing like it! As Brian Wilson and the Beach Boys said, "Catch a wave and you're sitting on top of the world." Once I caught the wave, all I had to do was make adjustments in balance and the wave carried me for an extended ride at an exhilarating speed. I didn't have the wave, the wave had me. It was terrific!

Marketing works the same way. In every industry there is a movement, a wave or a trend. Let's define a value first. For our purposes here, a value is the overwhelming trend in the market that results when consumers are buying a product, service or idea. The iPod rode the wave of a trend that swept the music industry. Actually the value was created by Napster with its unauthorized free downloads of music. It was eventually ruled in court as illegal, but as many predicted, the genie was out of the bottle. This opened the door for Steve Jobs to develop a platform and a device to legally download his iTunes. The rest is history.

The value is what consumers are buying en masse. It is what they are interested in. It's what they just have to have. The internet has only helped speed up this phenomenon. Remember when clicking through web sites was called "surfing" the web? In his book, *World Wide Rave* David Scott says, "One of the coolest phenomena is that when an idea takes off, it can propel a brand or a company to seemingly instant fame and fortune –for free."

Seth Godin says, "The best businesses and the best projects are a quantum leap ahead of their competition. This gulf represents a phenomenon labeled "competitive insulation", because others can't figure out how to catch up with you. Amazon is a leap ahead of other online retailers. Sure, their competitors might be able to mimic part of what they've got, but the gulf is so vast, it's hard to imagine overtaking them any time soon."

But how do you discover the value? How do you know what people are interested in or will buy in droves? There are two methods: Find a value that already exists and take control of it, or create your own value. We'll look at both methods and see which is best for you, for your company and for your situation.

The Pre-Existing Value

Marketing within a pre-existing wave or value allows you to save in several ways. First, you do not need to develop a new or creative concept. Second, it eliminates the need to educate prospective buyers about the value of your product, service or idea. In short, it's easier to sell something everyone already wants or is buying in huge numbers. Honda automobiles were experiencing this phenomenon in the middle 1980s. Consumers were buying so many that dealers literally couldn't keep cars on their lots.

So in 1982 if you are an automobile salesman, and you want to make a killing, what do you sell? If you sold Hondas, particularly the Accord model, you simply took orders from eager customers who were willing to wait for their car to be shipped from Japan if it was not available on the lot – and with the demand, it often was not. It really was that simple.

Of course, finding a pre-existing value sounds like the easiest ticket to success. But in reality, it isn't that easy. First you have to be quiet and listen to others. Observe what trends are developing in society, in your market, in your industry, in your competitors (Caution: if your competitors are already doing it, statistics show that the odds are against you doing it better). Has anyone "done" blended coffee better than Starbucks? Has anyone written a better "code" book than Dan Brown? But finding where a value exists is much easier than building a value yourself. Sometimes it isn't in your local community. Sometimes it is on the other side of the world.

It was Christmas, 1984. A group of popular British singers came together under the name "Band Aid" under the guidance of singer, songwriter and social activist Bob Geldof. They recorded a single record, "Do They Know It's Christmas?" to sell and raise money for starving children in Ethiopia. It was a huge success and spawned the Live Aid concerts for African hunger relief. The recording reached around the world. Quincy Jones got the idea to create an American version. He got two of the most popular entertainers in the country, Michael Jackson and Lionel Richie to write a song. Following the American Music Awards in January, 37 of the most popular American artists recorded "We Are the World."

The song outdid expectations – and its British predecessor. It was Number 1 on the US Billboard Hot 100 chart for over a month, Number 1 in the UK, Australia, Canada and France and the top-selling single in the US for 1985. So popular was it that on April 5, 1985 an unbelievable 8,000+ radio stations around the world played "We Are the World" simultaneously. The "value" raised millions of dollars for USA for Africa, the charity created to channel the money to the needy Africans. Quincy located a pre-existing value connected with a need previously established and took charge of it. To this day, "We Are the World" is what most people remember about helping starving children in Africa in the 1980s.

During the hard hitting winter months of the Recession of 2008-2009, I heard about a business in Florida that sold swimming pools. With the housing market at an all-time low, they weren't doing much business. The owner was looking for a way to sell pools in a market where the value wasn't supporting his product. Pools just weren't being bought. In fact many abandoned and foreclosed homes were being left empty with pools that were full – full of stagnant water, a perfect breeding ground for mosquitoes. My suggestion was to go to the city and offer his services in pool maintenance and upkeep on foreclosed homes. The result was a success! They had always featured pool maintenance as a continuation of their sales, but now it became the money-maker. The value was there, they just had to find a way to capture it and become the resource to solve the problem.

Not only does this work in the area of sales, it is true for customer service as well. If someone is meeting customer needs in an inventive way they can change the landscape and force the competition to meet needs similarly. Ten years ago less than half of the hotels you stayed in furnished a hair dryer. Many people packed them with their clothes on trips, taking up space in their suitcases. Now, you are hard pressed to find a hotel or motel without a hair dryer available, even in Europe.

It works the other way, too. If service is bad, find a value to correct it – tap into the mass of unhappy people and you can change a company's policy. Jeff Jarvis writes in his book, *"What would Google Do?"* that he purchased a Dell computer because of their great cabin (customer) service. When the computer developed problems, he couldn't get anywhere with Dell so he blogged that Dell sucked. It struck a tone with other disgruntled Dell owners and in a matter of months, Dell not only fixed his problem they changed their customer service policies and Michael Dell himself met with Jeff to make sure the good word got out.

Not convinced? Do you like the way your bags are handled when you fly? Most people don't. Many passengers have gone to carry-on luggage over checked bags. *Breaking News*, a source in London reported in March, 2009 that 1.2 million bags were lost by the airlines in 2008 – actually fewer than the year before. Everyone who has ever lost a piece of luggage while flying is angry, upset and wants to strangle the person at the Lost Baggage desk.

But more upset are the unfortunate few whose luggage is destroyed by the airlines. The carriers usually refuse to do anything about it claiming they "can't be held responsible." But one man, David Carroll, lead singer with the Canadian band Sons of Maxwell, in July 2009 finally did something about it. After United Airlines broke his guitar and refused to replace it, David wrote a song about the incident, "United Broke My Guitar," produced a funny video and put it up on YouTube. It was an overwhelming success – and a public relations nightmare for United Airlines!

In a few short days it was being viewed by over 2 million people on YouTube. David had tapped into the value of relieving frustration felt by every airline passenger. And not only passengers who have flown and had their luggage destroyed, but everyone who felt like some company was too big to care about their customers. The video was aired on every major news network in Canada and the US. Suddenly, everyone knew who David Carroll was and the Sons of Maxwell began selling their music in "record" numbers. The outcome: Within a week, United Airlines gave in, saying David's video complaint had "struck a chord" with them and the matter would be made right.

Conventional advertising and sales methods assert that you have to interrupt people to tell them how great your product is. The latest trend in interruption advertising is the animated characters that "walk on" the bottom of your television screen during your favorite show to advertise their message or program on the network. It interrupts your viewing and is irritating. Conventional advertising dictates that you sell consumers on value or pricing, whether actual or perceived. But did you really wake up this morning and want to be sold something? Probably not. We are bombarded through commercials on television, advertisements before movies in theaters, spam in our inboxes and junk mail on a daily (and sometimes hourly) basis.

Finding the value or the wave of enthusiasm makes more sense than interruption advertising. It tells you what people already want to buy and what they are interested in. You can be pretty certain what they will spend money on without thinking too much. Trends and values govern what people are already involved in and point the way to prosperity. Better yet, they don't just exist in sales and service only, they exist in societal values, too. Finding a value in society that already exists is easier than creating one, if you want to get your point across. History records times when an existing movement or value was used to catapult leaders to fame.

When Martin Luther King, Jr. took his children to a "whites only" amusement park in Atlanta and was turned away, he decided he had had enough of discrimination. The civil rights movement was well underway in the United States. But it lacked cohesive leadership. King became an activist and quickly emerged as that leader. Here was a man who embodied the struggle of his people, who was eloquent and who was persistent. He was beaten, stoned, spit on and jailed, yet never did he advocate violence. He made the movement his own, with his own style. Then he used his eloquence to gain support of the majority with his "I Have a Dream" speech in Washington, DC in August, 1963.

What movement or value already exists in your industry that you can become the spokesperson or resource for? What are people buying? What are they raving about? What wave can you ride in your community that would propel your sales? If you are in financial services, what are people already excited about that you can include in your marketing? In health care, what is the trend everyone seems to be moving toward without any advertising to push it? In automotive repairs, what are successful service centers doing that you can replicate in your community (that no one else is doing)?

Creating Value

Sometimes you simply can't find an existing value in your industry or geographic region. Which brings us to the question: How do you create a value or wave in which to sell when that value is not already in place?

You have the ability to create a value or trend where one doesn't exist. By performing some rather easy research with existing customers, you can initiate your own value proposition. Of course it helps to be creative, but don't excuse yourself by saying you're not a creative person. Creativity isn't always necessary. By asking the right questions and listening, you can allow your customers to do the creativity for you! Let's look together at how to do that.

We'll begin by asking a common question: "What is your customer's most frequent complaint?" What are they griping to you about on a continual basis that you could do something about but to date haven't. It doesn't even matter whether your excuse has been that you don't know how to fix it or you don't think it can be fixed. Just do something for your customers whether it is convenient for you or not.

Many times I have encountered companies that render poor service and don't really care about what I or anyone else thinks. I was even told last month by a supervisor at my bank, "We are successful and don't need any advice from you or any of our customers on setting policies." (This same bank has been on a government watch list for poor practices and was recently bought out by another bank before declaring insolvency. I won't give their name but it sounds something like "Watch-Over-Ya.")

The story of United Parcel Service (UPS) is a classic illustration of responding to the Number 1 complaint. They created a value trend that totally transformed the shipping industry, and as Thom Winninger, my friend and fellow marketing author puts it, got out of the shipping business altogether. Here is what Thom relayed to me about the UPS reinvention:

Do you remember what it was like in the 1990s to ship a package using any one of the commercial delivery businesses? You had to find out where they were located and go to their warehouse - usually located in an industrial part of town or near an airport. Once there, you stood in line with your heavy package in a non-air-conditioned room with everyone else shipping business supplies, widgets and canned preserves from Aunt Martha.

The attendants, who generally looked tired and impatient took your information, weighed your package, made you re-wrap it in their boxes and took your money. For that you received a receipt and the "promise" your package would be delivered in about 3 working days. If not you would get your money back, or part of it. Then you headed back to work, stopping off at your church to pray that the package arrived at all. The environment included a hot warehouse, cold employees and no guarantees.

All along UPS was bombarded with the same complaint: "Where is my package?!" Over and over again irate businesses and individuals would call and scream, "Where's my #@!%*@ package?!!!" It was a constant complaint that kept their dispatchers and public relations representatives busy night and day. Everyone was sick of hearing the same complaint that was occurring industry-wide. And no one was doing anything about it.

Then in the late 1990s FedEx decided to reduce their shipping costs to start a price war with UPS, who they knew couldn't compete at those rates. The president of UPS knew the company was at a crossroads. Reduce costs and probably go out of business, OR get out of the shipping business. He chose the latter! He decided that the complaints he and his staff were receiving weren't complaints, but suggestions from loyal customers.

So UPS created an unforgettable value based on what their customers were complaining about. They decided to get out of the shipping business and into the *"Where is My Package Business."* They developed a software program that could be installed in anyone's computer (now at their website on the internet for anyone to use) so people could ship and track their packages. No more "Where is my package?" Now it was "Here is my package and here is when it will get to its destination."

This solution totally re-aligned the shipping industry. Now, a shipper could go online, print the shipping label and UPS would come by THEIR air conditioned office and pick it up, leaving them with a receipt containing a tracking number allowing them to follow their shipments progress on the world wide web. It was ingenious! Soon everyone else followed suit or had to stay in the old shipping business where guarantees of on-time arrival were useless.

UPS didn't stop there. They heard their customers complaining about the expense and time of shipping their computers back to Japan for warranty service. It took time and wasn't cheap. So UPS built a factory in Louisville, Kentucky to repair computers for their customers. Now they work with people who don't want the expense or time of shipping broken computers halfway around the world. No one else in the shipping business did this.

UPS turned a complaint into an opportunity to listen, improve, and become the industry champion. They did it by developing ears that quit mistaking suggestions for complaints. Let me explain for a moment. Your complaining customers are loyal to you. If they weren't they wouldn't come to you with their concerns. They would go to your competition. But they don't.

They don't for two primary reasons. First, they like you for some reason or the other. They like doing business with you or they like some of the service you give them. Second, no one is meeting this known need. If they were, your customers would take their business from you and promptly go there. So in reality, your consumers are telling you what they want you to do for them that NO ONE ELSE IS DOING.

Wouldn't you agree that it's all in the way you view complaints? It's like a warning light on your automobile's dashboard. You can view it as a nuisance to be ignored and keep driving, or you can view it as your car telling you what is wrong and stop to complete the fix...or it will fix you by quitting altogether on you. Isn't it true that it's cheaper to repair a car that's running than to repair a car that's compounded one problem into several and stopped altogether? Replace the muffler hanger now or you can replace the entire exhaust after you drive over the railroad tracks!

As my auto mechanic regularly reminds me: "You can pay me now or you can pay me later."

I told a group of bankers to do what no one else is doing for their customers. It seemed to resonate with one of the attendees. A bank president to come up to me after the session very excited. She told me that her bank is located in a very rural area of western Nebraska. Her customers are almost all farmers and agricultural workers. They complain about having to come into town to do their banking. Often they leave some paper work back home when they come to town and their business can't be fully completed. She said, "After hearing you speak I told my officers at the conference with me that we are going to become *The Bank that Comes to You*."

She said they are going to start traveling out to the farmers to do business. They can take their laptop computers with them. Once at the farm they ask the farmers to show them their set-up...how well they run it; what shape their equipment is in; what their needs are. This solves the missing paperwork problem and makes the bank all about being accessible to their top customers. What a great vision for the future of the bank, and what a great way to connect better with her customers. She is now in the *Bank Delivery Business* (and the only one in her area)!

Seth Godin writes that giving things away for free is a way to create a value through scarcity. But be careful. "People look at the free revolution, "he says, "and say, 'oh, that could never work. If I gave x, y or z away for free, I'd fail.' They're right. They will fail... *If they keep the model the same and just give away stuff for free.* The way you win is by reinventing the model itself. So, for example, Lululemon is doing giant free yoga classes in New York. The more people come, the more clothes they'll sell... it'll become a movement. Or Crossfit, who publishes their insane work outs online. The more people do them, the better the scarce part (private coaching, etc.) does. When they give it and it is used, the real underlying need is uncovered.

Nothing makes you realize your need for professional legal counsel more than buying an inexpensive "Legal Wills & Trusts" computer program.

We spent a generation believing certain parts of our business needed to be scarce and that advertising and other interruptions should be abundant. Part of the pitch of free is that when advertising goes away, you need to make something else abundant in order to gain attention. Then, and only then, will you be able to sell something that's naturally scarce. This is an uncomfortable flip to make, because the stuff you've been charging for feels like it should be charged for, and the new scarcity is often difficult to find. But, especially in the digital world, this is happening, and faster than ever.

It's NOT About Price

Another way to create a value for marketing is to ask your customers what their changing need is. What need has been created by your service or product that is not currently being met? What need do your top customers have that you could meet and thereby recapture the lead in your market or industry? The answer will put you in the rare position of being the only one meeting the need and in a unique industry. Let me give you some examples of companies who became an Industry of One.

A credit union in New Jersey decided to answer the needs of their customers suffering with disastrous problems. In early 2010 Toyota owners were facing a crisis of catastrophic proportions. Under duress, the automaker was recalling many models because of either defective brakes or accelerator pedals. The credit union knew the "value" of its members was to "distance" themselves from their suspicious automobiles. They decided to offer "Toyota Recall Loans" designed to assist their members with reducing payments and selling their defective cars as soon as possible. They became known for this and became an Industry of One – the only financial institution in the industry of "assisting people with defective Toyota automobiles."

Remember in the movie "Miracle on 34th Street" how the store Santa Claus at Macy's Department store changed store policies nationwide? Santa did so by referring customers to competitor Gimbel's for toys that Macy's didn't carry or were more expensive. After receiving the gratitude and renewed loyalty of one mother, the store president tells his executives, "We will become the friendly store, the helpful store." If Macy's didn't carry it, but Gimbel's did, their employees sent them over there. The result was skyrocketing sales. Once Macy's started the practice, Gimbel's followed suit in their department stores nationwide. Macy's followed suit and it changed the way everyone did shopping. Sure it was a fantasy, but it illustrates the idea of changing the business you are in by meeting your customers' changing needs.

Here are some questions you should be asking your most loyal customers:

1. What are we doing that affects you the most?

2. What are we doing right that you would like to see us do more often or better?

3. What are we not doing that you wish we could do for you?

What a surprise I received when I began looking for a new air conditioning system for our house last month. Our old unit hasn't worked properly, so before it got too hot in Georgia, we began looking for a completely new system.

What a surprise. Who would think buying an air conditioner would be such a sales learning experience. One salesman tried to run down every other company in town. Still another tried to prove that his system and service was superior (oversold it to us is more accurate). Finally, one criticized us for getting bids from anyone else. They all seemed to have answers to questions *they* asked.

After several exhausting interviews, some friends suggested a local company who helped them after a storm. Hugh, the representative came on an incredibly hot day and immediately asked if we were comfortable at night in our home. We said we weren't. Then he told us what we had wanted someone to say (no one had yet), "Whether you choose us or not, I won't leave your system without enough Freon (refrigerants) in it today. You won't sleep hot tonight."

He didn't try to sell us a system (Features); he sold us on having a cool night (Value/Benefits)! Notice that he didn't have to get permission from the boss to satisfy us. He added Freon on the spot. He had the authority to make his company and boss look good by making us happy.

No slick presentation. No list of awards/accomplishments. No put-downs. Just *asked* what we really wanted… and delivered it.

We hired him. We didn't have to think about it. He won our business by asking us what we wanted and giving us what we needed.

Empowering Hugh to satisfy the customer made him the winner in the "Keep Our Family Cool" contest. By the way, his bid *wasn't* the least expensive. But it was the best because the value he delivered came with it. We would have paid almost anything to get cool without being ripped off.

Hold on! Doesn't this go against everything we've been taught about how to operate our businesses? Of course it does. Or at least it seems to. They don't teach things like this in most MBA programs. If they did, we wouldn't be competing with one another for the same customers so often. Instead they have frustrated former-marketing failures teaching students how to do cookie-cutter methods of marketing theory. No wonder so many graduates fail in the real world. They can't relate to actual customers and their needs because they aren't exposed to them in a marketing course in school. They don't know how to listen to customers because they aren't ever taught how important it is to their viability.

Let me illustrate. After speaking to an audience of financial services executives, one CEO approached me and asked if I could evaluate the needs of his customers to help him better compete (and dominate) in his market. "What is the most frequent complaint you receive," I asked, to which he replied: "That the hours of our operation aren't always convenient for our customers. By the time they get off work and can make it to the bank, we are closed. They can't cash their paychecks in time."

I agreed to meet with his team and coach them through the simple Reinvention Process. Together, we discussed the procedure and the alternatives. The consensus among his executives was almost unanimous that the bank needed to change their scheduled hours of operation. Then it came to the president: "But wait," he said, "we keep the same hours all the other banks in our town do. That would make us the only bank in town that...oh yeah, now I get it."

Suddenly he realized the difference that changing the hours of operation would make. His bank would become the town's newest industry – unique in its hours. Do you see how he had been lulled into the false assumption that he had to imitate his competition to stay in business? By concentrating more on what his consumers wanted and less on what his competition was doing, he was found himself listening to the right people for growing his business.

At another financial services conference I conducted an on-spot audience poll, asking again the most frequent complaint heard from their customers. The answer from over half the audience was a problem with location – their banking location was too far away from their normal travel patterns. Banking involved a "special trip" for these customers.

I simply responded, "If over 50% of my people are telling me something, I think I should listen. So why don't you go where they are?" It's just common sense. Convenience is relative to where *they* are (Value) not where *you* are (Features). If people complain about the same thing and you do nothing about it, you are just marking time before they find someone who will solve it for them…better than you. I asked, "Why don't you make yourself more convenient by a better online presence?" Any bank can buy or build another branch. Maybe "location" means they want to bank more from home than get in the car and drive to your "convenient-for-you" location.

What is stopping you from changing a policy or practice from the traditional way you have done it to meet your customers' needs? You would probably be the only one doing it and then you would be in unique in your community.

Now stay with me for this next part or you'll miss it – and it is important. Here's an all-too-often forgotten truth about success:

If you want to be outstanding you have to stand out.

That's right, you have to pay *more* attention to what the people paying you for your services or products are telling you than what the competition or a glutted market is telling you. You want to reach the people NOT being served well by everyone else in your industry or region. You DON'T want to reach them same people your competition is satisfying. Once you reach the unreached, you will see that there were more than you counted on who want what you have to offer. You can create your own value niche by just listening to customer complaints or evaluating the service you provide to your best buyers.

Why Do You Buy From Us?

Here is a challenge for you. Make a commitment to yourself to (before this week is out) ask your top customers why they like doing business with you. Ask them, "Why do you buy from us?" It might surprise you to discover what makes you popular instead of what you *think* makes you popular. Do you know what your top selling product or service is? Do you know what people like best about doing business with you? The answer will reveal a gold mine of potential profits for you and your organization.

I began asking this question of my top customers and found out what they liked best about me was NOT what I thought they were buying from me. I thought they liked my humor and depth. What I discovered was that in their eyes it wasn't that deep. While they were entertained by my presentation, I discovered that one of the top reasons people liked me wasn't me at all - it was my assistant Marti. My best customers were quick to say how easy my office was to deal with and how dependable we were in responding.

After many, many months of people praising my assistant, I began to really listen to what they were saying to me. I had not realized how many presenters are undependable or difficult to work with. On the other hand, Marti is very pleasant on the phone. She treats everyone as if they are our best client - the client who matters most to us - when communicating with them. She develops friendships with meeting planners and then makes me look great to them.

More importantly, she makes those same meeting planners look great in the eyes of the people who hold them accountable. For the first time, I understood that Marti was one of the most important elements that my business provided. In my reinvention process I realized her trustworthiness, and began to turn more responsibility over to her. Not surprisingly, our clients are even more delighted to do business with **The Mathis Group, LLC.**

If you start asking people why they are buying from you, you just might discover that you are selling something that you weren't even aware you had in your inventory. You might discover an untapped resource that is creating a wave or value for large numbers of customers choosing you and your company because they can't get it from anyone, anywhere else. What is the top product or service they buy from you? Companies spend fortunes every year trying to determine what will sell the best in a new market, but don't spend a dime on finding out what is already selling best. Oh, the big ones do this on occasion, but it is very rare. One major corporation was so angry that their customers were buying online, they waited for months before beefing up their internet presence. When they finally did, it was almost too little, too late.

I work with many small business people who feel they have an overstock of unwanted product that they must push to customers who neither want or need it but will finally capitulate and buy if only enough pressure is applied. How wrong! Customers know what they need. They already buy from you and I for a reason, but we fail to find out who is buying and why.

If people are demanding a product that you have or can supply them why wouldn't you want them to be able to give you money for it? There is a famous cartoon about an ice cream store with unhappy children walking by. There is an angry man in the doorway with his arms crossed defiantly and a sign next to him that says: "NO, WE DON'T SELL CANDY!" So many children have come in asking the same question, the store owner, who doesn't want to sell anything else, has posted a sign and an angry manager warding off potential customers. Many businesses do the same thing in their policies and lack of service to their customers and prospects. What is your business doing that ignores who is buying from you, what they are buying and what they want to buy?

Easy Action Step: To discover untapped markets and values ask, "If our service was provided just for you, what would you like to see us do?"

Chapter 8

GO OUT OF YOUR INDUSTRY

*"You can't be sentimental about nostalgia that hasn't worked.
And you have to embrace change."*

—Chef Ramsey

Movies vs. Reality

One of my favorite movies is "You've Got Mail" with Tom Hanks and Meg Ryan. Yeah, I know it is a "chick flick," but I like it nonetheless. In the movie, Meg's character owns a small children's bookstore called The Shop Around the Corner. She is competing with a huge new box store run by Tom Hanks' character. Tom's store, the mythical Fox Books, sells more than just the average book store. It has sections for everything and even specializes in books from local authors. The place where it burns Meg's store is the huge children's section. Fox Books does things a small bookstore would never dream of doing. Could Meg's store feature local authors? Probably. Could she sell something to her customers that they would buy from her and can't get anywhere else? Yes. Eventually The Shop Around the Corner children's book store is run out of business by the mighty Fox Books. Could Meg have saved her store by coming up with something that Fox Books didn't do for their customers? Definitely.

When something works, people first focus and then fixate on it. They lock it in as the only acceptable way to do things. They stop looking for alternative options. And this fixation creates an opportunity for those willing to reconsider the accepted approach.

Have you seen the kiosks in airports for Rosetta Stone™ the language learning tool? They decided to challenge the norm. In 1995, Rosetta Stone executives decided to bundle their language products and sell the package for $300, which was much more expensive than their competitors' price tag of $5 to $20. Their competitors sold product through bookstores and catalogues. If Rosetta Stone™ remained fixated on the notion that "the only way" to sell language tools was through bookstores and catalogs, it would be almost impossible to sell a $300 product. The idea was that people were unlikely to put that much money on their credit cards after only reading the product packaging.

Recognizing this, Rosetta Stone™ had to either give up its higher-priced strategy or diverge from conventional thinking. So they veered. Rosetta Stone™ headed for high foot-traffic areas like the mall and airports. It lined up its high-end language learning software with other kiosks hocking sunglasses and hair extensions. They seemed to be out of place - $300 software next to $20 sunglasses - but it fit their strategy. Creative thinking CEO Tom Adams later wrote "We needed to open places where we could demonstrate the products, so we opened kiosks. We bet that if we demonstrated it to 10 people, five would buy, because they'd get it." And it worked. In the last 5 years the company has grown an average of 50% in sales and is expanding more into markets outside of the USA.

About once a month, our family likes to go to a book store and spend a quiet evening reading and finding new resources. Our favorite place to go is Barnes and Noble. We like the atmosphere and the ambience. But we like going there for more than just a bookstore. Have you ever noticed what they have? Barnes and Noble is more than just a bookstore. They are a coffee and snack shop. They are a magazine store. They are a music and DVD store. They are a gathering place with comfy chairs. They are a children's place. They are a library. You can sit and read all you want.

I remember when I was about 10 years old going to a local drugstore and looking at the Superman and Batman comic books. You had to sneak a peak at them because if the manager caught you, he would always say in a gruff voice, "Hey kid! Buy it or put it back!!" Has anyone ever said that to you in a Barnes and Noble? Of course not. They let you read the books with the anticipation that you will like them... and buy them.

B&N is creating a place where people go to comfortably read and think. Isn't this what the local library was originally created to be? Some public libraries have morphed into being dry, dull storehouses of archived information. Only those libraries that have maintained this concept have prospered. Taking it one step further, B&N believes that if they create this environment, people will buy the experience by taking the product home as they go through the cash register. And they've proven the concept right.

Yes, Barnes and Noble is more than just a book store. This is why they are the industry leader. When they attend the booksellers convention you know how they are treated - either with a lot of respect or a lot of resentment. The ones who want to emulate them try to copy them. The ones who detest them do so because they can't replicate the B&N experience. Barnes and Noble is leading their industry because they are MORE than just a bookstore. They are all I listed above and more.

In the New World of Work, market leaders are at the top because they are more than their industry. They have cornered their industry market and have diversified into areas that enhance their services to become more than what they were at the beginning. Disney has become more than a theme park. Southwest has become more than an airline. Starbucks is more than a coffee shop. HBO does more than just show movies. Google is more than just a search engine. Apple does more than just sell computers. AT&T is more than a phone company. Wal-Mart is more than a discount store (more on that later), and so on.

As I go around the world speaking, I hear from time to time that many trade associations are saving money by hiring industry-specific speakers. They want to know everything current within their industry. I also notice that the industry leaders are usually absent from these association meetings. Why? Because they don't get the cutting-edge information at the trade association meetings anymore. The trade associations now cater to the smaller-budgeted and smaller mindset companies. The meeting planners have bowed to the fears of their members and hire only industry specific presenters. They fear the backlash from bringing in an outside opinion that goes against the industry standards.

It takes me back to when I worked in the church. Our denomination was arranged in local associations, state conventions and the national organization. The local associations were populated almost exclusively by smaller to medium sized churches. Smaller churches needed the association for support and funding of their programs. Their budgets were so small that they couldn't put together major training programs, so they relied on the association. The large mega-churches didn't attend because they had all the support they needed. Even they were resented somewhat by the smaller churches because of their size and the fact that they produced their own events and often their own material. Many of the large churches actually bought their training material and curriculum from outside of the denomination – heresy!

Look at Wal-Mart. Here is a major industry leader. What is their prime business? They are a discount store. But looking closer, you can see that they've become more than a discount store. Wal-Mart is a garden center. They are an optometrist. Super Wal-Marts are a grocery store. They sell massages and spa treatments. They are an auto care center. They are a health and wellness store. They are a beauty styling salon. They are a photo center. Put them up against the old world industry standard K-mart and there is no comparison. Target comes close with its super stores and groceries, but Wal-Mart is leading the way. They are even looking into banking – their own bank, not an in-store branch of another bank. Wal-Mart stays on top because they don't borrow ideas from the discount store industry. They ARE the new ideas for the industry. They shape the industry. Want to know the next big trend for the discount stores? Stay out of K-mart. Take a walk in your local Wal-Mart.

If you want to lead in your industry, get out of it. Look outside for ideas that work somewhere else and see how they converge with your message and product line. Get out of your cookie-cutter mentality and find a new way to provide services that no one else in your region does. Look for ideas that get your stodgy employees to say, "But companies like us don't do, or sell that." Can't you just hear someone going up to Sam Walton and saying, "But sir, discount stores don't do eye glasses!'"? Where would they be if he had listened to the people that told him (and you know they did), "Sam, discount stores just sell clothes, home furnishings and appliances.'"? They'd be... well, K-mart, or the old Target.

Notice that once a market leader picks up on an idea, it catches on and everyone begins doing it. UPS came up with a tracking system and got OUT of the shipping business and into the "Where is my package business." It became so popular that soon their chief competitor FedEx began offering customer-friendly package tracking. Now it has become an industry standard. Dominos began selling delivery of pizzas. Now their competition, namely Pizza Hut, Little Caesar's and Papa John's do the same. The challenge is to continually look for new ideas from outside of the norm and innovate ahead of everyone else.

An innovation that restaurants are implementing is to offer other services and perks for their customers. Some are making meeting space available during down parts of the day. Others have introduced a "Wall of Fame" of their most frequent and loyal customers. Some high-end eateries are featuring special menu items for those loyal customers that are "insider specials" for them and them alone. It makes other customers want to come back and be included. As one in a community introduces these services, others will follow. In a recent article in *Advertising Age*, Rance Crain wrote, "Companies hit by the recession can get back to growth by offering new services using their existing brands.". The publisher of *Better Homes & Gardens* used the brand to launch a home-repair service, while other companies have started side ventures offering wine groups, webinars and even trade shows. Are these products and services common to the home magazine business? No, but if successful, you can bet they will be the wave of the future in that industry.

USA Today ran an article on February 26, 2010 about hotels with a paranormal history marketing it to people looking for a "ghostly experience." Remember movies like Stephen King's "The Shining" and "Ghostbusters"? The managers of these haunted hotels wanted to keep matters private and hushed. For years paranormal sightings and rumors have been hidden for fear it would chase away business.

But many people are attracted by the possibility of seeing a ghostly apparition. Hotels are tapping into that desire. Charlyn Keating Chisholm, a travel writing who lists haunted hotels on About.com said, "It's a touchy subject. Some hotels fear it will scare off customer, and others worry guests who are looking for a supernatural even will feel cheated if they don't' experience one."

Hotels in Key West, San Antonio, New Orleans and Charleston, SC are part of city ghost tours. Author Bruce Raisch said that Arizona has 24 haunted hotels...so far. The Crescent Hotel in Eureka Springs, Arkansas is one who is proud of its reputation for being haunted. That reputation has driven their marketing. Likewise, the marketing director for the Hotel Provincial, near Bourbon Street in New Orleans agrees that the rumors are good for business. Bryan Dupepe said that years ago they would have shied away from mentioning it, "But I definitely believe over the past two years the fascination with haunting and ghosts has helped our business."

What Bryan and many others have found is that changing their attitude about publicizing paranormal history attracts those interested in the experience. Instead of hiding it, they are promoting it. They have tapped into a need by many travelers looking for a haunted experience. What are people buying in your market that you have been hiding?

This principle not only applies to products and services for your customers, it can be applied to services provided for employees. I worked with a hospital in Kansas that has one of the largest day care facilities for the children of its employees. As many times as I have worked with (or been in) hospitals I have never seen a stand-alone large facility like this. Market leaders who want to snag the brightest and best workers should think of perks and enticements that aren't industry standard. Look outside of your arena and find out what other organizations in other businesses are doing to attract and keep the best people. How would you fill in this blank?

"Our organization doesn't _____ *because no one in our industry does that for their people." That might give you a clue.*

You can also create your own industry by coming up with a new branding concept. Take as an example the story recorded on The Marketing Intern blog site of Greg Koch's efforts in marketing Stone Brewing Company's beer. Koch created a video about "Craft Brewing." The video comes from the site www.iamacraftbrewer.com, a site dedicated to the proposition that all beer is most certainly not created equal, that watered-down beer waters down the beer industry, and that it's high time people started drinking *what they like*, not what the television tells them to drink. While lots of brewers are featured in this video (and on the site), no one brand is featured more than any other. So when Koch featured in the movie and put "I Am a Craft Brewer" on his site, he positioned his brand (Stone Brewing) as a solution to America's beer problem. Rather than be like his competition within the industry, he created his own industry: Craft Brewing and set himself and his brand apart.

I did this in my own business and branding when I created "The Reinvention Strategist." At first I called myself a "reinvention strategist," but later changed to include the word THE in the brand. It set me apart from anyone else talking and doing personal and business reinvention. We will look into this more later when we discuss *Reinventing Your Brand*.

Trading Places

Another way to "get out" of your industry is to work someplace else to gain a new experience. Some executives switch places with someone from another industry to get inspiration and ideas that they can bring back to their organizations. Proven insights from one field can become a powerful force for innovation when they migrate to another field.

Case in Point: Build-a-Bear and the Container Store. Maxine Clark, founder and CEO of Build-a-Bear Workshop, switched companies for a day with Kip Tindell, cofounder and CEO of the Container Store. Bill Taylor tells this story about what happened. "Both outfits are big, fast-growing, passion brands in the ultra-competitive world of retail — although they have little in common in terms of target customers, in-store zeitgeist, or corporate missions. Yet those differences are precisely what made the CEO switcheroo so valuable: When the two leaders spent a day working on the front lines of each other's operations, they encountered all kinds of ideas about merchandising, employee motivation, and in-store communication that worked in one place, and might just work in the other if those ideas were exported to and adapted for the new environment."

To give credit where credit is due, the concept came from the editors of *Fortune* magazine, who were assembling their annual "Best Companies to Work For" issue. Build-a-Bear and Container Store both made the cut and the editors thought it would be a neat trick if two CEOs on the list traded companies for a day. They were right; it was a neat trick. Taylor writes, "It was more than that — it was yet another example of the power of a whole new mindset about innovation.

I've seen it time and again: Leaders who are hungry for new ideas don't just aspire to learn from the "best in class" in their narrowly defined field. They also aspire to learn from organizations *outside* their field as a way to shake things up and make real change. Strategies and practices that are routine in one market segment can be revolutionary when they migrate to another, especially when those ideas challenge the prevailing assumptions that have come to define so many market segments."

Reverse Innovation

Many global corporations are looking outside of their local market to bring in ideas to North America and Western Europe. They are taking advantage of their overseas success and bringing it back home. For decades companies in the US and Canada used a process called "Glocalization." This was the process by which an industrial-goods manufacturer developed a product in the rich Western countries and once it was successful, took it to the third world to sell. With glocalization, companies develop great products at home and then distribute them worldwide, with some adaptations to local conditions. It allows multinationals to make the optimal trade-off between the global scale so crucial to minimizing costs and the local customization required to maximize market share. With the rapid development of highly populated third world countries, those days may be coming to an end in the New World of Work.

Instead, companies like General Electric are taking products that have been very successful in China and India and bringing them back to the US to market. This process is called reverse innovation, because it is the exact opposite of glocalization. GE has two products, a handheld electrocardiogram device and a portable, PC-based ultrasound machine that were developed for those two countries where they were used in rural areas. Now they are finding new uses for them in the United States. In May 2009, General Electric announced that over the next six years it would spend $3 billion to create at least 100 health-care innovations that would substantially lower costs, increase access, and improve quality.

With this process, GE is taking its innovations from outside the US market and bringing them into it. They are effectively taking ideas from outside of their local market and bringing them *into* the US - a shift from the glocalization process that governed the old world of foreign-based enterprise. The success of basic products in Asia and Africa and the collapse of the Western consumer model (consumers based in the United States and Canada, primarily) are prompting more companies to try their hand at reverse innovation.

Other companies are creating formal processes streamlining ways to borrow from emerging markets. Telecommunications manufacturer Nokia researched how young people in Ghana and Morocco share handsets to listen communally to conversations. The company's aim was not only to come up with a more practical phone for Africa but also to work out where to put powerful speakers in the 5,800 Express phones released in the U.S. in 2009, enabling owners to share MP3 music and YouTube videos with others. "There has been a pull from emerging markets as much as a push into them," says Alastair Curtis, chief designer at Nokia. In early 2009,

Xerox hired two "innovation managers" who were tasked with hunting for inventions and products from Indian startups that Xerox might adapt for North America.

Selling emerging-market products in the U.S. or Western Europe carries risks. The example of the shoddy Yugo automobile is still stinging in corporate board rooms. The Yugo was a cheap car that was built and marketed abroad, then brought into North America as the cheapest car in the US. "The Yugo example has stopped so many people from doing this," says Harold Sirkin, a senior partner at management consultants Boston Consulting Group. "The key is that these products need to be what the U.S. market wants."

Convergence

Getting out of your industry is a double-edged sword though. You can't just go out and grab an idea or service and introduce it and expect to lead the market. A word of caution may be in order here. When looking to get out of your industry, make certain you don't neglect to include convergence. What is convergence? Convergence is the practice of several different ideas or concepts and bringing them together to make a perfect fit. It is a delicate technique that requires researching other industries to see what works there and introducing it here.

Former Coca-Cola CEO Donald Keough tells in his best-selling book, *The Ten Commandments for Business Failure*, that when Coca-Cola went outside of the soft drink industry and bought a winery, it was a disaster. First, no one at Coke knew anything about running a winery or the sophisticated alcoholic beverage business. Second, although a beverage owned by a beverage company, a winery didn't *converge* with the Coca-Cola message and product line. A family-friendly business, they ran into an identity crisis in the new venture. They lost millions of dollars.

Similarly, Dave Thomas, founder of Wendy's Hamburgers introduced the radical idea of the drive-up window, common at the time to the banking industry. Today, a fast-food restaurant without a drive-up window is unthinkable. Companies like Checkers feature the drive-up window as the primary location to purchase their food. Convergence sparked a whole segment in the fast food industry.

In the example at the beginning of this chapter, we saw where Barnes and Noble took the bookstore concept and combined a relaxed atmosphere to drink a cup of coffee, give the children something to do, buy other media (music and DVDs) and read any material they sell for free in almost silence. Libraries beware! The convergence of these services matches what their customers are looking for.

Disney produces family entertainment for every member of the family to extend a one day experience into a week-long vacation. It wouldn't make sense for them to add something so outside of the box that it distorts their image (although sometimes it looks like they spread themselves very far out). If they bought an airline that competed with other major carriers, it would diminish their brand and guarantee a failure. It just wouldn't make sense to fly Disney Airlines from Cincinnati to Fargo.

Ignore convergence at your own peril, as Reebok discovered. This consequence occurred when former athletic apparel leader Reebok bought Boston Whaler boats. In 1997 Reebok had a commanding market lead of 309 million to second-runner Nike's $164 million. Reebok had ruled the industry, but spreading themselves too thin cost them market leadership. Nike had run about half their lead in 1997, but the roles were reversed after fifteen years and two economic recessions later. Unrelated investments will sap your core strength. Beware spreading yourself too thin or getting involved in areas so "out of your industry" that you lack the core strength that maintains your lead. By 2002, Nike had a commanding lead of $1.1 billion in profits while Reebok's profits were a mere $247 million.

The same is true for trade associations. The association lobbies the state/provincial and national government on behalf of their members – often the smaller ones. The smaller companies belong because they need the support of the association. They get some of their resources and guidance from being close to others in their industry. But the problem this breeds is being so tight with your industry, that you become myopic to new innovations and ideas. The mantra swiftly becomes "Don't make waves". It's hard to get an outside idea into an industry – it's even harder to get it out. This is the main reason that the larger corporations don't attend and rarely join the state or national associations. They have their own training departments, their own resources and sometimes their own lobbyists. They have no need of the association because they have outgrown it.

I hear someone hiring industry-only speakers and I know right away why they have a limited budget. Their budget is limited by their abilities to expand their thinking. It is funny that the first thing many association meeting planners decide to do when monies are tight is go with industry speakers. Sure, they can get someone for next to nothing to make a presentation at the annual general meeting, but look at the lack of new ideas they will bring to the table. The industry speakers have very few ideas coming in from the outside. The large corporations look outside of the industry constantly for ideas and innovative ideas. They don't do business solely within the parameters of their business. They get out of it.

The future of your company lies outside of your industry. I speak across industry lines to organizations looking to get a leg up on their competition. Often I present to many of the trade associations who want the best ideas for their members because if their member organizations are successful, the association will benefit in the long run. My hat is off to the banking association from a Midwestern state who told me, "We want someone who has been successful in business apart from banking. We want to translate that knowledge to our people so they can rise above and be competitive."

Everyone sitting in the room is your competitor. You want to get ahead in your industry, look outside of the norm; outside of past experience; outside of the industry to get ahead. Your best way to get ahead is get out and away from everyone else. History has shown they will follow your lead.

Easy Acton Step: What are they doing outside of your field that will bring success inside your organization?

Chapter 9

REINVENTING YOUR COMPANY

"If everyone is telling you not to do something, it is very likely
the right thing to do. My theory is 'do the opposite."
—Tom Adams, CEO, Rosetta Stone™

Reinventing yourself is a tough enough decision to make. Reinventing your organization is a different matter altogether. You face the daunting task of getting a group of individuals on the same page who may have never even been holding the notebook before. You face working with a wide range of varying backgrounds, talents, generations and educational levels. On top of that, creativity and innovation aren't always welcomed with open arms in the corporate world.

Some people see innovation as a mystical process over which organizations have little control, whereas others see innovation as little more than a process that can be planted inside any organization and switched on or off at will. But while CEOs speak at conferences and annual meetings about the importance of innovation, very few of them can state clearly the direction that innovation should take. Fewer still are able to make this direction clearly understood throughout an entire organization. This key problem with innovation stems from a lack of definition. There is a tendency to confuse creativity with innovation, which by definition have different distinctives. Creativity is the ability to see things differently and develop new ideas. Innovation is the ability to take these new ideas and put them into action, or to take these ideas and extract value from them.

To create is to make something where once there was nothing. To innovate is to generate value where once there was raw material.

William Coyne, a Senior Vice President for R&D at 3M, says: "Creativity is thinking of new and appropriate ideas whereas innovation is the successful implementation of those ideas within an organization. In other words creativity is the concept and innovation is the process." One of the main problems with innovation is that companies fail to make this distinction. They embrace creativity (ideas) because it sounds like fun and expect (or hope) that innovation (action) will happen by osmosis. This is often where things really start to fall apart. The first stumbling block is your corporate culture. I've worked for many organizations that encourage creativity but frown on innovation because it threatens the power structure or tradition. Creativity without innovation builds frustration and robs hope within your ranks. As a boy, many of my friends would spend hours putting plastic models together – cars, airplanes, tanks, you name it. They would open the box, take out the stamped grids of parts, and then carefully assemble them, testing first for fit and then gluing for permanence. Creativity is testing for fit. Innovation is applying the glue. Even attempting to assemble a model airplane with no glue would be an exercise in futility and frustration.

Richard Watson says, "Most large organizations do not exist to create new ideas. Companies largely exist to manage a legacy, (existing) business, and to return a reasonable level of profit to shareholders - without putting the ongoing success of the entire operation on the line. In this context business is about order and control and managers are quite right to be [aversive to] risk. For example, if you are a shareholder or a customer of a bank, the last thing you want is creative accounting or radical experiments that endanger the very existence of the bank and your money. However, unless an organization can respond to changes in the external environment over time, it will eventually get into trouble."

Equally, if an organization does not come up with any new ideas at all, it will similarly wither. This is because products and markets tend to "commodify" over time and margins are eventually squeezed by newer, smaller, more nimble rivals. These rivals are able to embrace risk and uncertainty and cuddle up to the often messy, irrational and emotional business of coming up with new ways of seeing the world. For instance ice cream retailer, Coldstone Creamery, came out with stores where customers received customized orders. Inventive, but people are forced to wait while employees mixed each special order. The wait is crippling business. They are not doing as well as Nutella who is experimenting with a machine that mixes the ingredients for customers and serves them in half the time. What's needed, clearly, is a happy medium between maintaining business and creativity.

So what is the right level of risk and how should companies allocate resources between managing old ideas and coming up with new ideas?

Another problem is that we have just about eliminated the decision-making process for everyone in the next generation. They lack a sense of ambiguity. Internet management blogger, Jason Seiden, writes, "That doesn't just make [the next generation] more difficult to manage. It may require a complete rethinking of what leadership means. Companies will have to readjust their organizational charts to put decision-making power in the hands of the few people on staff who can handle it, while career paths will become more structured." He goes on to argue, "Take ambiguity away from leadership, and you take away tough decisions and responsibility. What you're left with is overpaid administration."

The present-day school system and deeply restrictive political and religious voices are taking away the decision-making process from our lives. Where uncertainty has not yet been eliminated directly, society has created such a vast network of teachers, specialists, therapists and over-involved parents that for many, ambiguity is an evil to avoid. No longer seen as a problem to be personally resolved, ambiguity is considered to be feedback indicative that some other party didn't fully do the job. Or the ambiguity is considered to be a sign that we need outside help.

We are not taught to think on our own. We are frightened away from making risky decisions. Corporate North America rewards those who play the game, hold to the company line, and don't stick their necks out.

Given this attitude, is it any wonder that your employees are afraid to serve your customers first without your permission or prior consent? Is it really a big surprise that an airline ticket agent can't make a decision to allow a loyal customer to check their luggage for free when it is one pound overweight? Creativity has been stifled and all ambiguity has been eliminated so employees don't have to make decisions – the expectation is that they just follow the policy.

The Intuitive Power of Thinking People

Here is a concept you need to wrap yourself around before returning to work on Monday morning. Your company is filled with creative individuals. They live, think and breathe without your assistance and they can solve almost any problem set before them. Win Wenger of Project Renaissance says, "We have profoundly underestimated the power of understanding and creative capacity in virtually everyone's mind. There probably isn't a problem which more than half of your staff is not capable of solving, given the right creativity techniques and some inducement to use them - including the focus on how to align personal interests with corporate and general public interests."

Your workforce is a goldmine of creativity and information. To begin with, they are on average in better contact with your customers than you are. They hear the complaints. And they hear the praises. They hear what you should be hearing to hone your skills in service and production. And they often know better, more streamlined ways of doing business. They come up with ideas that will improve your customer relations and delivery of services. Most employees are authorities on what works and what doesn't in your organization. They see the flaws in operations and delivery.

As companies grow, senior managers become physically separated from their customers. To combat this distancing, one major bank in Australia practices this approach: the entire board takes calls from customers every week. It's a radical and time consuming way to overcome this problem, and this board is a rare exception. Closer to home, I've had the pleasure of witnessing a JC Penney store manager in South Carolina who regularly assists at check out registers and bags the customer's purchases. When I asked him why he did this, he simply stated, "just to get to know our customers better." In each case, leaders are taking the initiative to reduce the distance between themselves and their customers.

Win Wenger, PhD says, "We all have seen things, whether we are consciously aware of them or not, which no one else has seen, and thought thoughts which no one else has thought. Use creative processes to draw on these unique resources to find ways to make unique positive contributions to your organization and your team."

You need to practice helping each person in your organization in realizing that he or she also has seen things, noticed or not, which no one else has seen and thought thoughts which no one else has thought. They need to discover that you believe that in them are also unique resources to draw upon. Make time for regular frequent practice of creative processes yourself, and support regular practice of such processes by your staff. The methods only serve you well if you practice and use them consistently and often in full view of your employees.

James Rogers, CEO of Duke Energy says, "I've always had a bias for being engaged and being on the frontlines. I think about the example of Normandy, where they had all these elaborate plans, and then when they landed on the beaches, the plans went out the window, requiring them to make it up as they went along. Particularly now, as I've been a C.E.O. for over 20 years, it's really important to be on the front lines and to remember kind of the sound of the bullets whizzing by, to be on the ground. It's one thing to make policy or direction or say, "Go take this hill." It's another thing to be there when the hill's being taken."

A recent survey by Bain & Company found that 80% of companies believed that their firm delivered superior service. Only 8% of their customers agreed. Perhaps senior managers are confusing profitable customers with happy ones. Departments like sales, customer service and customer complaints are usually close to the needs of customers. Hence they are close to one of the primary sources of innovation. Managers generally aren't - they are closest to the needs of the executive suite and the profit statement.

Zara, the Spanish clothing retailer, is a classic example of experimentation and innovation that comes from the front lines. Store managers send customer feedback and observations to in-house design teams via PDAs. This helps the company to spot fashion trends and adapt merchandise to local tastes. Just-in-time production (an idea transferred from the automotive industry) then gives the company an edge in terms of speed and flexibility. The result is a three-week turnaround time for new products (the industry average is nine months) and 10,000 new designs every year - none of which stays in store for more than four weeks.

How about old thinkers versus new thinkers? Old thinkers know that "it's all been tried (unsuccessfully) before." Their minds are made up. Their brains are set. On the other hand, new thinkers are filled with ideas and haven't had the opportunity to be told that their ideas aren't welcomed or won't work. There are plenty of reasons why the most innovative people in any organization are new thinkers. New thinkers make room for hope and inspiration, and tend to have the most energy and confidence. They're often seen as outsiders and have little regard for tradition or orthodoxy. In certain cases, their lack of experience might even work as an asset, unrestrained by history or preconceptions. But some companies still haven't quite caught up with the idea that it's new thinkers who are the most likely to invent their future.

Reinvention helps us in the process of thinking anew [or becoming new thinkers].

This lack of experience was something that Seymour Cray (an early designer of high-speed computers) seized upon. Cray had a policy of hiring newly degreed engineers because they hadn't yet been indoctrinated by old thinking. These engineers didn't yet know what couldn't be done. A company called Fresh Minds works on a similar principle. They supply freshly minted minds to some of the world's top companies. The longer you work for an organization, the greater the likelihood you'll adopt a "groupthink" attitude and the further resistant you'll become to real life needs of how customers think, feel, and behave.

As Motivational as I am Going to Get

There are two lessons every leader needs to learn and incorporate into their thinking, planning and execution. They are indispensable in maintaining a healthy perspective throughout the reinvention process.

The first lesson: **Market leaders need to embrace failure and be willing to take risks.**

As the Recession of 2008-09 began to approach, I watched as leaders, hesitant to make a decision, decided to cut back on everything. Many leaders were answering to boards and committees comprised of members having no experience running an organization that size. Yet these same boards still maintained an aggressive stance on decisions both made and not made.

That reminded me of my previous ministry experience: often working in churches with lay leaders without seminary training, having never prepared in how to run a church and without enough knowledge of the Bible to teach on these matters. Yet they exercised control of the pastor and staff and dictated programming and budgetary decisions that influenced how everything ran. I am reminded of this constantly when working with banks and credit unions that are run by boards of directors who don't have the faintest idea of how to manage a bank, pass an inspection or lead in financial services. I can understand why leaders get frustrated.

Market blogger Richard Watson writes, "I once worked with one of the largest automotive companies in the world who wanted to understand how people really bought cars. In one meeting we innocently asked a group of 35 senior auto executives when they had last bought a car on their own with their own money. Not a single person could remember. In contrast, those employees who were not given company cars had a much greater grasp of what factors were influencing a car-buyers thinking." Most companies - indeed, most people - fail more often than they succeed.

It is the proverbial elephant-in-the-boardroom. And yet by being scared of failure, we are missing a great opportunity.

A football coach once said he was relieved to lose his first game. It took the pressure of a perfect season off his shoulders. At the risk of being thought crazy, I'd like to suggest that you quit trying to avoid your first loss. Everybody (with one exception) fails at some point. Learn to anticipate failure with a positive attitude. Mother Teresa called Failure "the kiss of Jesus" on her life and looked forward to what her failures could teach her. Mickey Mantle was clearly one of the greatest hitters in the history of baseball. Did you know that he had the equivalent of seven seasons in times he got to the plate and never got a hit?

> *"You are never so close to victory as*
> *when you are defeated in a good cause."*
> —Henry Ward Beecher

That brings us to the second lesson: **Everyone is going to fail at something, but NOT everyone will pick up and learn from it.**

Humankind is prone to fail, cover it up and try to act like nothing has happened. Yet some of the most popular products have come from failures or accidents. Ivory Soap is the result of a chemical "flaw." It isn't pure soap. Rather than discard the results, they used it as a marketing campaign. Their advertisements proudly proclaimed that it was 99 & 44/100% real soap. By the way, as a result of the minor air that is in the soap, Ivory Soap floats. They turned that into an advertising plus, also.

When life shuts a door in your face, look for the window of opportunity you can climb through. By acting thus, we overcome our obstacles and move on to greater things. History teaches this lesson repeatedly. There is a difference between saying, "I failed," and saying "I'm a failure." Change your words. It'll change your attitude. Most people won't see you as a failure unless you project that image onto their mental screen. Both Henry Ford and Soichiro Honda founded automotive empires. And both men failed numerous times before attaining the successes they are known for. These men credited their successes to their failures. They knew how to pass their lessons on to those around them and on to future generations.

The point about failure is not that it happens but what we do when it happens. Most people flee. Or they find a way to be "economical with the truth." You hear excuses like "We launched too late." or "People weren't ready for it." No. You failed. Own up to it. This is a beginning, not the end. The problem is this: Most people believe that success breeds success and they believe that the converse is true too, that failure breeds failure. And to give these folks credit, they get it half right. But we must embrace this truth:

People who learn from failure move in the direction of success and away from the unlearned.

There are plenty of people every day who fail before they succeed. There is rumored to be a venture capital firm in California that will only invest in you if you've gone bankrupt. The reason this idea hasn't been popularized is that those who move in the direction of success find that failure begins to recede in the distance. And likewise, those who learn nothing from their failures also begin to recede in the distance. Those left behind can only look to excuses which self-validate their immobility and castigate the successful.

This is not to be confused with the mantra of most motivational speakers who urge you not to give up. "Success is 1% inspiration and 99% perspiration," they say, "and if you just keep on trying, it will eventually happen. And if it doesn't, you're just not trying hard enough." This is a huge lie. Doing the same thing over and over again in the hope that something will change is almost a perfect definition of madness. Although I have hit a hole in one in my life, I have a terrible golf swing. If I practice that same swing over and over again, will I shoot golf like Phil Mickelson? Of course not!

Do you remember Apple's message pad, the Newton? Probably not. It was a commercial flop, but the failure was glorious. Who is to say that the tolerance of failure embedded in Apple's corporate DNA is not one of the reasons for Apple's success with the iPod and iTunes? My friend George Campbell says, "You have to wade through a lot of "Newtons" to get to an iPod."

Does this mean you should abandon your failures? Yes and no. Your idea could be right but your timing, delivery, or execution could be wrong. Who could have guessed, for instance, that the one-time AIDS wonder drug AZT had been a failed treatment for cancer or that Viagra was a failed heart medication that Pfizer stopped studying in 1992?

As designer Alberto Alessi once said, anything very new often falls into the realm of the not possible, but you should still sail as close to the edge as you can because it is only through failure that you will know where the edge really is. The edge is also where real genius resides. So what you and I need to do is learn from failure and try again - differently. It is what we do when we fail that counts, not just repeating the same failures.

So here's an idea. Rather than putting up statues to people who did something that was successful, let's sometimes build monuments to the people who didn't. Let's celebrate the lives of people who took a risk, invented things that didn't work out or tried to do something just a little bit crazy. These are the people we all watch with perverse envy when we are too scared, too self-conscious, or too constrained to fail ourselves. Without these wonderful people, there would be no progress.

Develop a Multi-flavor Attitude

Failure IS an option! If you aren't willing to take a risk or make an attempt, you will remain in the same place forever. Risk-taking brings failures. Did you know that while Babe Ruth was leading the major leagues in home runs, he also led in strikeouts? Richard Feloni and Ashley Lutz wrote about famous designer Vera Wang. She failed to make the US Olympic Figure Skating Team. "Then she became an editor at Vogue and was passed over for the editor-in-chief position," Feloni and Lutz wrote. "She began designing wedding gowns at age 40 and today is one of the premier designers in the fashion industry, with a business worth over $1 billion."

Your organization should reward attempts and failures made in good faith. Stephen King became so frustrated with failure that he threw the early manuscript for "Carrie" in the trash can. Good thing his wife fished it out. Great leaders and managers know that the best innovation rewards creativity in any shape, form or fashion.... even if often it may wind up in failure.

What would you think of someone who failed over 5100 times in 15 years and lost their family fortune in the process? Would you support them to continue, or tell that person to give up and try something more attainable? If so, you would have discouraged Sir James Dyson, who developed the innovative Dyson line of vacuum cleaners. Today Dyson is worth an estimated $4.5 billion by Forbes. By the way, his documented failures were 5126, but who's counting, right? The attempt that made the difference was attempt number 5127, but it took the others to result in the best-selling bagless vacuum cleaner in the US.

Failure is an option if you have long-term results in mind.

Innovation and long term results are what count more than the number of successful attempts. Build your monument to the attempts your people make each day to make your brand and name remarkable. Find ways to push your staff to think not only outside the box, but instead of the box. Reward risk. Learn to say, "That's okay. I have failed myself. What we want is something different than anyone has ever thought of. That won't happen if you keep playing it safe."

When you discourage anyone to think independently you are demanding they choose vanilla instead of alternative choices. "Vanilla attitudes" will kill morale and creativity. Your competitor is looking for creative ways to run you out of business. The consuming public is looking for something unique to stand out and put their faith and money into for the long term. They are looking for a different "flavor" every day. Your vanilla attitudes will stifle growth and chase off business. Continual innovation should be what you are known for in your community.

Disruptive Innovations

There's been a lot of interest in "disruption" ever since Clay Christensen did his ground breaking work on *The Innovator's Dilemma*, which chronicled how incumbent companies were upended by competitors or substitutes who arose from "lower" markets to create a new cost and demand base. Southwest Airlines did it in air travel and Wal-Mart in retail. You know the story. Here are three examples:

Simultaneously simplify. When Southwest Airlines first launched, they flew only one aircraft — the Boeing 737. Today, they still have one aircraft. They have one class of service. They have simple fare structure. They sell direct to end customers. They go to the less frequented, second-tier airports. They have broad job descriptions and cross-train so that one person can do many jobs — including pilots handling luggage. Southwest Airlines created radical simplicity by simplifying many dimensions. They are not the only business where complexity has strangled the process of adding value. Likewise, new and radically simple business models can be created in everything from financial services to healthcare.

Give away the store. Craig Newmark of Craig's List is estimated to have about $100,000,000 in revenue — with 30 employees. That's $3.3 million per employee, and even if it costs $70,000,000 to run it (which it can't), that's a profit-per-employee of $1,000,000. (Compare that with Amazon's profit-per-employee of approximately $30,000.) Newmark's model is so disruptive because he gives away all the ads except those for jobs, thereby turning what was once newspaper profits into what economists know as consumer surplus. In China, Google is now giving away MP3's and sharing the ad revenue with the artists. Paid music is now all marketing promotion. Barnes and Noble and other bookstores have become libraries where people are encouraged to read books that they aren't necessarily buying. In addition, at *Wired* magazine's Disruptive by Design conference, a featured book was Chris Anderson's *Free*.

Reverse your focus. Michael Dell returned to the reins of the company that bears his name in 2007. Why? The company's market share was in freefall and they needed Dell to come back and restore their dominance. However, he announced that they wouldn't grow in the traditional way they had when he started the company. He had originally accomplished this by building a computer in his dorm room. Continuing effort turned it into the preeminent personal computer across the United States. Yet the personal computer giant had fallen on hard times. This returning CEO made his determination to change almost everything about the company he had started 25 years ago.

Dell's marching orders were simple: Create a profitable consumer business with designs to rival and overtake Apple's or HP's. The consumer business, long considered a professional dead end, was going to be a priority. Dell broke for good with its tradition of selling only direct to customers. It began to sell its machines at Wal-Mart, in what the CEO called a "first step" in using retail stores to reach customers. "We're not trying to become like our competitors," Michael says. "We're digging our own path."

Futurist John Sviokla says, "It is the leader's job to unlock this disruptive design potential so that it can be harnessed to help the incumbent make more money for its current shareholders, employees, and provide better surplus value to customers." Michael Dell is successfully applying this concept to a reinvigorated Dell Computers.

Customer-focused Innovations

The San Diego Zoo was hit hard by the recent recession. Zoo officials realized that to stay in business they would need to innovate. This wily nonprofit proved it's never too late to rethink your business model. They used a four step process to reinvent themselves which involved getting in closer touch with their customers. The San Diego Zoo & Wild Animal Park—one of the nation's leading zoos and a global leader in saving endangered species—came to a realization: despite more than 4.5 million annual visitors and $200 million in annual revenues, the organization itself was on an unsustainable path.

Founded almost one hundred years ago with the purpose of recreation, education, and conservation, the zoo was still on target to show an operating profit of $13 million despite the market panic that pushed many companies and nonprofits into the red. But as Chief Financial Officer Paula Brock told the executive committee, the long-standing model of funding conservation research and educational initiatives from entertainment revenues (tickets, food, and merchandise) and donations from their patron base couldn't be maintained—attendance simply wouldn't rise as fast as the costs of maintaining a 2,000-person enterprise.

The zoo had to innovate. They identified that their customer base, while interested in saving the planet, lacked the understanding of what that meant to the zoo's operations – their mission of conservation. The concept meant different things to different people. In order to connect with younger consumers, the zoo added more videos to its Web site; at the same time, it built a zip line ride at its 1,800-acre wildlife park north of San Diego that lets visitors soar across a beautiful natural landscape, offering them the same combination of thrill and reflection that has driven the "ecotourism" trend. In short, they tapped into an existing concern of their customers by communicating it in a way that the message would be understood.

Jessie Scanlon of Business Week writes this four step process used by the zoo:

1. **Ask targeted questions.** Consider all of the different ways that you can view the market. Different frames will reveal different opportunities.

2. **Look toward your base.** Talk to people throughout your organization in order to understand your various strengths and assets. The zoo found, for instance, that its facilities provided the space to host events and showcase new products.

3. **Understand (whose?) needs.** As San Diego learned, its visitors didn't necessarily use the word "conservation," but they did care about the planet and felt confused about how their actions were affecting the

environment. The zoo saw a chance to connect with those people and to get them more involved.

4. **Schedule and Prioritize.** Create a plan to grow over time. This will help you evaluate new ideas as they emerge. Some of those ideas might have merit, but you'll have to put them aside because they don't fall into the top-priority areas of the opportunity map.

Most organizations aren't willing to do this much work to get closer to their customers. When they do, they need to understand the customer experience from their perspective. The San Diego Zoo discovered that its customers cared about conservation, just not how it applied to the zoo's business. Many organizations have no clues about what their customers are experiencing.

How well do you really know what your customer experience? Probably very little. Delta Airlines, apparently in an attempt to make the job easier for their employees and cut costs, discourages its customers from making reservations by phone. They want us to buy tickets on their website. Rather than offering a discount to people who purchase online, they tack on an ever-increasing fee for tickets purchased by phone. Operators, who once were featured in television advertisements assisting service men and women in a pinch, now say frequently, "You know you can purchase your tickets online. Why aren't you using the internet to make this reservation? We charge $50 to make reservations on the phone, you know." Here's a good question: "What would the president of Delta feel like if he had to buy his tickets on the telephone?" Would customer-service-handicapped operators still have their jobs?

This begs the question:

How are you punishing your customers for doing business with you?

What are they having to do that is not being well-received or is chasing them to your competition? Do they have to wait in long lines, press endless buttons through voice mail loops, state their names five or six times to a machine that keeps saying, "I'm sorry, I didn't quite get that"? My cable company makes you enter your telephone number AND account number before you are allowed to speak to a live person, who then asks you for the same information. "We don't know why it asks you that, because it doesn't give us that information."

As the New World of Work dawns, the customer values dictate the benchmarks in services and products. It is most important then that the relationship built between your company and the customer is strong and built on trust. What consumers have to say about you will determine whether you stay in business or not. Wal-Mart founder, Sam Walton said, "There is only one boss: the customer. And he can fire everybody in the company from the chairman on down simply by spending his money somewhere else." Some corporations get this, while unfortunately, others don't.

Here are some questions to ask yourself as you begin the reinvention process:

1. What path are others fixated on because they assume it is the right one?

2. What ideas do I have to change?

3. How can I make things better, faster and more efficient?

4. How can I research my ideas without spending a lot of money upfront?

5. What mistakes are we making that we can benefit from?

Easy Action Step: To begin to reinventing your company, first you have to check yourself and your own values. Are they in line with creative and innovative thinking? Are you open to new ideas from your own people? How do you reward innovation in your organization? Are you dictated by a desire to never fail or only fail at no costs? Who is the most important person in your company? Is it your customer? In the chapter on Reinventing Your Customer Service, we discover what customers want and how you can tap into it.

Chapter 10

Reinventing Your Management

How to Lead a Change in Your Company Culture

"Once you learn how to change habits and get an organization to 'eat its peas,' you'll soon be ready to take on new challenges — whether that means eating tomatoes or eating the competition."

—Rutger von Post

Mr. Quick Fix

I have a habit that makes me want to fix things that are broken ASAP. It's just my style. It often helps me, but it often hampers me. If something breaks around the house, I am fast to fix it. My wife jokes that her "Honey Do" list never lasts that long. I am admittedly not very patient when a door or light or other fixture breaks or isn't operating properly.

In business this has made me very successful. If a customer or client has a need, I am quick to respond. My office is known for being in touch and returning phone calls promptly. I expect it of others, so I do it myself in my own profession.

But it doesn't always help to move quickly. Often my impetuous attitude lands me in more trouble. Friends joke that my impatience is both my strongest and my weakest points.

Let's face it, there are just some problems that can't be "fixed" right away and some situations that take a long time, no matter how impatient you are. You receive a bad medical diagnosis and you want to be cured immediately. But more often than not, cures take time and patience. You receive a bad report from your supervisor or executive board and realize that it will take time to change yourself or those you have offended.

And you can pretty much rule out a successful golf game if you have no patience (also baseball, football and any other athletic competition). You have to learn to slow down and look at the big picture and see what it is showing you.

We live in a day when people want to be serviced and served fast. Just a few years ago a 2G cell phone was all the rage. Now everyone is buying 4G and you can bet that 5G and 6G aren't too far off into the future.

We live in a one-click world on the internet. Customers won't tolerate hitting buttons too many times to buy or find out information from you. I coach fledgling speakers many times a week and I tell them when they send a proposal, don't make it an attachment to the email. People are suspicious of attachments and most executives won't open a file. They prefer it in the body of the message so they can read it when they open it. Don't you, too?

Your impatience can help you and hurt you both at the same time.

People have no patience for someone who comes in like the proverbial "bull in a china shop" and runs roughshod over everyone in the organization.

Your organization that needs to be reinvented didn't get that way overnight...and it won't be cured overnight either. I often ask executives who call me and want a keynote speech on reinvention, "How long did it take to get to where you need someone like me to come in to work with you? Do you think in a two-hour presentation that we will automatically correct that?" They think and most often say, "No."

They are right. Abraham Lincoln's Gettysburg Address was met with almost derision the day after he presented it. Franklin Roosevelt's "fireside chats" warmed hearts during the Great Depression, but the country didn't turn around for years. And Winston Churchill still inspires people today with the speeches he gave on the BBC during the bombing of London in World War II, but they didn't win the war.

Most major problems take time to resolve and a patient leader needs to know how to address them within the context and their specific culture.

Culture Clash

As I said earlier in the book, I am a former minister. I served under pastors who managed with many different styles. But this illustration doesn't come from the churches I served in. It comes straight from the Bible (I Kings, Chapters 11-14). I remember a professor of Religion in a college class telling us the story of King Solomon and his son, Rehoboam.

History has treated Solomon very well. He is known for his wisdom. He is also known for forcing the people into labor for the government, spending more than he had and burdening everyone with high taxes. (A problem we still wrestle with in many countries today). He is mainly known on the negative side for not listening to his own advisors who warned him of the dire consequences of his actions.

When he died, he left a large, disgruntled kingdom.

His son, Rehoboam was the natural successor. He was young, ambitious and wanted his reign to surpass that of his father's. Soon after his coronation, he was met with a crowd who asked him, "Are you going to lift the burden off of us that your father put on, or are you going to keep it on our backs?" My paraphrase.

Rehoboam sought wise counsel. But he didn't listen to it.

First he asked the older men who had tried to advise his father what to do. They warned him that that the culture of the kingdom couldn't stand anymore stress. They told him that the people would rebel if he continued his father's legacy.

Then he consulted with the young men with whom he had grown up. They told him basically, "Hey, you're the King. You can do whatever you want." So he did. "You thought you had it bad under my father? Just wait to see what I have in store for you?"

It didn't play well in Jerusalem, the capital. It played even worse with 10 of the 12 tribes of Israel. They rebelled, broke off and formed their own kingdom. Israel never completely recovered from this error in judgment and lack of understanding.

So what does that mean to you?

Not listening to your organizational culture can be critical. Acting without listening to your people first can be fatal. Making everyone do it, "Your way or the highway" will kill your leadership.

On February 17, 2011, Georg Szalai wrote in *The Hollywood Reporter*, "Time Warner chairman and CEO **Jeff Bewkes** told staff at the media conglomerate's Time Inc. magazine unit Thursday that **Jack Griffin**, who had taken over the division only a few months ago, is leaving as his leadership style didn't mesh with the company".

"Although Jack is an extremely accomplished executive, I concluded that his leadership style and approach did not mesh with Time Inc. and Time Warner," Bewkes said in a brief memo.

Why was Griffin fired? Because he was too overtaken by putting his own leadership stamp on the conglomerate and not paying attention to the culture that already existed there. In only four months he ran himself out of a job. Bloggers wrote about it for weeks. But the reality was that Griffin just couldn't (or wouldn't) adapt to the Time Warner culture that he was brought in to lead.

You can't reinvent the company overlooking its unique culture.

It just makes everyone more upset. The actions and accomplishments that made you attractive to a new position aren't necessarily the tools you need to change everything on Day One. I talked with a woman hired to transform the culture of her medical company. She was frustrated because the people who hired her had a hidden agenda that was only revealed after she took the new position as administrator. They hired her to crack *their* whip and thought she was the best to do it. But her frustration came when no one would obey her.

Starting a Revolution

Strategy+Business Blog carried an article in May, 2011 about British chef and television reality show host Jamie Oliver. On his program in 2010, Oliver came to Huntington, West Virginia to improve the dietary habits of the town. According to Rutger von Post, they had been voted: "...the unhealthiest city in the United States by the U.S. Centers for Disease Control and Prevention. The community of 50,000 led the nation in rates of heart disease and diabetes. Half of its adults were considered obese. Oliver had chosen this small city for an initiative (and subsequent TV program) branded *Jamie Oliver's Food Revolution*, with the idea of having a broader impact. If people could make themselves healthier here, they could do it anywhere."

Jamie started in the Huntington school system, thinking that changing the children's eating habits would change those of the rest of the city (their parents). He was welcomed by the administration, but not the dietary staff. He went on local radio to plead his cause. But his abrupt attitude was met with hostile opposition and he soon found himself branded as an unwelcome outsider. The harsh nutritionist was brought to tears in front of a live audience.

But he quickly recuperated his attitude and began to take small baby steps. He went more into the community and learned more about the people in Huntington.

Here is an example of how this applied in several situations in my life over the years. I was called to a church to manage (maintain) the Christian education program. It was steadily growing, but steadily becoming antiquated. Young adults were NOT attending and the

congregation was getting older with every day. It was so bad that our
only "Young Marrieds Class" averaged over 40 years old. Something
had to be done to stop the trend.

So I studied what churches were doing that were showing growth
in these critical areas. I studied churches who were stagnating, too.
Remember, a church is a volunteer organization supported by its members.
A leader can't walk in with a game plan and make sweeping changes. I
had to work with who we had and learn the culture.

First I met with teachers and leaders who were skeptical of me and
hadn't always supported new initiatives. I disarmed their feelings by
asking them what they thought we were getting right with our study
programs. Then I asked what they felt we weren't doing right. My goal
was to build unity by seeking out joint discontent. It worked. To my
surprise, the discontent circled around the same areas repeatedly. Now it
was easy to meet with the leaders who liked me and were on board with
anything I wanted to do. They agreed with the list of discontentment.

Next I carefully selected leaders from both groups to serve together
on a study committee to develop a plan of action. Every individual on this
committee had a long history with the church and had a vested interest in
its survival and growth. It was important that I be the lone "newbie" in the
group, so the culture of the church would not be threatened. The leader I
enlisted was very forward-thinking and respected by both sides.

Do you have leaders who you can trust with authority, or just with responsibility?

She and I would meet regularly where i received updates on the
committee's progress. My "co-conspirator" (as she dubbed herself) and
I had a great working relationship. The team worked diligently and soon
came up with ideas, a plan of action and a marketing method to "sell"
what they did to the congregation.

The transition was overwhelmingly successful. Although there were
similar instances, they were handled in the same manner – allowing

those from our church's culture to take the lead on the changes they were initiating. I stayed there longer than any Education Director before me.

On May 16, 2011 the Kansas City Star reported that Chief Jim Corwin was retiring from the police force after serving in various capacities there for over 32 years – longer than anyone in KC since 1973. They credited him with "changing the culture" of the police department.

How did he stay in the job so long?

According to reporter Christine Vendel, in an interview with former police board president Karl Zobrist, they were looking for "someone who could communicate effectively with the public and other community leaders." The story further said, "Corwin changed the culture of the Police Department by introducing a "holistic" approach to policing, where officers work with other segments of the community, such as schools, churches and non-profits, to solve problems." He promoted transparency and community policing…" "He conducted a top to bottom examination and introduced a strategic plan and vision for the department."

That is how a great leader who wants a long, long tenure stays in his or her job. By studying, listening and acting on a strategic plan that involves the entire community and its resources to turn the situation around. By changing the way people on the street view your organization and then building on that momentum to change it from within.

So Police Chief Corwin is retiring after 32 years as a successful public servant. He basically reinvented the way the Kansas City Police Department did their business of protecting and serving the public from outside and from within. Wouldn't it be wonderful if someone wrote *your* story of changing the organizational culture crediting you with your leadership?

They still can.

First you have to understand the culture. Then you have to understand people's reactions to change. You have to know where the landmines are before you go walking through the field.

Common Reactions to Change

What I have discovered is that there are usually a set of reactions every leader needs to be aware of when changing their management culture. If you know these in advance, you will be expecting them and can plan for the "surprises" when they happen. In fact, knowing them will keep them from being "surprises."

1. **Too much change can be too much.** If you come in with a sweeping overhaul, it will ruffle more than a few feathers. People will not tolerate change after change, after change, etc. You have to progress slowly. You have to put a few wins under your belt to move the program forward. I have led "Change Management Workshops" where we asked attendees to change their appearance in an exercise numerous times. You can watch them go from playful and laughing to outright frustration when you ask them to make the 3rd and 4th set of changes. In that teachable moment we say: "People won't tolerate too much change."

2. **People will feel they lack the necessary resources when change occurs.** Change causes that kind of pressure and you will find employees, managers, supervisors and whole corporations say, "We can't do that, it costs too much, takes too much time, or requires more staffing than we have at our disposal." They'll say this, though, before they really have sat down and counted the cost of the transition. Usually the detail-oriented people are the first ones to start counting the cost. You have to get them to slow down, take a breath (maybe several over a period of time) and encourage them to take stock of what they have. They'll be quite surprised to find that the change in question isn't as "costly" as they had feared at first thought.

3. **People are at different levels of readiness for change.** Some people can't wait for "out with the old, in with the new." They are excited to see change every day in their lives. By the way, these people are rare in an organization! They can be your greatest asset, but also will drive you forward sometimes faster than you can take the entire group. They seem to constantly be in "hyper-drive" mode.

Most people though, suddenly get blurred vision and remember the "good old days." Never mind the fact that those old days weren't really that good to start with. This will polarize the group and you'll have people running in all directions. Be aware that some people will have to be led through transition by the hand while others will have to be handcuffed to keep them with the pack. Pace yourself and your community of workers.

4. **When change occurs, people will feel alienated.** "Why is this happening to me?" they'll ask. "It's worse on me than anyone else in the organization." "It always happens to me—more than others." Well it doesn't, but those are the type of reactions that are typical when the world is being turned upside down. We don't notice the pain others are going through and crave attention for ourselves only. We also fail to look to others for encouragement, or ideas. It's interesting the different view you get of the world from 32,000 feet in the air. Most of your followers are limited to their view of the world on the ground. You can show them the total vision that affects more than just them.

These are times when it is good to ask questions like, "What are you feeling right now?" "What would make this experience less threatening for you? But you must maintain the pace, or you will lose valuable momentum.

5. **When change occurs people will think about what they have to give up first.** Most people aren't completely happy with their job or surroundings until you try to change them. Suddenly, what was a problem now becomes their most treasured possession. You mention change and everyone becomes a pack-rat not wanting to lose anything. It may not be material possessions. It may be status or power that will be lost when a new organizational structure comes along. They don't see the advantages of the new way of doing things, they are happy with what they have gotten used to.

You need to "sell" the *benefits* for them that will exceed the former system. Make sure they feel like they are getting something out of the transition. Make it fun for them! Keep them happy.

6. **When the pressure is off, people will revert to their old habits.** Remember the loveable character, Sneezy in Disney's "Snow White and the Seven Dwarfs?" Someone would try to hold their finger under his nose to keep him from sneezing, but the moment they removed their finger, he would let out the biggest blow you'd ever seen. The same thing happens when change occurs in any organization. People tend to fall back on what they are comfortable with and at the first opportunity, they will.

You have to continually re-cast the vision. Keep things moving in the direction of the new changes. I noticed in workshops that when we finished the "Change Game," people immediately re-groom and primp themselves *back* to their former appearance. The lesson learned:

The minute you take the pressure off, you'll see old habits resurface.

Knowing what to expect can avert a disaster. You can be the key to making a smooth transition. Problems in change can be anticipated and your organization will benefit from the time you put into preparation.

Seven Sweatin' Questions

But change has to come by *listening* to people. Not directing them. It begins with a leader who spends time learning the existing culture and changing *within*, not *despite* the framework.

Why should you "sweat" the details while your executive team sits back cool and comfortable? That's easy. You shouldn't. If you want to realize real change in your organizational structure and culture, you need to be the one making everyone around you sweat the answers. It starts with your leadership group, management team or executive board.

What are you doing to make your executive board stretch, innovate and lose bad habits? Are they cool and calm, while you are breaking out in a sweat?

Want to see *them* work up a sweat and come up with some great answers for a change?

First realize that it's not all about hearing *you* talk. Quit squirming and blathering away about your vision and enliven your executive board with some great questions.

Quit talking *to* your board and get them *interacting* with you in a dialogue.

What kind of questions should you ask? Ask questions that make them think. Ask questions that make them develop ideas. Ask Essay Questions (Stay away from "Yes/No" answers). Ask Story Questions (Generate great stories).

Ask Sweatin' Questions!

1. **What don't you think customers/members like about what we are doing in our business right now?**

The wisdom behind the question: It starts everyone in the room thinking about people other than themselves. It gets them to see your organization from the customer's or member's view. It gets them out of their cocoon – maybe for the first time. I asked this question of a banking group in a strategic planning session. One of the managers signed up for an account as a "regular" customer. After three months, he still didn't have an ATM card. Needless to say, the senior leadership was unaware of the difficulty in simply opening an account. What would happen if the president or CEO tried to call in for themselves on the customer service line? What hoops would they have to jump through to get to a live person to answer?

2. **What has changed in our customers' buying habits in the past two years?**

The wisdom behind the question: This question gets everyone in the board room thinking about the changes in culture, the economy and their territory and how they have affected business recently. It helps them start making constructive comments about the changes (good and bad) that have affected their business. If you allow them to talk about them to the group, it begins the process of group coaching. They will say, "It's not just affecting me." Again it focuses on the customers' habits and expectations. You can use this to motivate people to change their way of thinking about pricing or value-less selling. A group of construction leaders noticed that they had more people emphasizing the price points than the value of their services when we asked this question. That was the moment they realized their sales people were trapped in a loop of falling back on price instead of delivering value and benefits to their customers.

3. **How have we become "different" to match those changes?**

The wisdom behind the question: Now you are focusing on what your organization is doing to match changes your team has already observed in your customers and members. This question asks, "Okay, you know the problem. What are you doing to fix it?" The finger-pointing now is turned inward. It makes people realize that not only are their customers and members doing less business with you, we aren't doing anything about it. I love this question because of the smiles I see on people's faces, who moments ago, were proudly proclaiming how bad the customers have had it with these challenges. It forces your leadership to seek solutions, not just gripe about problems. Now the pressure is on them to say, "Here is what I think we should do to resolve this situation for our people's best interest."

4. **How do people feel punished by our policies or practices?**

The wisdom behind the question: This is the favorite question I ask of every board or leadership team I do strategic planning with.

Even the CEOs like this one. If you thought your management group was customer focused before, this will target specific practices and policies that aggravate people who do business with you. On a call to American Express about a disputed charge, I realized that membership *doesn't* have its privileges as they used to say. When I told this to her supervisor, the sympathetic supervisor said, "I know. I am so sorry. Your same complaint is the top complaint we get from our all of our loyal members." Then why not change the policy if that is what is provoking the most negative feedback?

5. **What habits are we holding on to that are holding us back?**

The wisdom behind the question: Your organization has policies, practices, inventory (and yes, even people) that are holding you back from making a profit and achieving the results you desire. They come across to you as necessary, but to many of your staff, employees and financial advisors they are perceived as deficits. They cost you more than they are returning to your bottom line. They are keeping the organization stagnant. You think that one day they will come around, be bought by someone or come back into fashion. They won't...ever. Ask your team about every item on the agenda, "What purpose does this serve?" "How is it achieving the results we want?" Stand back and be prepared. You may not like the answers, but it will deliver hope to your leaders that you are serious about streamlining processes, making changes and getting results. It will also free them up to release some items and practices they have wanted to be freed from.

6. **Where are the "dinosaurs" in our organization/office/ policy manual?**

The wisdom behind the question: This will begin to close the loop on the practices your customers or members dislike and what you are doing to justify yourself as an organization. Your dinosaurs are extinct, but you are maintaining them. Rather than taking care of a living, breathing organism you have become the curator of a museum, limited to polishing dead bones. It is time to bury the bones. It is time to reinvent your policy manual (if you even have one). Your policies are probably outdated and not very friendly (either in practice or in delivery) to the people who mean the most to your bottom line...your customers and members. They don't care what your "manual" says. They don't care how you deal with everyone else. They care about how you deal with them and them alone. Don't you feel the same way in every business relationship, too?

7. **What are you most afraid of losing most in a change or transition?**

The wisdom behind the question: Here is the "meatiest" question you can ask a group of secure leaders. They fear losing something in a transition. They fear conceding control to someone else whom they don't trust. If you demonstrate that you are willing to release some authority to them early in the process, they are more likely to follow your model. Yes, there will always be those who can't give up the power and prestige they have worked so hard to attain. Your own board probably wouldn't come out and say it, but they like their positions and their security and don't want to share it with anyone who has new ideas or directions.

What do you think is at the root of this?

POWER in the hands of unwavering leaders is fatal.

When the pain of giving up power becomes less than the pain of extinction, they will change. They will suggest ideas that call for everything except granting control or authority. In the end it will be about surrendering their power to avoid their own demise.

Building Community at Work

Your company produces a unique culture. Leaders who invest time in their people reap rich rewards. Happy employees are productive employees. They are loyal employees. Loyal employees invite frequent customers. Customer frequency is the goal - not customer satisfaction. Solidifying a value-based relationship is the essential step in assuring customer loyalty and repeat business. Frequent customers breed other frequent customers by referrals.

Do you want to build community and profits simultaneously? You don't have to work in the private sector. You can be a public servant like retiring KC Police Chief Corwin.

How do you begin?

First, stop building a "power structure" and start building *community* among your leadership team. Celebrate the passages of life together. Make your workplace a safe harbor for people to enter and work in – to grow and share their pains and joys. Spend time walking the floors and the aisles. Go out where your people work. Come in through the front door and greet the greeters. If the reception desk is the gateway to your company either by phone or in person, invest time each day making sure that person is the most cheerful, compassionate individual in the corporation. Let them know how important they are to the success of the whole. Find ways to reward them for a job unnoticed until now.

For years people have attempted to build community in our schools, but we are a disjointed society without a lot of free time to get involved in our children's school. They have tried in neighborhoods, but most people can't name families that live two doors down the street from them. They have tried in churches, but when the most active people only attend 2-3 hours a week, you can't build a very consistent community. The place we work is where we spend most of our time every week. It contains the people we interact with more than anyone else in our lives. It is the perfect ground to grow community.

How well do your people love your company? Look at the spirit of community at Southwest Airlines. Why? They have great employee morale. Fly Southwest Airlines and you are treated great because the employees love working for Southwest. Their planes take off on time more than any other airline can boast. They don't charge you for extras. They put the customer first. Is it any reason they rank at the top of every customer service poll in the airline industry?

Apple is a company that fosters innovation and creativity within its corporate culture. Go into an Apple store and you are met with employees who love working for Apple. They have reinvented the tech store. Umair Haque, Director of the Havas Media Lab writes, "The goal of Apple Store employees is simply to show off their awesomeness, and let you share it. Love for what we do is the basis of all real value creation." Love of your company builds community at its basic level.

Community is the pathway to a successful future. Leaders who spend time studying and building community will reap the rewards of increased productivity and performance. Coach your people to be the best they can be. Reward them often and publically. Stimulate their achievement.

Easy Action Step: How can you transition to a supportive community in your workplace that encourages achievement for the group or organization? How can you reward a generation of workers who have little loyalty to you or your company? What "Sweatin' Questions" can you start asking to turn your peoples' creativity into a community of support for common goals and productivity?

Chapter 11

REINVENTING YOUR CULTURE

"The product of a company is its culture."

—Jim Mathis

The "Cult of You"

When I was in seminary studying for the ministry, the most popular elective on the campus was "Cults." Partly because of a charismatic professor and his stories about groups he had encountered, students flocked to this class. He was popular off campus as well. Constantly being sought for interviews, he was on the radio several times each month. He had something of his own cult following on campus too. His electives were the first to be filled each semester. He not only taught about cults, but pretty much had a cult following. In his class, cults were defined as "smaller groups whose beliefs differed substantially from the mainstream."

In that sense, successful corporations and organizations that reinvent themselves can be defined as cults with cult followers. Apple computers have a worldwide cult following, even though Microsoft PCs are more popular. Jaguar automobiles have a worldwide cult following, despite the price and service problem rumors that abound. Publix grocery stores have a cult following in the US, when in direct competition with less expensive stores. Tim Horton's doughnut shops have a cult following in Canada because of name recognition and national identification.

Each of these brands has individuals devoted to buying from them exclusively. Even though some have reputations that would make the average person question their value, people follow them almost religiously. And there is a religious overtone to the relationship between the brand and the followers. Have you ever noticed that the word "cult" is at the root of culture and cultivate?

The product of a company is its culture. The culture is the result of what you are putting into your organization within and what is being produced for consumers. Together, the internal "customers" and the external customers are your culture – your product. The lives you touch in both groups are your product in addition to the goods and services you provide. To bring about a positive culture, you need to see the culture as your true product, with the goods and services supporting the culture and vice-versa.

To have a positive culture you need to start with your own cult. It means you need to form your own cult. You can begin internally with your small group of devoted employees and customers and build on that. You can begin externally with social media as well. Social media is the place many people are forming their tribes and cults today. LinkedIn groups, Face Book Fan pages, You Tube and Twitter are attracting groups, fans, subscribers and relationships. Aren't people who decide to become a part of your group on "Twitter" called "followers?" Twitter already has the "cult of you" structure in place for you to build a following. What do you have in place?

To have a positive culture you need to start with your own cult. It means you have to form your own group. You can begin with your small group of devoted employees and customers and build on that. You can begin externally with social media (aren't people in your group on "Twitter" called "followers?"). No matter what the mainstream is saying, your "cult" stays with you. John Maxwell says, "A leader who says he has followers and doesn't have any is merely someone taking a walk." How do you keep yourself from "merely taking a walk?" To cultivate relationships within and from without your organization, you have to start with a cult of followers who are devoted to "the cult of you."

Not all cultures are started the same way. Many companies will generate a following by signing customers up for their membership club or rewards/loyalty program. I am a member of several from my bookstore, to my office supply distributor, to my grocers and even to Starbucks. They offer rewards for doing business with them. Delta Airlines gives Skymiles to frequent flyers. Hilton Hotels gives Honor Points to their most active travelers. Office Max has "Max Perks" for business rewards. Hertz Rental Cars have a Number 1 Gold Club for their loyal customers. All of these companies are rewarding faithful service and generating a cult of followers.

But not everyone has a perks program for their followers. Not every company can afford to give away free trips, rental deals or a cup of coffee. Some of us are just working within the company and can't come up with a perks program (and accompanying budget) to reward our top consumers. We have to rely on how we treat them to build our follower list.

If you want to cultivate customers and have them faithfully follow your brand, products and services you need to develop culture that meets peoples' needs - both internally and externally. A company's culture is the traditions and practices that it is known for by employees, staff and customers. It is the product of the company in the truest sense of the word. What is the culture of your company? It goes beyond your name. Every year, *Fortune* magazine chooses the best places to work. Smuckers is a fun place to be employed and they were chosen several years ago as the Number 1 place to work by *Fortune*.

How do you know you need to reinvent your culture? Easy. When your system gets so costly or oppressive that people start leaving or distancing themselves from you as workers or customers, you need to reinvent your culture. It is that simple. When it is costing you more in any way to keep the culture as it is than to change it for the better, it is time for a cultural reinvention.

Case in point: In 1986 the Soviet Union under Mikhail Gorbachev suffered the fatal accident at Chernobyl – a nuclear accident that killed hundreds and critically injured thousands. A cloud of uranium-laced dust swept over Eastern Europe and threatened the West. In the wake of this terrible tragedy, Gorbachev called for Perestroika (Openness). The Soviet Union had become so oppressive and hushed in its culture that people were dying to keep cover-ups.

The Soviet economy was practically busted and the Soviet leader knew he needed to reach out to others in order to survive as a nation. In essence, he reinvented the Soviet Union. The upside was the fall of Russian communism. The down side was his own leadership. Gorbachev fell victim to the openness he insisted on and was forced from office in a few years. The changes he advocated helped millions but were more than he could handle personally.

You won't be forced from office if you stay ahead of and drive the changes in your culture, but the warning is that you have to play an active role as a leader or you will be swept out as irrelevant when the changes come. It is important to know the territory and the players at each step of the way. It is important that you remain the visionary and be seen out in front taking the lead and personally making the changes. Otherwise you will lose credibility with your following, be they internal or external. The people you appoint to be in charge must be trustworthy and have faith in you and your vision. Your cult must follow you and the vision you continually cast.

I have identified two methods you can use to develop the "Cult of You." First we will deal with generating it from within – that is developing the cultural reinvention inside your organization. Then we will examine external cultural reinvention with your customer base. So how do you promote culture from within?

Internal Culture Reinvention

Even if you aren't aware of it, your company has a culture with traditions, habits, taboos and unwritten policies. There are subjects people just don't discuss openly. There are stories told about former employees, former supervisors and even you. There are vendettas, resentments and unappreciated contributions lurking around certain corners in the office. There are rules that aren't in writing, but they are more powerful than the ones that are recorded.

Your people tell them to each other year after year and pass them along to new employees, once they have checked them out and approved them (another unwritten policy) to stay. The new crop of trainees has already been indoctrinated with them.

But much worse, these are most often revealed to customers both verbally and non-verbally. They are given away with looks, glances, rolling of the eyes and outright truth-telling. The most dangerous employee is one who is assisting your competitors by driving your business away. They are sabotaging your customers with stories that support their claims of poor service. "You think this is bad? Let me tell you what it is like working for him…." Get the picture? You can do what you like, but these stories persist.

Believe this: your customers know whether your people like working for you. Have you ever been tipped off by an employee as to how they don't like their job? Has anyone ever complained about their company to you? What was your reaction as a customer? Did you keep the same opinion of the company or their boss they told you about? Constant nagging, complaining or poor attitudes with customers are signs that your culture is terrible and in need of reinvention. If you don't know it yet, trust me, your customers do. They get it regularly from your own people.

Adding new employees either enriches or discourages this culture. It adds to the stories and takes away from them. But it continues the traditions and tales just like a family passes its heritage along to each new generation. Like it or not, this is your company culture and it permeates the relationship every employee has with one another and the customers.

However, companies who generate openness and positive feedback from their employees have positive cultures. They have people lining up to work for them. They have staff who enjoy what they do and supporting the CEOs and company's goals. It can be felt by everyone who calls in, comes in or visits their web site.

A successful organization I worked with who made an internal cultural change started by holding town hall meetings with employees and staff. They were asked to tell what they felt would improve customer service based on their experiences with the customers. After all, who knew more about what customers want or feel than the people dealing directly with them? Often the suggestions of sales and service personnel are ignored when they have more actual experience with customers.

What does all this say about what you can do to transform your company culture? It says that you need to be in tune with the goings-on in your own organization. It says that you need to connect – not merely communicate. It says that you need to wander around to get a clue about what is happening on your watch. It says, "Wake up to the real world of your company culture!"

First what type of self-examination process do you perform? Do you do it on a regular basis? Do you have any idea what the people working for you know or do? Do you have their pulse? How well do you know your culture? What research have you put together to gather insider information from trusted sources within your own organization? Do you connect with your people on a personal level?

While strategizing with a group of sales leaders and CEOs in Toronto last month I asked them to discuss habits and beliefs they need to let go of to move forward. One sales manager reported after the discussion that he was going to let go of the weekly sales meeting. With a sad expression he told the group that he found out that his sales people hated the weekly events. They told him the weekly meetings were stifling their creativity.

He never realized what a drain it was on the morale and efforts of his account executives. Following the meeting he decided to start holding regular "town hall" meetings to get feedback he had been missing.

CBS Network premiered a new television show in 2010 airing immediately after the Super Bowl that had corporate board rooms trembling. The name? Undercover Boss. It is based on a British series of the same name. Each episode of the show features a senior executive at a major corporation, working incognito as a new entry-level hire in his or her company for one week, to find out how the company really works (including the impact of "corporate policy") and identify some of the unsung heroes among the employees. CEOs of Waste Management, Hooters, 7 Eleven and White Castle were some of the first to slip out of their suits and work the front lines.

What they discovered about the company culture and their own reputations shook their corporate world. Their policies weren't being implemented. Their people didn't respect them. "I always thought everyone liked working for me." several bosses said. "I never cared what they thought…until now," another admitted. They learned that they hadn't been communicating because they weren't connecting with their organizations. They learned through the Undercover Boss experience to connect with their people.

Lack of connection is a major culture killer. Iain McMath, managing director of services firm Sodexo Motivation Solutions Ltd. of England, says his company's revenue grew 19% last year because of a faster delivery of products as a result of changing the culture around communication within the workplace. By identifying the different ways individuals in his company preferred to communicate, Mr. McMath says his team has been able to speed up decision making. "I do things based on intuition, so when I meet with my financial director I only need a one-page summary.

She, on the other hand, was coming to the meetings with a file of 600 pages. We were coming to the same conversation but with different angles," Mr. McMath says. He was miscommunicating because they weren't connecting on what he really needed from her. What ways are you forcing people to communicate rather than connect within your organization? More was discussed about this in the chapter on *Reinventing Your Management*, but suffice to say that your own people know what will make it a better, more efficient workplace. They are brilliant and intuitive. Release their creativity and you will tap an untold wealth of experience and knowledge. It will relieve them to know that their input is making a difference as well.

External Cultural Reinvention

The second method for reinventing your culture is changing how your followers view you, your product and services. Your customers have a culture as well. They are your followers, your tribe, your devotees. They either love doing business with you and your style or can't stand it. If they like you, they follow you. They create their own stories about how you helped them or solved their problems. They also tell stories about how bad you treated them. The good news though is that as long as they are talking to you, be it complimenting or complaining, they are part of your cult of followers.

Your movement is at the heart of your external cultural reinvention. What is the movement you are creating among your followers? It may be as big as the desire for independence in Tiananmen Square, or as small as everyone who likes whole bean roasted coffee in Little Rock, Arkansas. It may be only a micro-movement, but you have a movement that people want to follow. So how do you reinvent your culture to identify the followers for your movement? There are four easy steps every leader can take to reinvent their culture.

First, to develop your culture, you need to publish your beliefs – your manifesto. Give it away. Allow others to spread it for free. Use social media to expound on your ideas and mantra. I publish a monthly e-zine and allow anyone to sign up without giving all of their personal information to me. I also allow anyone at any time to reprint my articles each month for free, asking only that they give me original credit for the material. This makes culture reinvention easier for my followers and gets my message before more people with each contact they make.

"Cult" leaders make it easy to add followers. It could be as easy as connecting with you on Face Book or subscribing to your newsletter. I use every opportunity to subscribe to my monthly newsletter (subscribe@ jimmathis.com). They do more than just communicate. How well do you connect with your customers? The big buzz today is social media. Everyone is trying to get an edge in communicating with their customers. I don't think the name of the game is communicating. It is connecting. When you know what people are buying from you and what they are saying about it, you are connecting with them. When you know how your customers feel and what is in their hearts you are connecting. How well do you connect with your people?

Third, make it easy for your followers to connect with each other. Allow them to communicate and connect with each other. It is a great experience to meet someone in the Hilton Honors lounge or waiting for their automobile to be serviced in a Lexus dealership. It creates community within the culture. Cultural reinventionists create those moments and make them available for everyone in the community to connect with each other.

Fourth, what are you doing to make your cult exclusive? Can just anyone get in? Exclusivity makes your group more attractive to outsiders. People want to feel special and set apart. The move exclusive the group, the more people will want to join and be a part of it. It's as if who isn't part of your group is more important than who is…for instance, we stayed at a resort in Mexico on vacation one time. We got a deal through our timeshare. When we got there, my wife noticed a "caste system" in place. There was a hierarchy of services available to people based on how much they were willing to pay. Almost everyone wanted to be in the "Select Club" regardless of the increased sales pitches you had to endure just to join. Exclusivity was the goal.

Here are two examples of cultural transformation: one negative, the other positive: Comcast Cable the United States' largest cable television provider, long maligned for poor customer service announced in February, 2010 they were changing their name. The giant monopoly decided it would simply change its name to make things right with consumers. Why not? After all, the name "Comcast" has become nearly synonymous with poor service. There is an entire web site called www.comcastsucks.com. The February 2010 issue of *Consumer Reports* gave Comcast the following poor marks:

- No. 14 out of 16 for television service

- No. 19 out of 23 for phone service

- No. 23 out of 27 for Internet service

- No. 11 out of 12 for bundled services

So rather than reinvent their business model, implement cultural change within the corporation and improve their customer service, Comcast planned to only change its name to Xfinity later that year! A name change didn't work for tobacco giant Philip Morris (now Atria) or the SciFi Channel (went for the name "syfy," which they found out was a slang term in most parts of the world for syphilis). Will people forget their surly and inconsiderate representatives? Probably not, but the web site disgruntled customers purchased to protest their rudeness will probably now be changed to xfinitysucks.com.

Your culture is either promoting you or killing you. It is driving people closer to your brand or driving them away. Merely changing your name won't help. It has to come from inside. Your culture is both what is within and without of your bounds. It has its own identity. It breathes life into you and inhales your creativity.

The Grateful Dead rock band knew something about cultural transformation. They remain one of the most popular musical groups. Their tours sell out huge arenas. They made over $100 million in their lifetime. They have a following, the "Deadheads" who will go to any lengths to attend their concerts. Yet they only recorded one album that was listed in the Top 40. They weren't selling records though; they were creating a cultural phenomenon. Remember what I said earlier about allowing your cultural followers to interact with each other? When one Deadhead says "2-14-70," it's like a secret code that only other members of the movement understand.

As I write this I am listening to a Jimmy Buffett concert broadcast live on "Radio Margaritaville." The culture that Jimmy has stays with him and grows every year by leaps and bounds. Everyone seems to know the words to the songs. When he says, "Fins up!" everyone knows what he means to do and what song is coming next. Although he writes new songs every year, his community loves the culture he has developed around his brand.

Jimmy Buffett has throngs of followers called "Parrotheads." They know the motions to specific songs, dress like a day at the beach for the tailgate parties that precede his concerts and know all the words to his hit songs. Yet Buffett has only had one Number 1 hit song (and it isn't *Margartaville*). He has only been awarded one Grammy award. But he sells out arenas the day his tickets go on sale. His chain of international restaurants and gift shops are as strong as ever. He began Radio Margaritaville as an internet phenomenon and has carried it to satellite radio and Dish TV. His cult following is well entrenched. It is more than an experience, it's a feeding frenzy!

I know from personal experience what it means to reinvent my culture. I spent a miserable year with a high-speed internet provider. I called the company at least once a week to complain because our high-speed internet wouldn't function properly. They tried to fix it on the phone, in person and over the line. Each time they blamed my equipment, not there's. Finally I had enough of being told that there was nothing wrong with their system (an excuse several friends told me they got as well) and I quit complaining to them. Do you know why? I took my business elsewhere. Their culture of blaming the customer finally ran me off. I quit communicating and connecting with them and it ended the business relationship. I hear they moved on.

But sometimes you have to reinvent the message. I had to reinvent my message a year ago. I was blessed that three book publishers approached me within a few months about writing a book on reinventing yourself (you see who won the race!). It was a struggle to reinvent the message. It would have been easier to find a new audience to hear the same message, but I was restless and wanted to change the message. I am glad I did!

The Whole Foods grocery chain has a cult following. They rarely build one of their green, earth-friendly grocery stores in areas where there isn't a base for support for their message of organic foods. Yes, they charge a lot (in fact, in Atlanta their nickname is "Whole Paycheck."). But their followers will go miles to shop in their big box-style grocery stores. They reinvented the message of grocery stores. Now they have acquired a cult following that will pay more and drive farther to shop and protect the earth at the same time. Are they a big corporation? Yes. They have followers who hate big corporations, but like what this one is doing for organically grown plants, unfettered animals and environmental-friendly business practices.

Social media has taken the front seat at most conventions and conferences I have attended. Most people who are using it aren't making much money, but it is a new and different method of connecting with your followers. You can use Twitter, LinkedIn, Face Book and a newsletter to connect with a set group of followers who give you permission to market to them. Once they follow, link up, befriend or sign up for your service you have them in your database and your culture.

I have even gotten into the act. Several years ago I developed my monthly newsletter list (subscribe@jimmathis.com) which continues to grow as you read this. In the past year I created both a Face Book Fan Page and LinkedIn group for my followers (The Reinvention Strategist). Why create a Fan Page or a LinkedIn group? It's a way to identify your loyal customers and friends. It also allows you to market to a direct group of people who have given you permission to interrupt them with your information. These are just some of the basic, easy tools you can use to begin to develop a following or loyal customer base to connect with.

So what is the culture that you generate with your followers? Are they followers or merely clients? I spoke with an office products sales account executive in Canada who decided after a strategy session that she no longer wanted to look on her "cult" as simply accounts but as people who depend on her problem solving in their lives. She gets it.

Ford Motors' Cultural Transformation

Your culture is determined both by you and your customers. It's not one or the other, but both. What you do internally directly affects what your customers and the general public perception about your business culture. For instance, Ford Motor Company has undergone an amazing transformation recently under the guidance of CEO Alan Mulally. If it continues, Mr. Mulally will be credited with one of the great turnarounds in corporate history. It all began internally.

Pulitzer Prize winning author Paul Ingrassia noted in the Wall Street Journal, "Ford's recent success is already amazing considering the prior half-dozen years of near-fatal decline. Mulally's method has been to simplify, relentlessly and systematically, a business that had grown way too complicated and costly to be managed effectively.

"Improve Focus, Simplify Operations," reads one of Mr. Mulally's many charts, which he repeats like a sacred mantra in staff meetings. Soon after his arrival Ford began shedding brands—Jaguar, Land Rover and Aston Martin among them—that the company couldn't afford to support. At the time of this writing another brand may be in line to go (Ford announced in June 2010 that Mercury would be the next company to cease production within the next year). Meanwhile, the core Ford brand got an investment infusion to replace aging cars and revive a model lineup that had been heavily tilted toward gas-guzzling trucks.

In the process, Ford reduced its number of global platforms (known as "chassis") from more than 20 down to eight, and the number of nameplates from 97 to 25. Each platform and model involves hundreds of millions of dollars of engineering costs, which translated to billions of losses because Ford couldn't sell enough of each model.

But the real cultural transformation occurred at the top, where Mulally overhauled the "often-contentious culture" in Ford's executive suite. Most of his appointees are company veterans, but they're the sort of people who typically got overlooked when style seemed to count more than substance, as in the past history at Ford.

Product-development chief Derrick Kuzak, for example, was not as charismatic as the very flamboyant Bob Lutz, who held the same job at GM for most of the past decade. But Mr. Kuzak is methodically implementing a strategy of developing cars in a single region (say Europe, or North America) and selling them globally, instead of developing slightly different cars in each region at enormous extra cost.

And what is the result in company culture of Ford? Internal surveys show 87% of Ford employees believe the company is on the right track. President Barack Obama would love numbers like that. What CEO bringing his company back from the edge of extinction wouldn't? And the public has noticed and loved the fact that Ford did all this without taking any government stimulus aid or bailout money. Ford seems to have caught the wave of self sustainability while its rivals were begging for public tax dollars to stay afloat.

Ford also has gotten big boosts from the missteps of its major rivals. GM, in contrast to Ford, insisted on keeping all of its eight brands until the government, who held the "lien" on the company forced it to shed four of them last year in bankruptcy. And Toyota's safety problems in early 2010 assisted Ford as well. The Japanese company's legendary quality has been slipping below Ford's for the past few years, according to Consumer Reports magazine. And this was before the furor over sudden, unintended gas pedal malfunctions.

Culture Reinvention Strategy

Cultural reinvention leaders concentrate on building a culture of positive affirmation and support. They work within their organizations to listen to the hearts of their people and generate positive stories. They encourage story telling among their followers.

If you want to reinvent your company culture you have to start with your style and attitude. Are you attracting positive people and positive experiences? Remember, the more eccentric you are, the more the animosity you create among your followers. The more eccentric you are, the less you connect with your followers. When cults go bad the connection between the leader and the followers falls apart.

We have all heard of cult leaders who failed to connect with followers and the real world at the same time. They either connected with their people and not the real world, or connected with the world and not their people. You can do both. Great leaders always have.

Winston Churchill had a cult following because he connected with the people of Great Britain and they felt the connection. He could paint a true and positive picture of the real world to everyone. He never said conquering the Nazis would be easy. "We shall fight on the beaches, we shall fight on the landing grounds, we shall fight in the fields and in the streets..." But he went on to say, "if the British Empire and its Commonwealth last for a thousand years, men will still say: 'This was their finest hour'." That message connected. Notice that he related it to what people would say about their place in history - in a thousand years.

Finally you have to tell the stories of your successes to get your people to start telling those stories. Marketing is all about telling stories. Marketing used to be about expensive advertising. It was determined by who had the largest budget and marketing team. The internet has broadened the scope and leveled the playing field. Today marketing is much cheaper. It tells what we make and whom we serve. It elects presidents, fires CEOs, raises money for earthquake victims and drives the market. Today, marketing is engaging your culture and delivering products and services with stories that spread.

What are you doing to generate great stories within your culture? Instead of useless meetings, many leaders today are using the power of positive stories and experiences within their organization to generate a positive company culture. Use gatherings like awards banquets to tell the stories of victory and success within your organization.

Finally, generate positive stories among your customers. Energize your base and give them permission to energize others. Get testimonials. Put them on your web site. Put them in your marketing materials. Plaster them in front of your people. As the stories are told and re-told, they will generate the same momentum the negative ones have been generating. Consequently, you will have a positive culture of people who will follow you anywhere.

Easy Action Step: How can you develop the "Cult of You?"

Chapter 12

REINVENTING YOUR SALES

People Buy Where They Perceive Value

"Who can say what a competitor will be in a couple of years, in a world where Apple is a dominant force in music, Wal-Mart is a doctor's office and Amazon is your source for supercomputing?"

—Quentin Hardy

Controversy at the 2010 Winter Olympics

I enjoyed watching the Olympic Winter Games in Vancouver, BC. The men's ice skating competition this year featured a stirring upset by American figure skater Evan Lysacek over many great skaters, including Russian Yevgeny Plushenko. Plushenko had come out of retirement to try for his second consecutive Olympic Gold Medal – an unprecedented accomplishment for over 60 years. His signature skating move was the quadruple jump. "You can't be considered a true men's champion without a quad," the 27-year-old told worldwide sports reporters.

But win gold without a quad you can.

Why? The quad wasn't what the judges looked for alone. Sure it is impressive to anyone, but these judges used ALL of the skaters' moves to make their decision. The judges weren't buying Plushenko's quad as the differentiator. Instead, Lysacek "sold" them what they were "buying."

Rather than attempting a quadruple jump, Lysacek instead wowed the judges with artistry and flawless footwork.

That's when it occurred to me, "Duh!" The judges had well-publicized their expectations for what they were seeking in a Gold Medal performance – and it wasn't being determined by the skaters. The judges set the standard, not the competitors. In doing so, they did what customers do every day when they make decisions about purchasing what they want.

The truth is that nobody buys what you and I sell. They buy on the value they perceive.

Customers determine what they want and all the interruptions you and I throw in front of them don't sway them from knowing what they want. A reader emailed me after I wrote a blog post on this subject, arguing that "customers are dumb and don't really know what they want". I regret that he feels this way, but he has fallen victim to the lies that terrible marketers tell to try to convince us to push our products harder and harder.

When was the last time you saw an advertisement on television that attempted to push you into buying a product or service? Most advertising is called 'interruption advertising." It interrupts our daily routine. We are watching a television program or listening to the radio. It comes into our computer inbox as SPAM. It comes in the form of a telephone call at an inopportune moment. In the interruption, we are enticed to change our thought or belief patterns to buy a product or service that the advertiser wants to convince us we need. Suddenly we are made to feel inadequate, unattractive, incompetent or incomplete without this "necessary" item. Whether it is a car dealer, a time-share telemarketer, a beauty aid consultant, a grocery store or a girl scout selling cookies, we find ourselves being forced into their way of thinking.

The reality is this process is the hardest way to sell a product or service. The easiest way to sell is to find out what people already want to buy and sell that to them. What if you got out of bed and knew what people wanted to buy from you? What if you marketed a product that people would hand you money for without even thinking about the cost to them? What if you knew for certain what people buy?

What Do People Buy?

I was talking with some leaders about six months ago in the Closet and Storage industry. They were discussing a new product they offer to customers. It's called "A Closet In A Day." The idea is that you need a closet, you call them on the phone and within 24 hours you have a fully constructed closet in your home. We were discussing how they could market this unique service to their customers. It started us to think about what they are really selling. I may need a closet, and having a one-day response time is great. But when you tell me you are going to install a closet in a day, it conjures up images of sawdust, dry wall pieces, nails, paint and guys with dirty shoes tramping in and out of my bedroom all day long. "Now," I said, "you tell me that I can call you on the phone and within 24 hours I will have a nice, neat, organized space to hang my clothes, I would buy that." Are these both the same thing? Yes and no. We also got the idea of servicing the closets – offering consulting in organizing and un-cluttering to their customers.

People buy the value they perceive. We have become very resistant to high-pressure sales. We are bombarded by ads from every direction. NBC television network now puts advertisements in the shows they televise. On the hit show *The Office* it is common to see the crew sending out for Subway sandwiches, or drinking a Coca Cola with the label turned in full view of the camera. Our mailboxes are filled with direct mail flyers almost on a daily basis. Our email inboxes are glutted with unwanted SPAM ads for high income home-based job opportunities, sexual enhancement, and promises of miracle weight loss – both real and bogus. The average consumer doesn't like having their daily routine interrupted by someone trying to make a fast buck at their expense. We have become so hard shelled against sales techniques that we use the terms: sales weasel, used car dealers and sleazy salesmen to describe the bad experiences we have had.

But people do buy things every day. So what do people buy? Well, for one thing, it isn't what we sell to them. No one likes to be sold something. Did you wake up today and say, "I hope someone tries to sell me something today."? Our initial reaction to a sales situation is resistance. Whether it is a telemarketer on the phone, an advertisement on television, a SPAM email message or even a girl scout at your front door, we don't like being sold something. It is an interruption and often a product that we really don't feel we want or need. We just don't like to be sold.

The problem is that as market leaders we get so involved in our product and trying to push it to customers; we don't see what people are really buying. Consumers will buy what they buy. Academics have described this different concept of a market as 'a market space'. They buy what they want. For instance, children's playtime is a market space; a doll is a product. Family market space is affordable transportation; a car is a product. Pet owners want companionship (market space), not a dog or cat (product). Travelers want a comfortable bed and local experience, not a hotel room. Executives want a superior image, not a suit of clothes.

Economist.com, an internet blog says, "When IBM was king of the mainframe computer market, it came to understand just in time that 100% of a market that was rapidly shrinking would soon be 100% of nothing." What its customers really wanted was not mainframe computers as such, but rather the power to process information electronically. That is true market space.

It's not about price. It's about the value of your product to the customer. I had an office products leader in Canada tell me after a strategizing session, "You can't beat me on value." He understands that pricing is a trap that you get into with your competitors and lose on every time. If the discussion is down to price you will lose the battle. If you can provide better value, you will win, no matter what the price. While speaking with a group of building materials dealers I heard one say in a panel discussion, "I will pay more for an item, if I have a good relationship with the vendor." He buys on the value of his relationship, not the price. His vendor was in the room and couldn't have paid for a better endorsement in front of his peers.

Don't allow the customer to turn the conversation into a pricing one. Sell the value he or she is looking to buy and you will always produce success. Understand that people aren't always buying your product; they are buying what it does for them – the value. They aren't buying car parts; they are buying "Keeping their clunker running." They aren't buying a health care facility; they are buying "Great food in retirement." They aren't buying a camera; they are buying "Memories for years to come."

Interviewing chamber of commerce executives last summer, I asked what they sell. Their answer was memberships. They constantly seek out new members to join the chamber and pay their dues to keep the chamber solvent. But as a chamber member, I don't buy membership. I want to network with other business leaders who would be interested in hiring me for their businesses. I want access to the chamber directory of members so I can network and target my marketing. To the chamber executives this is membership; to me as a business leader, it is potential business. No, I don't want to join. Yes, I want access to a superior list of business leaders in need of my services. See the difference?

One of the latest movements to surface has been Customer Relationship Management, commonly known as CRM. CRM is a way of designing structures and systems so that they are focused on providing consumers with what they want, rather than on what a company wants them to want. It usually involves a restructuring of the company's marketing systems and a reorganization of its staff. Market leaders have to ingrain the notion in their employees' minds that the customer's wants supersede their desire to just sell the product.

Go into any HH Gregg and you will see an organization bent on hard selling and making a profit - where salespeople attack you out of greed. Or you get the other extreme, as editor Sarah Green put it, "Best Buy - where you wander around for a full half-hour unable to find anyone to help you before you finally get the attention of some blue-shirted 12-year old who turns out to know nothing about the products she sells and ultimately end up committing hara-kiri with a Wii controller". *Their* goal is to sell.

Last month I was in a meeting of small town newspaper editors. They had met to discuss how to improve sales during economic hard times. These really are tough times for newspapers. With the advent of cable news and up-to-the-minute reports, fewer people are subscribing to their services. The internet has made a major dent in the newspaper industry. Their main source of income has been corporate advertisers and individuals who buy personal ads. The Craig's List internet site has dealt a major blow to the newspaper industry. They told me their greatest concern in selling ads was that their clients don't buy ads from them as much as before.

The publishers though get bogged down in selling advertising space. They spend most of their valuable time trying to convince businesses in the community that advertising is their best value. Often this is futile. Companies say they don't have the marketing money, the vision that a newspaper can assist them or they aren't looking for "advertising." "What are your customers looking for?" I asked. "Our customers buy access to a subscriber base that wants to use their service," one of them responded. "Then sell them that!" Concentrate on WHY people buy your product or service, not the product or service itself.

Marketing Value

We buy the results of what a product provides for us. Marketing leader Thom Winninger says that people buy the action (what a product does), not the service. When we call a travel agent, we don't buy an airline seat, we buy the destination. This is why smart travel agents are selling the destination now to stay in business. Leading Travel agencies are coming up with lists of things to do when they book a trip or vacation. They say, "When you go to _____ there are five things you HAVE to do there." Now that airline seat has become the delivery of the destination, rather than the end in itself. The value of the seat has just increased exponentially.

This would have worked great for the spa my wife and I went to at a resort in Mexico. They are being beat out by a cheaper group, not associated with the resort and located directly on the beach. Instead of a value-based marketing campaign the beach is littered with warnings that these people are not official staff and not guaranteed. The spa owner could instead publicize his/her services at check-in as one of the "must-dos" at the resort and sign people up before they ever get to the beach. They could even offer discounts for signing up at registration – a much better alternative than negative warnings on their own beach. It also occurred to us that the *owners* could have furnished their services on the part of the resort's beach as well. "Want to relax after your long trip here? We can help you begin NOW." Unfortunately they are selling a spa and not relaxation – the top reason most people go to a beach resort in the first place.

So the better you can convey what your product or service does for people, the better chance it has of selling. This is where value marketing comes in. You need to learn how to describe what your product or service does for consumers in a unique way that nobody else is doing. If it does something extra, then so much the better. When everybody else is doing it, then you have to be different, or find a distinction that sets you apart.

Really, what is the difference between screw drivers? Yet Craftsman and Stanley have been at it for years trying to convince you that their products are different and better. So they guarantee them for the rest of your life. When was the last time you needed a lifetime guarantee for a screwdriver? On the flip side, though, we buy appliances and electronics that have certain features on them that others don't. Why? Because they differentiated themselves from the rest of the pack.

Umair Haque, Director of Havas media Lab says, "Nokia, Motorola, and Sony tried for a decade to 'add value' to their phones — yet not a single feature did. Food producers and pharmaceutical companies claim they're 'adding value', but mostly they're just mega-marketing. The vast majority of companies — in my research, greater than 95% — can only create what I have termed thin value. Thick value is real, meaningful, and sustainable. It happens by making people authentically better off — not merely by adding more bells and whistles that your boss might like, but that cause customers to roll their eyes." Excitement generated by consumer wants and needs is your goal. Customer satisfaction determines the ultimate value in the end.

You can do all the fancy marketing you want to do, but people still buy on the value they perceive. So you have to reposition your service or product to match what they are buying. People buy automobile insurance because they want to have a safe bet in case something bad happens, not because a lizard told them to do it. They buy film because they want better memories, not because the package was brighter. They buy from McDonald's because their kids are hooked and it is fast and convenient, not because they felt the quality of the food was an epicurean's delight.

I bought the services of a web designer last year. I interviewed a half dozen. I went with him not because of price or elaborate designs; but because he could do exactly what I wanted and communicated that to me in a short, easy-to-understand manner. He got my business. If few people are buying your service or product, you stink as a sales person. Really. You haven't tapped into what people are buying. You are trying to get them to buy your service/product based on YOUR opinion of it – not theirs. Why do you think that the more you force people to hear what you are selling the more they will buy? It won't happen. Find out what people want to buy and orient your product or service to their buying habits or desires.

Who is Directing the Marketplace?

Remember the reader at the beginning of the chapter who emailed me saying "blah blah blah?" When assuming that your customers, and/or the general populace are stupid, you indicate your sales approach. The dumber you assume people are, the more you will push what you want over their needs and desires. The smarter you know they are, the more you will endeavor to sell what they tell you they want.

A market leader's goal should be to design their marketing and sales approach to what the customer values. This is contrary to the product-oriented way in which most firms grew up, when divisions and business units were built around products and product groups. It was not then unusual for each group to have its own service department, its own IT unit and its own marketing team. People who worked for these vertically integrated "silos" were often competing as much against other silos within the same organization as against outside rivals in the marketplace (us vs. us). Their loyalty to their silo frequently blinded them to the wider interests of the company and the consumer as a whole.

What about putting structures and systems in place that cut across the vertical lines of the traditional firm and focus on individual customers? Before CRM was introduced, customers might be approached by the same firm in several different product guises over a short period. No one department or divisions within the firm would know (or care) what any other was doing at any particular time.

Today the focus on the customer's need for a service and not just a product is influencing more and more companies. These organizations want to regard their customers as customers for life and not just as the one-off purchasers of a product —it is far less expensive to retain an existing customer than it is to acquire a new one. It then becomes important to measure a customer's lifetime value, and to think about cross-subsidizing different periods in their lives. Banks make little or no money out of their student customers, for example, in the hope that they will become more valuable in later years.

Customer value satisfactions dictate the market, not the sellers' opinions or concerns. Customers determine what is successful and what isn't. In 1958, the Edsel was one of the most luxurious cars Ford ever built. It came with options that only the most discerning and wealthy Ford customers would want. But the public thought it looked ugly. Perception became reality. The car wound up being a major flop and embarrassment for the Ford Motor Company. Today the car named for Henry Ford's son is synonymous with failure.

A few years later, in 1964 under the leadership of Lee Iacocca, Ford premiered the Mustang, the world's first fully customizable sports car. It was (and still is) an overwhelming success. The public bought into the image of a car for the "me" generation that they could customize and call their own. The car became a collector's item, still featured in movies and television. An entire industry has been built around buying and restoring mid-'60s Ford Mustangs. I know; I restored a classic Mustang myself.

Customer values dictate the market, make no mistake. And customer purpose helps determine what will succeed and what will fail. So WHY customers buy your product is more important than whether they buy. Because if you know why your product sells, then you can sell more to people who want it. Let's look at the takeout pizza industry, for example. If you want a *good* takeout pizza, you order from Pizza Hut or Papa John's. If you want a *fast* pizza, you order from Domino's. Again, Thom Winninger tells that Tom Monahan tapped into the idea of fast pizza delivery over quality and cornered the market. If you ask him what he does, he will answer that he is in the pizza *delivery* business, not the pizza business. He sells only to people who want their pizzas hot and now!

What is the difference between Hershey's chocolate bar and a Ghirardelli chocolate bar? As far as the chocolate consistency is concerned, there is no difference. Both are milk chocolate in about the same consistency. The difference is in their purpose. We buy a Hershey's bar to eat it. We buy a Ghirardelli bar to give it to someone as a gift – so it is wrapped in nice packaging…with a bow on top. Hershey's is for people who want to eat chocolate. Ghirardelli is for people who want to give chocolate to someone special. Basically, Ghirardelli is giving the chocolate away. They charge for the bow and nice wrapping it comes in. Hershey's sells to anyone who wants to eat chocolate. Ghirardelli sells only to people who want to give chocolate in a nice package. Specialization allows them to charge more. In a sense you could say that their target market is only people who want to pay more for the same chocolate. Who do you sell to "only"?

Lady Gaga on Buying Trends

If a market leader can find out what people are buying and why, success is guaranteed. A friend in the speaking business was telling me that she taught executives how to dress for success. She helps leaders create a great first impression. She said that her greatest challenge lies in convincing her prospects that her service is needed and that *she* is the best one to deliver it. But what if you marketed only to people who already saw the value in your service? What if you targeted those people who were already of a persuasion to know the importance of a great first impression in dress and demeanor? Wouldn't that make the sales process easier? All you would need to do then is convince these people that you were their best choice. This cuts the sales process in half. Sell what people already want to buy and stop selling what you think they should buy.

The pop singer Lady Gaga is phenomenal at selling what people want. I took my daughters to a Lady Gaga concert a few months ago. Wow! What a show! I didn't go in with them, of course, but their description was phenomenal. They were tweeting during the concert - in a day when we are told to turn our cell phones off during presentations. She called a lucky fan out during the presentation who texted her (it was like a prize drawing) to meet with her after the concert for "hot cocoa."

As Andrew Hampp put it in a recent article for <u>Advertising Age</u>, "Lady Gaga, with her army of nearly 2.8 million Twitter followers and more than 5.2 million Facebook fans, can move product. Since fall 2008, her digital-single sales have exceeded 20 million and her album sales hit 8 million, all at a time when no one under the age of 60 buys CDs anymore." She delivers what the public wants… in waves. The premiere of her video for "Bad Romance" debuted on LadyGaga.com *before* MTV or any other service outlet could play or publish it — resulting in a server crash, a Twitter trending topic that lasted a week and 110 million (so far) views on YouTube, more than any viral music video in the past.

What makes Lady Gaga so popular? Simple. She sells what she knows people want to buy. Music fans are buying the extravaganza (did you see her intro at the Grammy awards with Sir Elton John?). They are buying the image. They are buying the show. They are buying an onstage performance that would make Alice Cooper say, "Wow!" They are buying what she delivers. Why aren't more performers selling as many albums or digital singles? Because they aren't selling what people want to buy.

What can you take away from this? As in sales and business, knowing what the client/customer wants to buy and is buying is what determines the Gold Medal of success. It's not what you or I think they want. You don't get the opportunity to determine what people are buying. They buy what they buy. You get to determine what you sell them. Sell them what they are buying and you are successful. Sell something else and you are a footnote in history.

The Olympic judges were buying artistry and great footwork, not quad jumps. What are your customers/clients buying? Are you selling that to them? Don't get in their heads. Get in their hearts.

You need to find the movement, or wave that people are buying in. Architect Frank Lloyd Wright designed a college campus. On the day the school opened, students flooded the new campus. The president noticed something was missing: there were no paved pathways to get from one location, building or facility to another. He called the ingenious architect to report the omission and asked why he had left out such an important detail. Wright told him that he had not left them out; he simply was waiting to see where the students were walking. Then he would pave those trails. This way they wouldn't have to put up signs telling people where to walk. It made the campus more attractive and more accessible. He simply found out where people are already walking and paved the trails they were already making on the grounds.

Where are people already "walking" in your industry or community? Are you reading the signs of their habits to pave the way to your own success? What would they put money down for without even thinking about it?

Easy Action Step: Where are people already "walking" in your industry or community? Are you reading the signs of their habits to pave the way to your own success? What would they put money down for without even thinking about it? What are customers valuing that you already sell? What changes did you observe in the list you made earlier in the book? How can you orient your selling strategy to the buying trends you observe?

Chapter 13

REINVENTING CUSTOMER SERVICE

How Have You Been Punishing Your Customers?

*"Customer service and retention are paramount in this age.
If you're not listening to them, you're missing an opportunity."*

—Jim Steele, Salesforce.com president for worldwide sales

We bought a new HD (high definition) television several months ago. I couldn't wait to hook it up and watch the clear picture and special programming. Our cable company swapped me for a new decoder and I thought I was ready. However, I soon discovered that my skills in electronics were no match for HDTV. There were more wires and places to plug them than I had ever seen on a television or a cable box. It was against my nature to read the instructions but I spent one fruitless evening going over them. They were written for someone who already knew what they were doing--not me. So I called the cable company...12 times.

After suffering through the endless voice loops and choices each time I would get advice or promises of assistance that never worked. Finally a lady admitted that she didn't understand it either. She handed me over to Technical Support (after 11 calls for help). Latrell answered the phone. I remember his name because he is the only one who actually endeavored to help me. "How can I help you Mr. Mathis?" he said. I began telling him my story. He began quoting the concerns and problem I had back to me. At last I found someone who understood! It only took a few minutes but Latrell pinpointed my problem and came up with a solution. The things he couldn't solve, he agreed to research and call me back in exactly 24 hours. He did.

How Are You Punishing Your Customers?

What do people have to do to buy from you? How many forms must clients fill out? Are there restrictive policies that favor your employees over the customers?

I am a Delta Airlines Elite Plus Platinum Frequent Flyer. Impressed? Delta doesn't seem to be. From a very frequent flyer's perspective, they seem more interested in making their employees more comfortable than the passengers. In 2008 they purchased Northwest Airlines and took on their routes, employees and terrible business practices. They added kiosks to check in to give the ticket agents a break from having to deal with customers in person. Delta also decided to push its internet sales by adding an additional cost to customers purchasing over the telephone. When you call the number to buy a ticket, rather than tell you that you can save money by purchasing online, they tell you that it will cost you a penalty of $50 to buy from the person you are speaking with. Crazy!

It's not like they are doing so well in business (Delta and Northwest both lost over 4 billion the first quarter of that year) that they can afford to anger their most valuable customers. In the summer of 2009, Delta decided to combat declining passenger numbers (and add insult to injury) by charging for checked luggage. In October they announced that their passenger numbers were still decreasing so they were adding a $10 surcharge per ticket to all holiday travel purchases. Two weeks later they raised it to $20 per ticket.

What was the reason? They announced that they were charging the holiday travelers to make up for empty seats during normal flight days. In other words, if you choose to fly with us during the peak times, you must pay for the ones who DON'T fly with us the rest of the year.

Oh by the way, to further accommodate the flight attendants over the customers, Delta went "cash-less" in December, 2009. It meant that you had to use a credit card on flights to purchase food or beverages and good old American legal tender was no longer acceptable. Again, it makes you ask, how are you punishing your customers for doing business with you? What hoops are they being forced to jump through to either accommodate you and your employees or to just get through to someone with empathy?

Remember my 12 calls to the cable company? Each call I was asked electronically to punch in my phone number and account number. When I finally got a live person the first question I was asked was, "What is your telephone number and account number?" When I asked why I had to punch them in to the recording the customer service individual would say, "I don't know, all I know is I don't have access to your account without you giving me this information." There is nothing more annoying than having to push button after button to get to a live person. Wait, there is. Some companies (okay, Delta Airlines is one) have a voice recognition system where you speak your information to a recorded person. Have you ever heard the phrase, "I'm sorry, I didn't quite get that."? You do if have ever called and gotten this system. I don't know about you, but if the machine makes me angry, I can only wonder what speaking to a real person is going to do for my blood pressure.

Is your customer service marked by these types of policies? It is causing you to lose business, whether you yet recognize it.

Is it any wonder that customer ire is on the rise? By the time you get to a real live person, you are fit to be tied. Statistics bear out that most people aren't persistent and will just hang up if they have to go through more than one level of pushing buttons to get to a person. From the customer angle you can usually take one of two actions to get around this: Push 0 three times and it will sometimes disable the system and take you to the operator. Another solution is to go to www.gethuman.com. This creative web site lists numbers you can call from private corporations to government institutions to get a live person on the phone - even IRS!

Another great way customers are getting back at poor service is through social media. Case in point: In 2009 a woman went through a popular drive-in restaurant on her bicycle. She placed her order and was told to pull up to the window to pay and receive her food. But when the attendant noticed that she was on a bicycle, he refused to serve her. He told her that their company policy was to only serve people in automobiles and trucks. She left angry and began to tell her story on Twitter. Within 3 hours of the incident, her message had been broadcast to over 10,000 people. She received a phone call from the the management offices apologizing and telling her that their policy had just been changed. She received compensation for the inconvenience. With blogs and social media skyrocketing, you can be sure that more companies are being attentive to customer complaints on the internet. Comcast Cable now has an individual who answers complaints on Twitter for the company.

I received excellent service recently from Alaska Airlines. The gate agent went out of her way to rebook me on another airline when bad weather grounded my flight in Portland. I made certain to take down her name and ID so I could write a commendation letter. Upon my return home I discovered that you have to join their frequent flyer program to call or email in a compliment on an employee. Is anyone listening? How much longer is the public going to stand for this "punishment?" Not much longer if you look at sales of companies that treat their customers badly. Corporations have gotten so large they seem to have forgotten what grew them in the first place.

Reinventing Your Customer Service

Today the customer is king (and not you). It was supposed to be that way in the old world, but convenience for the employee (known as "our Policy") seems to have superseded that mandate. I asked a group of over 100 telecom customer service representatives to name the most important person in their corporation. They named the CEO, the President, and the top sales account executive. Not one said, "The customers." When I asked the CEO the same question, he knew it was his customers. Sadly, that message had not reached the people who came in contact with them on a daily basis.

Do you have a group of "Latrell's" handling your call center? So many organizations just do not get it. They do not show concern or empathy for their customers and they certainly do not go the extra mile. It is maybe a little thing, but it means everything. What are the characteristics of quality service? What keeps your customers coming back and telling others to come to you? It begins with quality customer service.

1. Quality Service is Responsive to Needs. Quality service involves being courteous, asking the right questions, suggesting only what is right for the customer, and not promising what you can't deliver. It is not characterized by saying you *can't* do something. We switched our cell phone company. The former company never responded to our needs. They often acted like it was an imposition to help us. We were made to feel like we were the only individuals experiencing problems (I've since found out that almost everyone I've come across who was with them left for the same reason). They kept telling us that the problem would be fixed with the service and it never was.

In retrospect, it appears they finally let us go simply to get rid of us. Either way, we got out of our contract and a into better cell company. Their reception isn't better, but there CSR's are. Truth be known, I was a week away from paying the former company's penalty just to get out of the contract. Sometimes the service can be so bad that you'd be willing to pay just to get away. Do you have customers that would pay anything if they knew there was a better service provider out there?

Quality service is characterized by doing what can do to satisfy every customer with a smile on your face. That's it. It really is that simple. It's NOT characterized by having to get permission from someone above you to make people happy. What are your customer's needs? Have you spent time interviewing your customers to get their stories of successful service? The more stories you can get your consumers to tell, the more they will start telling them to their friends and associates.

I flew Midwest Airlines on several legs to Green Bay. Every person I spoke with associated with them was courteous and went out of their way to make my travel smooth and satisfying. They give warm chocolate chip cookies to passengers on every flight, except the shorter ones. On the Milwaukee to Green Bay flight the attendant announced that the flight was so short that he wasn't supposed to pass out the cookies but he liked us and was going to search for some. He took extra time looking and produced a fresh warm batch for all passengers. You can be certain that I am flying Midwest in the future!

2. Quality Service is Timely. Timely service doesn't mind taking an extra 5 or 10 minutes to satisfy the customer. It means finding ways to streamline the process and working more efficiently. Now quality service doesn't always have to be speedy. In a conference a few months ago, a participant said she thought her supervisor might not like her taking the needed extra time being concerned about the needs of someone calling in. I answered that her boss would love it if the extra time mitigated the concern, rather than postponing it. The supervisor, who was in attendance agreed. Do you as a leader prefer to have customers satisfied or dismissed quickly? Timely doesn't always mean right away, but it does mean in a reasonable or agreed upon period. Latrell promised to get back within 24 hours and he did. He agreed to research my questions and come back with answers. He set attainable goals for good service and delivered.

Is your CSR team handling customer concerns in a timely manner? Are your valuable customers hanging up because no one is being paid to answer the phone promptly? Do your customers know all the words to the bumper music (the music your phone system plays for people on hold) because they've been on hold for so long? When someone does finally answer the call, are they empowered to satisfy the customer first and above all?

3. Quality Service is Accurate. Accuracy is doing precisely what either you said you would do, or what the customer needs you to do. It involves actively listening. It is paying attention to what you are being told by your customer. It is asking the right questions to find out precisely what the customer's problems are: What do they really need?

Do you remember a television program in the 1970's called "Columbo?" Peter Falk played a detective who was one of the messiest, most disorganized appearing personalities you've ever seen. He wore a rumpled coat, drove a beat up old car and smoked ratty cigars. He was characterized, though by incessantly asking questions. Question after question he would drive the "killer" crazy until they were willing to confess to both the Kennedy assassination and the Manson murders.

Enduring the course of the each episode, he would turn back to interviewees after ending the conversation to ask "just one more question." It was Detective Columbo's method for finding the key that would unlock the mystery and bring the truth to light. Unfortunately too many customer service representatives are trying to solve the crime in the first few minutes without delving into the real mystery.

Great CSR's aren't problem solvers. They aren't Mighty Mouse, saying, "Here I come to save the day!" Rather like Columbo, they are investigators. Only after you have posed the questions can you find out what the customer needs. Don't be too quick to solve problems. Start asking about them. Practice active listening. The person asking the questions is always in charge of the conversation. Asking your customer questions puts you in charge of the conversation and lets the customer give you information. Look on your role as an investigative reporter doing an interview. If the customer is forced to ask all the questions they aren't getting their needs met and they are in charge of the conversation. And by all means, when asked a question by your customer, give as brief and direct answer – followed by a question of your own. Can your Call Center team be relied upon to do some investigative research? Are they trying to solve the problem too quickly? Are they investigators? Do they go out of their way to give accurate service?

Along the same note, are you asking the right questions? Tim Brown, CEO of IDEO says, "As a designer, I'm always looking for solutions to the problems I see in front of me. And the big trick to being a successful designer is always making sure you're asking the right questions and focusing on the right problems. It's very easy in business to get sucked into being reactive to the problems and questions that are right in front of you. I do think that's something that we forget — as leaders, probably the most important role we can play is asking the right questions. Those right questions aren't just kind of lying around on the ground to be picked up and asked." When you go back and look at the great leaders — Bernard Marcus, Sam Walton — one of the things that stands out is they somehow had the ability to frame the question in a way that no one else had previously done – and in such a way that started their audience thinking from a different perspective.

4. Quality Service is Complete. Complete means everything was taken care of. It also means finished. The problem is remedied and the customer is satisfied. The needs of the customer are put ahead of policies.

No one wants to hear your company policy quoted back to them. They aren't doing business with you because of your policy. While checking in at an airline counter I was required to show my frequent flyer card to a gentleman. This wasn't a problem until it created a "bottle-neck" of angry customers trying to get to the desk. When a passenger asked why they were doing this, the attendant answered, "Hey, it is what it is. This is for YOUR convenience." No one in the upset crowd felt convenient at that moment. They felt inconvenienced by an airline with more policies than service.

I have found that whenever anyone is telling you, "This is for your convenience or security," they are generally trying to appease you for the inconvenience or insecurity you feel. It doesn't usually work to your advantage. How do your customers feel inconvenienced when your policies are quoted to them for not doing what they want you to do? Does satisfying their needs outweigh your policy manual? I know we can't do everything for our customers, but they can tell when you are trying to not serve them in the best way to serve yourself.

Quality service means that you deliver what you said you would in a memorable manner you want to be known for. Sears was once the top selling appliance dealer because their service was impeccable. Even if an appliance cost more, people bought from Sears because the service contract was the best in the business. But they began sending out "repair" people who were no more than surveyors. It took twice as long to get a repair done because someone had to come out and "survey the damage," before anyone with a tool box could actually start work. It may have made sense in the board room, but a woman waiting on the washing machine to be fixed, or the man with a broken television was forced to wait longer and longer for service. Soon the word was out that Sears was slow to repair.

Quality customer service means that the matter is taken care of with a minimum amount of fuss, and with courteous and empathetic service. The result? A very happy and grateful customer, ready to sing your praises. Too often CSR's are trained to deal in volume and they don't take the time to make sure that all the needs were met. Again, asking questions is the best way to make sure everything has been taken care of. Specific follow-up is arranged to make sure that everything was taken care of. Have you ever taken your car in for service and had the dealer call you back several days later to make sure everything is okay? I've even had my doctor's office call me a day or two after a sick visit to see how I was improving. Does your CSR team get the job done? Does it take several calls to get to the remedy of your clients' needs? Are they good at asking, "Is there anything else I can do to help you"? If not teach them now.

On a final note, how well do you allow your customers to praise your company's employees? I received great service from an airport information service representative. But after two hours of searching for a way to recommend her for her selfless aide to me, I gave up trying.

Give your customers something to praise;
then give them an opportunity to do it!

Do you provide a place for people to sing your praises? How responsive is your organization to the boom in social media feedback? Are you taking advantage of this wonderful tool? Can your customers use Facebook, Twitter or another social network to allow them to praise your company and its people?

What Makes You Different?

You can do all of the above to attain quality customer service. But often that isn't enough. You have to be different. What makes you excellent is how you differentiate yourself from your competitors. It is important to know what sets you apart. Ask yourself why anyone receiving excellent service from your competition would, in a head-to-head challenge, choose you over them?

I met with a group of building materials dealers in Florida earlier this year. Their businesses have taken a terrible hit in the recession. They were talking about what kind of future they were facing. One of the challenges we tackled was differentiation. If person A sells the same lumber or siding to builders, what differentiates them? It isn't products. If you answered pricing you were wrong there, too.

We came to the conclusion that the difference between them was this: They deliver greater VALUE to their customers. One attendee said, "You might can beat me on price, but you can't beat me on value." His buyers and contractors knew who he was and what he stood for. His integrity and value are his brand. Most leaders would give anything for that reputation in their industry and among their customers.

There are likely to be lots of people on this planet doing what you do. It is your brand that differentiates you from all the rest. Your goal is to develop a brand that is so unique that consumers immediately associate you with it. Gourmet coffee? Starbucks. Superior electronics? Sony. Upscale menswear? Brooks Brothers. The best branding you can have is when the product is associated with your name by almost everyone. Facial tissues are typically called Kleenex. Gelatins are usually referred to as Jell-O. Making copies is now known as Xeroxing. In the Southeastern United States, almost all soft drinks are called Cokes or at the very least cola's (as in Coca-Cola).

What did it take to crown these brands? The frequency and loyalty of your customers. It wasn't necessarily an action the company had direct control over. Most often, the customers are the ones who bestow the honor. Kleenex didn't set out with a campaign to make everyone call the product by their name. It occurred as people became loyal to the brand and after the performance of the product was proven to be excellent they called it by that name frequently. Frequent use in service and products is the best branding you can get. Why do people shop at Publix grocery stores? Their prices are often higher than their competition and they don't give out as many coupons.

Actually, Kroger grocery stores have one of the best frequency programs in the business with their "Kroger Plus" card. Publix doesn't have a discount card at all. But they deliver great service on their products in addition to the occasional sale. A friend told me when we were moving to Florida in the middle 1990s: "Once you shop at Publix, you will never want to go anywhere else." He was right.

I heard an advertisement for Direct TV the other day. It said that you should choose Direct TV over Dish Network because Dish has always had a poor customer service reputation. But that isn't true. Direct TV has been the one with the most complaints. In a visit to Consumer Advocate Clark Howard's web site the majority (a large majority) of respondents told about the problems they had with Direct TV's customer service. Even Clark weighed in on the discussion saying that Dish Network had the better reputation. Listen to the stories people tell about you. They tell about your brand.

Your brand may be chosen by you or your customers. A smart reinvention leader chooses their battle grounds. He/she chooses what they will be known for. They know that every buyer tells a story. They know what they have earned a reputation for. The brand should tell about what you do better than anyone else.

I once asked my top customers what they wanted more of and they responded, "We want more interaction." So as a result I began to incorporate increasing amounts of interaction in my presentations. By early 2010 I was incorporating dialogues, known as "Strategizing Sessions" into my presentations. Other speakers offer to simply give a lecture or motivational talk; I was giving clients what they were asking for – because I listened. It completely reinvented my speaking career, ultimately branding me as a "strategist." This is what we discussed in the chapter *Get Out of Your Industry*.

So what makes you different than your competition? What are the stories people tell about you and your brand?

There's a lot of competition out there! You have to create, define, and publicize the difference you bring. The difference is what will make you interesting and marketable. Seek to identify whatever it is. Ask others what makes you unique in your market and to your customers. What can you do that sets you apart from the crowd? Is there a service you can render that no one else does in your industry? Once you define that difference then you need to share that with everyone in every way you can. That difference will put you ahead of the pack and lead others to you.

Remember how earlier we noted Home Depot's practice of having employee's "walk the customer" instead of "point the customer" when asked where an item was located? This training by co-founder Bernard Marcus and the practice of this idea in stores kept Home Depot at the top in customer service polls throughout his tenure. But did you know that after he retired, the company got away from enforcing this policy? It wasn't "convenient" for the employees to walk customers all over the store. So the practice ceased. Pointing replaced walking – and Home Depot's earnings nose-dived. In short order the board of directors met in emergency session to change the customer service policy and restore their competitiveness in the market. It worked.

Easy Action Step: Ask yourself: "How am I going the extra mile for my customers/clients today?" In fact, going that extra mile does not have to be restricted to your professional life. Think of someone who you can make a difference for today in your personal life by going that extra mile. It will become your brand.

Chapter 14

REINVENTING YOUR BRAND

"Changing your brand strategy means becoming a different company ...
it's not just changing your name or your logo."

— Rob Frankel

In this day and age, you have to confront the present reality: The world has changed, and consumers are seeking an experience that's markedly different from what your organization has been offering. Your company may be the first name in Boss 302 engines, but now you're dealing with a marketplace that no longer needs them. You may be famed for making spacious gas-guzzling SUVs, but car buyers are turning to hybrids and compact gas sippers. You may be selling daily newspapers to readers who increasingly look to the Web for their news.

Or your company may be a family oriented casual-dining chain trying to succeed in a crowded and intensely competitive market where all brands sound alike. What actually differentiates an O'Charley's restaurant from an Applebee's? Just calling yourself the "Neighborhood Bar" doesn't cut it anymore. Familiar names are facing enormous challenges that threaten their continued existence. The parent company of Bennigan's filed for bankruptcy protection in 2008. Sales at other chains are down. Even the popular Cheesecake Factory reported a significant drop in same-store sales.

Increasingly we are seeing products and services coming to market designed to appeal to the momentary attention of shoppers on the internet.

It is worth noting that most internet web surfers are scanners, not readers. But most internet web sites are designed for readers. Some companies have picked up on this and made changes. In some cases they've started down the path of reinvention.

The Huffington Post has evolved by pushing investigative stories down the page in exchange for "bait and link" stories and sensational celebrity briefs. This strategy gets page views. But it leaves you wondering if they really have any readers who stay for the copy at the bottom of the page? We no longer live in a day when you write a catchy headline and everyone reads your complete story.

Time magazine faced a similar problem with their newsstand copies. They began manipulating the magazine cover and then the article contents in order to boost newsstand sales. They may have found a short-term solution, but the magazine is doomed precisely because their audience isn't paying attention and the audience they've reached isn't one that is attractive to their advertisers. Either way, the world and economy has changed so much that their brand is now becoming obsolete. It is on the brink of becoming extinct.

Ignoring your brand leaves you in danger of becoming extinct, too. You need to reinvent your brand. Check to see if it is obsolete. Dwindling sales and attention are driving your customers in another direction. A speaker came up to me after a chapter meeting and said, "You are killing my dream with this reinvention talk. Why can't I speak on what I want to speak on?" I told him he is more than welcome to speak on whatever topic he wants, but if no one is paying to hear it, he might consider changing topics.

Maybe you need to come up with something so new and innovative that it sends the market in a new direction. Look at these three successful brands.

When The Nashville Network realized their target audience wasn't tuning in to watch fishing shows 3 times a day, they changed their name and brand to Spike TV and focused on a wider range of male viewers.

he was worked with on reinventing their brand, was founded by George Eastman to create memories for people, not to just sell film. When they re-identified with their purpose, they were able to fend off lower film prices by their chief competitor Fuji Film. Do you know why your company was founded?

Who is Buying From You?

If you truly know your target audience and customers, you are close to defining your brand. An example is your friendly neighborhood credit union. The credit union movement has been around for over half a century. Credit unions once were formed to serve a select group of consumers who had something in common – like where they worked or the organization they belonged to. It was easy to distinguish their members from anyone else by the common ties. This gave them a target market that was easy to identify and reach.

Then came community charters (opening up to anyone who lives works, attends church or school in the immediate community). Once they became community chartered, it became a double-edged sword. Where they once targeted a very select group to heavily market, the expansion of charters widened membership far beyond the original group. The message and branding became diluted to the point where they don't know who they serve specifically. Many have lost their uniqueness in the process. Their diversity requires of them a new brand identity.

Does your company need to create a new brand identity? The solution to creating one is to begin by asking a few strategic questions that will help you on your way.

What are people buying from you now? Who is buying and what are their changing needs? You need to do research on your consumers. This is a case where "profiling" is used properly for its originally intended purpose. What is their profile? What is their demographic? Their age? Their gender? Their family situation? What is their income level? What are the typical needs of anyone in your community or industry who fits this profile? Also ask who buys from you the most? Who are your customers and what do they most often buy? That tells you who your target has become and why they choose you for your business.

A friend met me for lunch in Philadelphia. He had a unique "problem." He was receiving frequent phone calls asking if he booked speakers for a living. He received calls of this nature several times each week. His problem was that he doesn't handle booking for speakers. His question was a good one: should he start offering the service? "Why are they calling you and asking you the same question?" I asked. "What are you doing for them now that leads them to believe this is also what you do?" There is a reason he is getting these calls about a service people want to buy from him – even though it isn't a service he provides...yet. I pointed out to him that he has tapped into a movement that people want to buy from him without knowing it. He found that his brand was in an area that he could make a lucrative living in. All because he asked *who* was buying from him, *what* they were buying and *why* they wanted to buy from him in the first place.

A Simple Reinvention Story

I once received a request from the owner of a chain of auto repair shops, seeking assistance with reinventing his brand. He was losing many regular customers and wanted help in retrieving the business. During the appointment we reviewed his business model, including his clientele and what they bought when they came to him. It turned out he primarily repaired cars for families. So we looked at who usually came in for the repairs, developing a demographic and buying profile for his average customer. Each service center created a profile of their "Joe Customer".

After careful analysis we discovered that his average client was 34 years old, had 2 children (toddlers), drove a sedan, and brought the car in for recurring work like brake repairs and oil changes. Oh, yes. One more interesting demographic: the majority of the people coming to his service centers were women. And it was the women who had been previous customers that were no longer using his shops. I asked him what the customer service lounge in the shop was like.

Have you ever been in a repair shop's customer lounge or waiting area? Do you think his was female-friendly? It turns out he was losing customers because the waiting area was filthy. It had little reading material for women to read, a terrible odor, a television that only tuned to ESPN, and a grimy floor. In the corner were two old coffee pots (only one worked), snacks for the repair technicians (they shared with customers), and the women's restroom – which was only cleaned "at least once a week!"

Once he looked through their eyes, he could see how the environment in his waiting area was running off his top "buyers." He took a field trip – and wisely took his wife. I coached him as he left, "If you want more women to come into the shop for repairs, then clean up the customer waiting area. Also, get ideas from a business in your area that caters to women successfully." They went to an upscale dealership and observed everything they saw being done differently than was done at his business. He returned from the field trip and said it was "eye-opening."

Immediately he implemented several strategic and inexpensive changes in the customer waiting area. He sent out invitations and coupons to attract his former and prospective customers in the community. The changes made a difference. His target customers, the women, came back and brought friends. They began making appointments in groups. Soon his business was again growing, finally surpassing its previous revenue records. He had more business than he knew what to do with.

He reached into his demographics and pulled out some amazing facts that put him back in business. His discovery during his reinvention process was what the customer valued. Before reinvention, he THOUGHT his customers were buying auto repairs – because that was all he was selling. What he learned was that they were ACTUALLY buying the service environment. They wanted a nice place to wait while their repairs were being completed. There is a big difference in what you THINK you are selling or producing and what the customer actually perceives it to be. The difference is crucial and will make or break you in the highly competitive global market place of today.

During another exercise, I posed this question to the executive leadership team from a community bank. Research uncovered that their average customer was a patriotic 42 year old woman, mother of three children, attended kids sporting events and wanted future security for her children. These bankers realized that they weren't reaching their target. The answers were simple and cost effective, but not before they'd already spent a chunk of money.

It turns out that before contacting me, they'd hired a "slick" firm from New York to redesign their logo. The president was told to "update" their logo and brand. That advice came at a tremendous price. Yet despite their exorbitant fees, the firm failed to profile the average customer who was already satisfied with the bank's business. It sold them a logo and brand that didn't reach the people they were already succeeding with. While their core business was with the 42 year old mothers and families, their new branding logo was targeted to a 23 year old man who was very internet savvy. The problem was that while this played well in New York, it fell flat in this family-friendly bedroom community.

No one in the target audience or the company liked the new logo – except the CEO who had spent all the money on it. It looked like the Pringles logo had crashed into a word processor. The result wasn't appealing to the people they had built a relationship with over the years. Their local community would support the brand change to the 42 year old mothers, but not the 23 year old men. From the outset, their bank brand needed to be reinvented to reach the people who already were loyal and faithful customers. The president would never have realized this unless the right questions were asked and the demographic profiles were studied.

OK, so who are *your* customers? What are your customers buying? What are you known for by those who are willing to spend money to get it? Knowing this will make you an overwhelming success. Your success is tied closely to what you are popular for doing. You need to be *The One* who does it better than anyone else. It reminds me of one of my favorite movies.

"City Slickers" is a movie about a 39 year old man at the halfway point in life who goes out on a cattle drive with two friends to find his smile and satisfaction in life. A central scene in the movie involves two characters played by Jack Palance and Billy Crystal. Jack and Billy are out alone on the range looking for a lost cow. Jack is a crusty old cowboy with little emotion other than anger as far as Billy can tell.

During their conversation, Jack remarks, "All you city-slickers come out here about the same age - same problems. Spend fifty weeks a year getting knots in your rope then--then you think two weeks up here will untie them for you. None of you get it. Do you know what the secret of life is?" Billy shakes his head no and asks what the secret is. "This!" (Jack holds up one finger). "One thing - just one thing. You stick to that and everything else don't mean anything." he says.

"That's great, but what's the one thing?" Crystal asks. "That's what you've got to figure out," replies Jack. These are not elegant words but they speak volumes to your place in the global market. What's your "one thing?"

What Are You the THE of?

When you find yourself atop the top of the heap in any industry, you're known as the *"THE"* of that industry. Elvis wasn't "A" King, he was THE King. The best always holds the distinction of being THE. Not being just another A. It differentiates you from everyone else doing what you are doing, but puts you on top. It is THE name of THE game. What differentiates you is moving from being A at something and moving to the THE. People don't hire you or buy from you because you were A, but because to them you were the THE of it. It takes you out of an ordinary category and places you in the industry of ONE. There is only ONE THE in any field.

Famous individuals throughout history have used "The" to set themselves apart from all others: Louis XIV of France was known as "The Sun King." Richard of Great Britain was known as "The Lion Heart." Ivan IV of Russia was called "The Terrible." Peter of Russia, Catherine of

Russia, Ramses of Egypt and Alexander of Macedonia were all known as "The Great." How many "The's" can you think of throughout the pages of history?

In my ministry days, I met Dr. Ed Young, Sr. At the time he was the very charismatic pastor of Second Baptist Church in Houston, Texas. He was one of the most practical marketers and creative people I met in the ministry and helped inspire my marketing. When Ed first came to Second Baptist, he immediately branded the church: The Fellowship of Excitement. Their staff wanted the church to be not only a true fellowship, but to be the exciting one. Notice they weren't "A Fellowship of Excitement," they were "THE Fellowship of Excitement." This set them apart because no one else could claim this brand once they took it. And they took it in a big way. It was an exciting church. They even answered the phones: "Exciting Second!"

Modern day celebrities know that to corner a movement or market, you have to be more than just another A; you have to be the THE. So

- Aretha Franklin isn't A Queen of Soul; she is THE Queen of Soul.

- Although the sun definitely shines on all 50 states, only Florida is THE Sunshine State.

- Coca Cola isn't A Real Thing it's THE Real Thing.

- Mohammed Ali wasn't A great boxer; he was THE Greatest (putting him above Peter, Catherine, Ramses and Alexander).

- Fox News commentator Bill O'Reilly doesn't call himself A Factor; he is THE Factor.

- The best university in your state or province is called THE University of _____.

What can you be the THE of in your industry? How do people identify or differentiate you from everyone else who probably does the same thing you do? How do you create unique value they can't get from anyone else or in any other place?

Most of us by becoming THE… could take first place in our business just by changing the branding phrase. After all, colleges have done it for years to distinguish themselves from their rivals: Auburn University in Auburn, Alabama even co-opted (nailed it before their rivals in Tuscaloosa could use it in their branding slogan) by calling themselves THE University of Alabama.

Is there a "THE" in your brand? Want to become the THE in your field? Do you want to be in an industry of ONE? This type of branding can't be beat.

I mentioned Elvis Presley earlier. Here was an artist with a distinctive brand that seemed like it would endure forever. Elvis' career and brand were rocking right along, then BAM! He was drafted. "The King" had to serve in the United States Army. While there, his career came to a screeching halt. The whole entertainment world wondered if he would ever come back. When he left the service, Elvis came back, but he had changed. He had matured and the old Elvis wouldn't sell to people anymore. He needed to make a change, so Elvis and reinvented himself and his brand in his post Army career. It was a different Elvis and it attracted not only his old fans, but a different group as well.

Your brand distinguishes you from everyone else in your industry. You can take just one product or idea that you are known for and turn it into your brand – if it is popular enough with everyone. Jimmy Buffett, a very creative artist has basically taken one song (that was never even a Number One hit) and built it into a worldwide brand of apparel, restaurants, gift shops and one of the first internet radio stations – Margaritaville. His followers are so devoted. They call themselves "Parrot-heads" and dress outlandishly for his concerts, which are more like parties with Jimmy as the "CPO" (Chief Party Officer).

It is the same all over the world. A brand is reinvented and the new identity becomes a sensation. In Canada, a hockey player retired and reinvented his brand as the doughnut king – Tim Horton. You haven't been to Canada unless you buy doughnuts and coffee at Tim Horton's. It is similar to Dunkin' Doughnuts and Starbuck's but it is distinctly Canadian and is a source of national pride. That is their brand – Canadian doughnuts and coffee.

Verbal Branding

Without a doubt the best way to get the word out about your company or name is verbal branding. It can help you or it can kill you in the market place. Verbal branding is when your brand becomes a verb for what you produce or do. When using your product becomes synonymous with the act of the product you have struck gold. Xerox became so associated with making copies that the action became known as *"Xeroxing."* The room the copier was stored in became known as "the Xerox room." DO you have a runny nose? Then you reach for…Kleenex. The brand is named *"Kleenex."* The product is facial tissues. People don't ship items in many companies, they *"FedEx"* them. You don't look up a subject on the internet, you *"Google it."* The brand name has become the verb for getting the product or service done.

In 1811, Governor William Henry Harrison won a major victory over Chief Tecumseh and his Native American confederation at the Battle of Tippecanoe in the Indiana Territory. He was the hero of the day to the citizens of the United States. This made him so popular that when he ran for President 1820, his campaign staff referred to him simply as "Tippecanoe" to remind voters of the victory nine years earlier. His victory on the battlefield became his brand.

Some companies come close to verbal branding. Many people get a "Starbucks" when they go to coffee outlets selling a different brand of coffee. Sony is known for superior audio products, but no one "Sony's" something when they want to make the most accurate audio or video recording. We do, however refer to most mp3 players as iPods. More will be on the way!

There is negative verbal branding as well. Bad mistakes have their negative marketing as well;

- Every political scandal in the US since 1974 has been named "Something"-gate after the Watergate scandal and controversy. Remember Spy-gate, Travel-gate, Lewinsky-gate, etc.?

- Major defeats in battle have been known as "Waterloos" since Napoleon's defeat there in 1815. In an article the day after the US House of Representatives voted to approve the American Health Care Bill, Author David Frum referred to Obama's victory, saying, "Republicans might have thought this was going to be his *Waterloo*, but they messed up."

- Traitors in the United States have been called "Benedict Arnolds" for the famous General who tried to sell out West Point to the British in the American Revolution.

- While Volvo is Latin for "I roll," Nova means "Won't go" in Spanish.

Roll With the Changes

The world has changed forever. In the time you picked up this book a multitude of changes have taken place that affects your life. The speed of service is getting faster. People are clicking on web sites (perhaps yours) and moving beyond at incredible rates. They are making decisions and deciding "No" faster than ever before.

Sociologists tell us that the world reinvents itself more frequently now *and* at a faster pace than at any other time in history. Everything around you has changed and is changing. It's a relevant question: Have you? Most of us bury our heads when change comes and pretend the changes won't affect us. Get your snicker on and read some famous statements in the face of change:

- "While theoretically and technically television may be feasible, commercially and financially I consider it an impossibility, a development of which we need waste little time dreaming." -Lee DeForest, "Father of the Radio," 1926.

- "The ordinary 'horseless carriage' is at present a luxury for the wealthy; and although its price will probably fall in the future, it will never, of course, come into as common use as the bicycle." - *The Literary Digest*, 1889

- "What can be more palpably absurd than the prospect held out of locomotives traveling twice as fast as stagecoaches?" -*The Quarterly Review*, 1825

- "The energy necessary to propel the ship would be many times greater than that required to drive a train of cars at the same speed; hence as a means of rapid transit, aerial navigation could not begin to compete with the railroad." - *Popular Science* magazine, 1897

- "The abolishment of pain in surgery is a chimera. It is absurd to go on seeking it today. Knife and pain are two words in surgery that must forever be associated in the consciousness of the patient. To this compulsory combination we shall have to adjust ourselves." - Dr. Alfred Velpeau, 1839 (anesthesia was introduced seven years later)

- "At present, few scientists foresee any serious or practical use for atomic energy. They regard the atom-splitting experiments as useful steps in the attempt to describe the atom more accurately, not as the key to the unlocking of any new power." - *Fortune* magazine, 1938

- And my personal favorite: "No woman in my time will be prime minister or chancellor or foreign secretary - not the top jobs." - Margaret Thatcher, 1970

How are you deceiving yourself? Your brand needs a re-work; a reinvention, if you will. It is passé and on the road to becoming extinct. If you look to your top customers you will see the direction you need to take. If you continue to look at the past and what worked back then, you are doomed to stagnate. You can either roll with the changes or be rolled over by them. The choice is yours. Seize today. Catch the wave of what your customers are buying and verbalize what you do into an action. Reinvent your brand and keep ahead of those who predict a dire future.

Easy Action Step: In the first chapter you were asked, "What changes have you seen in your business, your customers, your industry and your geographical area in the last two years?" You were asked to make a list of 20 changes. Did you do it? Now I want you to add 20 additional changes to that list. What do these changes mean to your brand? Can you adequately meet the new challenges of today? What can you do to better communicate your brand to a forever changed market? Ask your top customers what you can do for them that no one else is doing. Meeting that need is what you will be known for.

Chapter 15

REINVENTING YOUR TARGET MARKET

Developing a New Message

"Business has only two functions -- marketing and innovation."
—Peter Drucker

"Culture defines community."

Marketing Matters

My introduction mentioned that in January 2009, I was faced with a crisis, one identical to the crisis that almost every speaker I knew was facing. No one was buying what I was selling! For years I had given presentations on teamwork, personality differences, time management and excellence in management. I even had a book that was selling fairly well on excellence. But now, it seemed nobody wanted to be excellent. They wanted to survive, endure, maintain or just make it through the day. In large measure, I had to sadly admit that so did I.

But on a presentation in Nashville the following month, I had an epiphany. If no one wanted to buy what I was selling, trying to sell it *harder* wasn't the answer. The solution to my problem was to reinvent my market. Then I reached the conclusion that once I reinvented my own market, I needed to help others. It's all about marketing. Without marketing I talk to no one and they don't talk to me. Without marketing communication, and more importantly, connection breaks down between me and my customers and prospects. Marketing is what makes everyone on the planet different in one form or the other. It made me think of a t-shirt I read: "You are unique: just like everyone else."

In the movie Apollo 13 the Director of Electrical Operations says, "It's all about power. Without power we don't talk to them, they don't talk to us." He knew that the remaining battery power was the key to rescuing the three men in space and bringing them home safely. In your business it's all about marketing. Marketing is how people find out about you and what sets you apart from everyone else who does the same thing you do. It's not about looking the same. "Same" doesn't get you paid. The key is *difference*. And the more different you are, the better you are in position to stand out.

You can have the greatest product in the world, but without good marketing, it gets bumped aside. Most of us have heard the expression, "If you build a better mouse trap, the world will beat a path to your door." Did you know someone actually built a "better" mouse trap in the 1930s? It was so ingenious that the homeowner didn't have to bait it or touch the dead mouse to clean it. But the superior product was marketed poorly and the company went out of business as a result.

For years I had been told that it was easier to get a new audience (buyers) than to get a new message (product). But now I was facing the unavoidable and seemingly unattainable. I needed to produce something new that everyone already wanted. Instead of looking at what others were doing (pretty much the same thing they had been doing for the past 5 years), I was going to have to look ahead to "one step beyond" for everyone I wanted to market to. And my overwhelming question was "How"?

For the Birds

Richard Mammone, Rutgers University Business School professor tells a great story about two birds. "The nuthatch and brown creeper are different bird species that look a lot alike and eat insects in the same wooded areas in North America. You might think they compete, but they don't. In accordance with a common arrangement in nature that ecologists call the competitive-exclusion principle, the brown creeper starts searching for insects at the bottom of a tree while the nuthatch starts from the top."

It isn't common in the business world to look at other markets. The common practice is to compete in a death match of price wars or copying the other's innovation. Business competitors will normally go at each other relentlessly unless one finds a new market niche or a new process to address the existing market. Dan Brown wrote <u>The DaVinci Code</u>. Thereafter a whole lot of authors wrote books about codes. One airline added in-flight wifi service then others scrambled to follow suit. In the 1970's the Ford Motor Company produced a car with intermittent windshield wipers, then GM, then Chrysler. Are you getting the picture?

Reinventing your market means finding something new that no one is attempting or addressing and meeting that need. It is leading instead of following. It is original instead of copied. Reinventing is going in a purposefully different direction than you or anyone has gone before. Just like the nuthatch - looking up instead of down. Entrepreneurs can learn from this evolutionary process.

For years, coffee was coffee. They all tasted pretty much the same. Then Starbucks turned the coffee-drinking world on its ear by *blending*. The answer was blending different flavors and labeling it "gourmet" coffee. They reinvented coffee and changed the playing field. Suddenly everyone who was anyone was getting into the blended coffee business - Seattle's Best, Newman's Own, even Dunkin' Donuts!

To reinvent your market, you need to invest a sizeable amount of energy into innovation. To start the <u>innovation process</u> that could lead to such a breakthrough, you should perform a detailed <u>competitive analysis</u>. Pay attention to all the market intelligence you can get. Use your competitive intelligence to make good, innovative decisions. What areas are your competitors covering? What areas are they not covering? What are they leaving untouched?

First, keep track of your competition. You need to make yourself aware of moves large and small that your competitors are making so that you aren't blindsided or materially outmaneuvered. You can do this by collecting information about your competitor's activities, using Google alerts and other services such as social media site monitor <u>Radian6</u>. A recent McKinsey <u>survey</u> shows that most executives conduct this type of ongoing competitor-intelligence analysis using many of the following sources: Web sites, press releases, job ads, Securities & Exchange Commission filings, ads, annual reports, industry market share data, and industry pricing data.

Reinvention strategists can then analyze the intelligence they've gathered and estimate the impact of each potential move on short-term and long-term market share, earnings, and cash flow. They should also look into what steps other industries might be taking. After that, it's time to make a list of possible defensive and offensive responses to each identified threat. Businesses have gone bust by focusing on the wrong improvements while their competition blindsides them by marketing the ideas they've been developing.

One business leader concentrated on his voice recognition software, when BAM! His competitor blindsided him with a large marketing campaign for its product. That competitor now owns the voice recognition company he started—and got it at a considerable bargain. It can happen to anyone.

Moving Up the Tree

I know two professional speakers who chose to leave their market when the recession hit them hard. Both spoke in the real estate industry – hard hit by the recession in 2008-2009.

Michael, an experienced presenter had made a name for himself on the West Coast of the US in the real estate market. But the recession caused him to reassess his target audience. His research showed him that health care was an industry where he could find success. He already had a method of approaching potential clients using good marketing principles. He used the basic principles that had brought him success in real estate to enter the health care industry. He also used his skills in negotiation to produce a successful book on the tactics he used.

Rich, another former real estate speaker, found success in overseas markets and speaking on keeping his body in shape. Just so you know, he is a great physical specimen. His very presence before an audience is proof that he stays in great shape. All he needed to do was talk about what every audience saw as he stood before them. His market research had audiences telling him what to talk on, rather than asking them. Like the nuthatches, Michael and Rich both moved up the tree to find their sustenance.

It is okay to be innovative when the market isn't going your way. Some of the greatest inventions and innovations have come out of economic recessions. Air conditioning was invented during the Great Depression of the 1930s. It made migration to South Florida and other warm climates possible. In fact you might argue the case that it moved the Southeastern United States upward on the market's desirable list, since people could now work comfortably in warm, humid climates. The iPod, Xbox, Kindle2 e-book reader and Jet Blue low-cost airfares all came out of recessions.

What tree is standing before you? What is your industry? Where can you move in that industry to capture a different target? While watching ABC News in March, 2010 I saw the story of the Mississippi community bank that had moved up its own tree. It is a perfect example of a recession driving an innovative CEO to move his market to an area that no one else is targeting.

Mendenhall, Mississippi is a town of a bit more than 2,500 people. Peoples Bank of Mississippi has stood since 1908. Just as in the movie "It's a Wonderful Life," the Great Depression tested its strength. Bank president and CEO Dennis Amman can recall how his grandfather fought to keep the bank solvent. "He was 19 years old and he said, 'This bank isn't going to close,'" Amman said.

Nearly a century later, Peoples Bank faced another test. In 2009, when lending to small-town businesses was at a record low, the bank kept giving out loans. It kept lending even though new loans backed by the government stimulus offered little for the bank -- no interest and deferred payments. It became known for making more interest-free loans than any other bank in the country. While other banks were shutting their doors to such loans, Dennis and People's Bank kept their doors open.

What were the results? Peoples Bank is now third in the entire country in offering small business owners loans. "We looked at it and said it's going to take work on our part; we might not even make money off it in the short run, but in the long run it's going to be good for customers, so it's going to be good for us," Amman said.

"I consider them all to be my friends," says this forward-thinker. "They are our neighbors. We go to church with them. I see them at PTA meetings. I see them at the ball fields." Dennis lives this out in his personal life as well. On his email's Out of Office Auto Reply, Dennis puts his phone number if you need to contact him and who to talk to about your loan. Direct access is something almost no bank president or even a large church pastor would be willing to do. But Dennis does!

There are other simple ideas that could be a big help. As the president of People's Bank, he has fostered a culture of asking customers what he can do to make their experience better. Asking questions like this has attracted some intriguing suggestions. Most bank customers are frustrated with long forms to fill out loaded with disclaimers. Right now, multi-page mortgage documents often are an inch thick. One of Amman's clients suggested three-page mortgage agreements and one-page credit card agreements become the norm, with penalties and fees marked clearly in the same big font. That's an idea that appeals to Amman at Peoples Bank.

"Documents could be streamlined," Amman said. "It would reduce the paperwork to not only the lender, but also the consumer, that they could have something they could read." They're some smart ideas from a small town, but the question now may be: Are any of the bigger banks willing to consider them? Dennis has moved up his tree and is reaping huge benefits. Is anyone watching or listening?

Perhaps the tree you need to move up is your geographic region. USA Today carried an article in 2010 about Proctor and Gamble CEO Bob McDonald's major foray into the international scene. Eight months into his tenure at the top of the world's biggest consumer products company he was planning his global strategy. It's not enough that almost every home in North America probably has Tide in the laundry room, Pampers in the nursery, Pantene in the bathroom or Bounty in the kitchen, Bob wants to be in every home in the world (This is not an unusually unique goal. The president of Coca Cola wanted a Coke available throughout the world, so he made sure one was in the hand of every American soldier in World War II. He just about succeeded as Coca Cola went worldwide in the 1940s).

McDonald knows that his culture defines the community he will reach. So this CEO is planning to reach into China, India and the nations of Africa in a strong thrust to increase P&Gs income by $20 million (an increase of 1 billion customers) within the next five years. It is not enough that every person on the planet already spends $12 per year on P&G products. He wants to increase it to $14 per year. Bob sees the tree he needs to move up and it is the world.

Bob McDonald's style of leadership breaks conventional molds of people in the largest companies. He leads unlike most other CEOs. He regularly eats with employees. When he first started working for Proctor and Gamble, Bob often rode the bus to and from work. When he travels abroad, he visits consumer homes to see how they are using Proctor and Gamble products. He believes so strongly in diversity that he said at a recent leadership summit, "We are never going to be able to serve the needs of 5 billion people if we are not diverse ourselves." Bob has a great understanding of global markets, having observed them for many years. His peers admire him for his global outlook and goals. Mike Duke, CEO of Wal-Mart says, "He (Bob) is a true global executive. He has a great understanding of markets around the world."

McDonald wants to use a two-pronged attack to increase his company's global standing. First, continue they plan to provide the best products at premium prices. Some of P&Gs products are at the highest level of costs to consumers; however the second prong involves basic products that present great value for minimal prices (Proctor and Gamble markets both Pampers diapers and Crest toothpaste at the high end of the market, while also offering Tide Basic, a low-priced version of its mainstream product, Tide). This goes against a decade-long campaign to convince consumers to pay *more* for P&G products because of their quality.

To make the transition, McDonald says he is listening to customers. The year 2009 was a terrible one for the company, losing over 3.3% in revenues. To overcome the deficit in 2010 he took the corporation in a more global direction. He is on an "innovation tear," adding 30% more in core products than in 2009. How many companies would follow a dismal year with expansion? Bob McDonald would – and he will.

Changing Products and Services

The easy answer to moving up your tree is to just change your product or your service to meet demand. This works on some levels, but isn't always the best or most successful solution to reinvention. The McKinsey survey I mentioned earlier also found that most businesses do not innovate to counter a competitor's threat. Instead senior management reacts with a knee-jerk response, moving "down the tree" and matching a competitor's price change or imitating its new product or feature. Entrepreneurs should aspire to be more like the innovative nuthatch and step up.

Ford Motor Company is well known for producing the Model T in only one color for years. Henry Ford himself said, "People can have any color they choose, as long as it is black." Eventually they were forced to change when General Motors introduced a variety of colors and automobiles to compete with the aging model.

But just changing products doesn't always work. Heinz and Hunts have been at war over ketchup for decades. In the 1960s Hunts produced both pizza and hickory flavored ketchup. In the 1970s Heinz produced green ketchup. Neither was a hit. In 2006, Nestle introduced a wide variety of selections to their popular Kit Kat candy bar in the United Kingdom. Some of the new flavors were mango and passion fruit. But the result was much less than they expected. Customers didn't like so many choices and sales declined 18% for the year.

Gathering market intelligence is the first step. You need to discover what people are saying about you. Do you honestly know WHY your customers buy from you? Do you know what is your top-selling product or service and WHY? Innovative leaders who want to know what others think of their companies ask their customers why they buy from them. What polls have you taken to determine why you were hired and why you are successful? I worked with a CEO who was shocked to learn what the company web site said was the reason she was hired to run the company. "That's not what they told me!" she said.

What are you known for among your customers? What is your brand? Your purpose, your culture and your personality all define your brand. More on that later in this chapter.

But what does your marketing say about who your target is or will be? It goes back to meeting customer needs. What is your slogan saying about how you meet people's needs? The Cooking Diva, the Pain-Free Dentist and, yes, the Reinvention Strategist.

Crate & Barrel sells furniture to people who want to assemble solid furniture unlike IKEA who targets a different community altogether. Rhodes and Ashley sell to anyone who walks in the store meeting minimal credit requirements. The same is true for the difference between high end electronic stores like Best Buy and low-end dealers like HH Gregg. Go in each and you will see the difference in the way they treat their customers. One allows you to browse; the other pounces on you in desperation to make the sale. Look at how their culture has defined their community of customers. They each attract their own style of customer. The problem for all these companies may be that their target market is so narrowly defined that they lack a large enough population to sustain their business!

What is your promise to your customers? It is in the target you choose. Who is your target?

- Motel 6 only markets to anyone traveling on a tight budget.

- Tide only markets to people who want to target stains and dirt (they use a bull's eye on their logo).

- Wear leather? Think you're tough? Big power? You buy a Harley-Davidson.

- Want to fly, have fun and not pay luggage fees? Southwest Airlines.

- Martha Stewart? Women and homemakers.

- Steve Jobs? Cool computer users.

Your customers have a problem and no one else is solving it. They will willingly give their hard-earned money to anyone who can identify it and make the problem go away. It is within your power and means to make it go away? If you can identify the problem your customers face, you can provide the solution or (better yet) be the solution to their problem...and you will have more business than you know what to do with. So get out of the "servicing people" business. And get out of the self-service business and instead, get into the problem-solving business.

Easy Action Step: What key problem within your target market do you solve?

It's Not Always About Pricing

The key to meeting the needs of your customers is providing value better than anyone else. Think of it as "surpassing value". It is value that outdistances other companies in your field. As an attendee to one of my reinvention strategy sessions tweeted me later, "Someone may beat me on price, but not on value." He gets it. He gets it while others around him don't.

In times of economic change, companies often try to re-energize their sales by slashing prices. Please understand that when you choose to compete on pricing alone, you have already run up the white flag of surrender. Price cuts, discounts, rebates, and fire sales all leave you vulnerable to competitors who can give more value for less profit. In 2001, Saks Fifth Avenue met the recession head on by drastically slashing its prices. At first this seemed like a good idea and their profits jumped – but only in the short term. Meanwhile, competitor Neiman Marcus kept their identity as a luxury leader with its target consumers. The deep price cuts implemented by Saks increased revenues, but decreased luxury consumer confidence in them. By the end of the recession, Neiman Marcus was the clear winner in the eyes of luxury shoppers. Unfortunately it seems that Saks returned to this same strategy again in 2008. Time will tell if they can make this work for them.

Discounts are a bad idea that worsens with time. Apple has gained a reputation as a culture of innovative designs and products. Innovation also defines their target community. In April 2010, when Apple unveiled the new iPad in what was easily the year's biggest buying frenzy, it seemed everyone WANTED, NEEDED, MUST get their hands on the latest gadget the very day it came out…before the price had a chance to drop to normal levels.

Yeah, the price dropped. Why? Apple knows you want to beat the rush and are willing to pay the most, so they didn't discount their latest and hottest product. They never do, instead using this phenomenon effectively to their advantage – and their bottom line profit! Remember the long lines for the new iPhone? The long lines for the new iTouch? The long lines for the iPod (okay, that was a while ago)? The newest, hottest products are never discounted and they sell out because the perception is planted in everyone's mind that they are valuable. Watch how inexpensively you were able to buy a Kindle a couple of months after the iPad was introduced.

Conversely, the more valuable the product, the less likely the discounted price. Can't you just see the ads? "Pick up your new BMW today while the introductory prices are in force." "Be the first to purchase a Yumi

Katsura wedding gown during our special discount days program." "Dr. Turner offers brain surgery for 50% off at his new practice!" Yeah, right. Line me up for that one.

An author friend of mine introduced her book on the market. To promote it she offered free copies to the first 50 people who answered an online survey. Then she sold it for an "introductory price" on her web site to sell more. The price was reduced. Her problem was, by discounting the book price, she de-valued her product. And her book sales reflect it - they aren't selling so well. The ugly back end of this practice is this: the price can only go.....DOWN. It is highly unlikely that my friend will ever get full price for her book after introducing it at a loss.

Value-Based Marketing

The move of the brown creepers into the environment of the nuthatches was really the best thing that could have happened to them. It forced this species to seek new food and helped them survive and grow stronger. Yes, the competition actually strengthened the birds. Competition is your best friend, if you view it with the right attitude.

In a capitalist system, competition also serves to keep costs in check. Competition is great for your business. It keeps your company healthy and on its toes. I worked with a marketing and sales company that owned its market – literally. The CEO had bought out his competition and business was booming. Then the recession hit. And to compound matters, a competitor moved in. His sales staff feared the worst and began actually cutting prices in order to keep customers. His salespeople were in panicking. He called me in to stop the hemorrhaging. So I talked with them about how having healthy competition was good for business.

We talked about the rescue of the elk herds in Yellowstone National Park by introducing the grey wolf into the ecosystem. For years the elk population had declined in the park. Park rangers, biologists and veterinarians pondered over what was killing off the animals. Then someone realized that without the grey wolf – killed off and run out of the park, the elk had no natural predator to keep them active. After the wolves were introduced, the elk began to "toughen up" and experienced an increase in population. The presence of their natural enemies made them stronger and more prevalent.

The same is true for your competition. The brown creeper is the best thing that could have happened to the nuthatches. Norm Brodsky writes: "Competition is great: When rival start-ups began to pour into the records-storage business, Brodsky was thrilled. "In a young industry like ours, you have to spend an inordinate amount of time and money just explaining what you do and why prospective customers should pay you to do it," he explains. "The more competitors you have, the easier that task becomes. Competition makes comparison-shopping possible, which simplifies your sales pitch. All you have to do is explain to a sales lead why you're better than the next guy."

Competition creates a value that is hard to beat. And when put in perspective, value beats pricing every time. When they understand what they're getting, people will pay more for great value over low prices. Most discerning consumers will overlook the cheaper store brands for a trusted brand value. They shy away from deep price cuts in the long term in a recession. That's what Neiman Marcus discovered. I discovered it, too.

In my own business I allowed some flexibility with certain customers who were long-time friends and loyal to me. I wanted to foster a culture of loyalty in my client base early on. I knew most of them were going through rough times and wanted to provide them with substance for their money. But at the same time, I knew I would never rise above as a professional speaker if I cut my fees and ran a fire sale. The problems I faced in the turbulent economic crisis were made worse by my new status as a Certified Speaking Professional. I had just earned this prestigious designation in 2008. Less than 7% of all speakers worldwide have attained this honor. To cut my fees immediately afterward would have cheapened my status in almost every meeting planner's view.

The point is that I didn't need to drop prices – I needed to reinvent myself and my market. Pricing was a distraction that would have kept me from the real issue. Speaking with clients and prospects, I found a need and a niche in the area of marketing and reinventing. It seemed that folks were looking for a new angle, a new pitch, a new focus. Everyone was suddenly interested in how to reinvent themselves amidst the economic challenge.

When I started talking about the economy not being down, but different, it struck a chord. At first people bristled when I made statements like: The recession will never end. But explaining how they have lasting effects on us forever, people began to say, "Aha! Now I see what you mean." Stating that "Teamwork doesn't always work" seemed to resonate with leaders who had exhausted themselves trying to make dysfunctional teams function together. Saying outright that "people don't buy what you sell" reached every sales executive who was tired of pushing valueless product on unwilling customers.

The result was that more and more CEO's and meeting planners were calling me and asking me to say what others wouldn't say to their people. Bold statements that made leaders re-assess their approaches to customer service, marketing, management and sales. It paid off. My bookings year over year went up 150% and the evaluations indicated that my topics were hitting home and initiating reinvention.

Netflix, the mail-order movie store has surpassed Blockbuster Videos and just about single-handedly put them out of business. Ludwig Von Mise, an Austrian economist once wrote that the entrepreneur who fails to use his capital to the "best possible satisfaction of consumers" is "relegated to a place in which his ineptitude no longer hurts people's well-being." Successful businesses are successful because they fill an unmet need. If they're unsuccessful, it is often because they have failed the consumer. In that case going out of business or bankruptcy is an economic good for relieving those the market has left for dead of any further capital to destroy.

John Tamny writes for Forbes.com, "The demise of Blockbuster Video offers some lessons about Schumpeterian creative destruction, the necessary role of short-sellers in making markets transparent and the role of capital in rewarding winners and losers. Once a popular growth stock among investors, Blockbuster is now viewed on Wall Street as a sick company teetering on the edge of bankruptcy. While it would be foolish to cheer Blockbuster's decline, its descent speaks to the importance of allowing companies no longer fulfilling market needs to go bankrupt."

In its heyday, Blockbuster's customers gained from the lower prices for movie rentals that this volume buyer could command. Blockbuster had "pull" with the major motion picture studios. But as often happens as companies grow, Blockbuster concentrated on perfecting its existing service while beating competitors offering the same *instead* of looking into ways that outsiders might destroy its business model altogether. Great entrepreneurs disrupt. In this case the entrepreneur "disrupter" in question was Netflix.

Tamny goes on to say, "Popular as the Blockbuster brand was, getting to the video store in order to take advantage of its services was a hassle for customers--as was returning videos on time to avoid paying late fees. The rise of Netflix from well outside the traditional retail space meant these problems were solved in one fell swoop."

Netflix entered the market offering a monthly fee for movies, DVDs by mail and no limits on how long their customers could keep the movies in question - real value-based marketing. Netflix out-maneuvered a former innovator with a service that solved the late-fee problem and didn't require customers to leave their homes. They solved a problem and offered a value that Blockbuster wasn't willing to offer until too late. Netflix moved up the tree to solve a problem and gained the edge in value.

What community has your culture defined for you? What do consumers value in your offerings? How do you give value better than your competitors? Cavett Robert, the late sales expert and founder of the National Speakers Association said, "The best type of market growth comes from making the pie larger for everyone, rather than just making your slice larger within the pie." Reinvention strategists look for ways to increase the pie for their customers and clients. The nuthatches managed to reinvent themselves by moving up the tree. I think by now you've seen how that strategy is rare in business – making more room for you at the top. Where are you moving on your tree – up or down?

Easy Action Step: What key problem within your target market do you solve?

EPILOGUE

Getting into Your UNcomfort Zone

Some people never discover their passion in life. They wander through this world without a purpose and are therefore, left unfulfilled, aimless and without ever knowing their full potential. Still others do discover their passion but never pursue it because they are either too discouraged from life's pressures or too distracted with temporal pleasures to regain their focus and start the pursuit.

The truly fulfilled and contented individual is he or she who not only discovers his or her potential but who lays everything else aside to pursue it unabashedly. They live in an "UNcomfort Zone." Do you have one? They constantly scan the horizon for a better way to pursue their dream and be more productive. I respect everyone who has found what they can do to make life better and this world a better place for all of us to live. They have found their UNcomfort zones.

These men and women go out every day and try to be better. They realize that the world changes daily and they do their best to keep up with it. They don't blame others, their environment or their life situation for why they can't succeed. They can't afford to be comfortable with maintaining the status quo.

The world of work has been changed forever. Consumers are more savvy, less patient and have higher expectations. You can't dish out the same products and services you were offering just two years ago and expect to succeed. Medical facilities and companies are facing a set of changes from the government and patients unparalleled in history. Banks and financial lending institutions are facing new compliance laws and restrictions on lending that they know will change their business models forever.

Constant improvements in communications and media are changing the way we receive news and making them more answerable to a more intelligent customer. Book publishers are facing the advent of electronic publications that could spell the end of the hard and soft cover published book in the next 10 years. Municipal, county, state and national governments can't do business the way they traditionally did through increasing the tax base. People are more mobile than ever and will simply move where they aren't taxed as much or have more voice in the same services. You can't afford to be comfortable with these changes in consumers and the public.

Your employees know they are valuable to your business. In a survey I read in Delta's Sky Magazine it was reported that the millennial generation (born 1982 - 2000) has a better knack for finding creative solutions to workplace challenges, and for turning to their social networks for assistance. They feel they are entitled to ask for and expect more from their work. They are more prone to seek a job they find more fulfilling and not care for one that doesn't fulfill them. You can't manage them according to the old team standard. They don't fit the mold. Forcing them will only make them look elsewhere for the position that fulfills them. They are independent and have no loyalty to outmoded and outdated systems and strategies. You can't afford to be comfortable with the changing workplace expectations.

Consumers know more, care more and want more than ever before. If you can't supply it, they will find someone who can.

My wife and I sought a plumber to install a bathroom fixture. Rather than just call our friends, we went online, we sought references, we value-shopped the internet and conducted interviews. The one who got the job wasn't the slickest promoter. He wasn't the cheapest. He was the one most in touch with our needs and wanted to serve us best. He differentiated himself. He created a value that trumped his price. Customer values dictate the market, not pricing.

Reinvention works on a corporate and individual basis. It prospers in a marketplace and personal environment. Equipped with this knowledge you are now able to move forward in a different way for a different day. The economy isn't down; it's different. You can whine and moan, or wait for the climate to recover, or you can determine how the difference has affected your market and start differentiating yourself today. The choice is yours. Today is a new day with new challenges. No one can make you move forward. It is your choice. You can either embrace the changes or cheerfully wave to them as they pass you by. Bon voyage!

Easy Action Step: What have you seen in this book that inspired you about reinventing yourself? What statement, example or idea made you think, "Yes, I can do that!" How can you take that list of 20 (expanded now to 40) changes you have observed in your personal and business environment and put them into action today? What will be your first step on the road to your personal reinvention?

It's D-Day!

On the night of June 5, 1944 over 100,000 allied soldiers (British, American, Canadian, French, Polish, Dutch, and many more nationalities were represented in the attack) were flying, sailing and moving toward the shores of the French coast. It was the night before D-Day, the greatest invasion in history. It was the event that spelled the end of the Nazi occupation of Europe. What must it have been like for those soldiers, sailors, airmen, medical officers and paratroopers? They were about to change history. They were about to re-take the European continent and make it free. They were about to do something totally unexpected.

They carried the hopes and dreams of millions of oppressed people around the world. The expectations were the highest in recorded history. President Franklin Roosevelt described the purpose of the invasion was "to preserve our civilization and to set free a suffering humanity." Succeed and the world war is over. Fail and die. The stakes don't get higher.

Like the first wave that ran out of the landing craft or jumped out of the airplanes, YOU are the first soldier on the beach of the enemy territory. YOU are taking fire and people are dropping around you every minute. Your culture of employees and customers look to YOU for leadership, support and encouragement. Will you hesitate? Take a "wait and see" position? Will you find fault or find a solution? Will you call a meeting? Will you fight the way your father did? Or will you fight a new enemy with new tactics? The uncomfortable choice is yours.

Much of this book has used historical references. Not to use them as the way to move forward, but to illustrate how people changed and made history by being different. Many examples have been observed of companies who faced challenging economic conditions and conquered. These companies are making historic decisions that are changing the economy for them, their customers and their competitors forever.

Through the course of this book you've read examples of famous leaders and battles – George Washington, Napoleon, Abraham Lincoln, Teddy Roosevelt, Montgomery, Patton and Eisenhower. Why? Business is a daily battle to take the territory. It is a minefield and you have to know where to step. You learn best from those who walked before you. You learn best when you take on the competition in a way that confounds – rather than matches – their tactics. You don't win by imitating them. You win by defeating them in a way they aren't expecting. You win by outflanking them.

On the lighter side, there is a great moment of irony in the movie *Airplane*. Just as the crippled jet is attempting to land, the tower chief refuses to turn on the runway lights. When asked why, he says, "No, that's just what they are expecting us to do." Funny. What is your competition expecting you to do? Do something that makes you different from the norm and you will put them out of business forever. What are your customers expecting you to do? Do something different and you will secure their business (until somebody else does something different). It worked for Netflix, Starbucks, Apple, UPS, Dominos and many, many more.

Just making the one-time change shouldn't make you feel comfortable. It should inspire you to stay on the cutting edge. Never, never, never settle in! Leaders with a reinventive attitude constantly look to improve their services and products, knowing that otherwise their difference will become the new norm and they will again be left out. Don't be left out – again (it worked *against* Circuit City, CNN, the Lehigh Railroad, Blockbuster, the Gap and many, many more).

You can't reinvent yourself one time and hope that settles it for the rest of your life. My life and my business are constant efforts on my part to reinvent myself personally and professionally. The reinvention process comes easy. The decision to DO it is a choice I have to deal with daily. It doesn't make me comfortable, but the challenge is exhilarating! It keeps me on the cutting edge and hopefully more in touch with my customers, clients and fellow strategists. It keeps my competitors very uncomfortable. That is my job. The stakes are high.

I hope that doesn't make you feel comfortable. I hope you aren't "settled in" to "stay the course." This is not the time to get comfortable. This is the time for you to reinvent yourself; and to take on the challenges in the new normal of the global market. It is time to - by your actions - *define* the new normal. Are you ready? The economy has changed as you read this. The market is moving forward. Your competition and your consumers are studying and watching you to see what you will do next.

Pursue your Passion: Some people never discover their passion in life They are left unfulfilled, without ever knowing their full potential. Still others do discover their passion but never pursue it because they are either too discouraged from life's pressures or too distracted to regain their focus and start the chase. The truly fulfilled and contented individual is he or she who not only discovers his or her potential but who lays everything else aside to pursue it unabashedly.

I urge you to take the beach. I call you to take the challenge. It is time to take control of your life, business and future. It's your choice. I'm pulling for you. Make the UNcomfortable decision and

Reinvent your life forever.

Appendix A

Speaker's Evaluation & Feedback

I use a special evaluation at the conclusion of my speaking engagements. My purpose is to elicit honest feedback to use in crafting my message for ever greater impact. It is only natural that I tell listeners they should use this same list of questions as their standard for improving or reinventing their business models. Below is the questionnaire. I wish for you the same discovery that it has brought me:

1. ***What did you hear me say that affected you the most?*** Often people will be affected by some remark, quote or story that I use in a presentation that I didn't think was that significant. On occasion, they will say they heard me say something that I don't recall saying or in fact didn't even say! I want to know this so I can better tailor what I say the next time. I can also determine what people who hear me are being motivated by. Have you ever thought of asking your top customers (and you *must* ask only your top, most loyal customers this) what you do for them that affects them the most?

2. ***What did you hear me say that you wish I would have said more about?*** This tells me where they are engaged and how I can elaborate more to assist them. Often in the space of one hour, I don't have time to go into detail on a particular point, but the answer to this question tells me what they want more of for next time. When service stations became convenience stores over 35 years ago, owners recognized that they were making more money on the products inside the store, than the gasoline products sold outside. They saw a trend and movement

and sold to that. Today, gasoline may be the commodity that attracts customers into the store, but the most money is made from convenience items like soft drinks, alcohol, tobacco products, candy, snacks, small grocery and household items. Ask your customers what service or product they like best and what you can do to improve it or produce it better for them. What do your customers want more of from you? What nugget does your service provide that people like enough to buy in multiples?

3. ***What did I not speak on that you wish I would have spoken about within this topic?*** Am I asking for trouble? No, certainly not. I am asking the audience to tell me what I didn't cover that is a problem to them. It helps me refine my presentation and helps me sell my services in the future. Ask your top customers what service you are not doing that they wish you would do for them. This heads off complaints and actually tells you the business your most loyal consumers wish you were in for them. The Hertz Corporation reinvented the airport car rental service by asking their top customers what they wanted them to do for them. The answer was a clear, "Get us out of the airport faster." The result was the Number 1 Gold Club. You join by paying $50 one time (which is refunded after four rentals). Then when you rent your car online or by telephone, it is waiting for you in the garage with the keys in the ignition, trunk open, parked going out and the contract hanging from the rear view mirror. That gets their top customers out of the airport faster.

4. ***If I came back to speak, what could I speak on to YOU that would help you?*** This tells me (and the meeting planner who hired me) what they want to hear from me next time. It is an appeal from the audience to bring me back in to hear me speak to them. Often I work with trade associations who, as a rule, don't hire speakers in back-to-back years. However I am re-hired to speak the following year at a better-than-average rate because of the feedback we receive to this question. No one objects to me coming back if they like me and want to hear me speak on a particular problem or subject. Ask your people what you could do if you marketed just to them. What could I or we do if you

were the only customer we served? Imagine the possibilities. Imagine the positive word of mouth this question will generate among your most loyal fan base. In my line of work, it moves me from being a "voice" to being a consultant, analyst, and advisor.

I once asked my top customers what they wanted more of and they responded, "We want more interaction." So as a result I began to incorporate increasing amounts of interaction in my presentations. By early 2010 I was incorporating dialogues, known as "Strategizing Sessions" into my presentations. Other speakers offer to simply give a lecture or motivational talk; I was giving clients what they were asking for – because I listened. It completely reinvented my speaking career, ultimately branding me as a "strategist." And I wasn't just any strategist; I became "The Reinvention Strategist." This is what we discussed in the chapter *Get Out of Your Industry*.

APPENDIX B

50 Changes in Customer Behaviors and Expectations Today

Customers are different today than they were just two years ago. Your customer is more intelligent and discerning than ever before. He/she knows more, is more adept at finding information and has much less patience with poor treatment. The business game has changed and the customer is directing what is and isn't relevant in business.

We're Not Gonna Take It!

Your customer:

1. Is OVER you telling them how important their call is while they wait on hold.

2. Is OVER your lame recorded hold message/advertisements/Muzak and pitches for more business.

3. Is OVER your voice mail telling them what the day is or when you will be back – when both are incorrect.

4. Is OVER you telling them that you will call right back...and you don't – ever.

5. Is OVER your off-shore call centers - "help desks."

6. Expects someone to answer the phone when they call who knows how to help them then and there.

7. Probably doesn't FAX anything anymore – but scans.

8. Is using a debit card and cash more.

9. Is now using smaller banks, credit unions and personal bankers and online banking from their smart phone.

10. Is now using their own resources for internet and marketing purposes.

11. Will not be buying gas-guzzling cars, Pontiacs, Mercurys or Saturns.

12. Is not able to purchase a no-money-down loan for their home.

13. Is not investing in the market like they did before.

14. Is SCANNING internet web sites – *not* reading your lengthy copy meant for readers.

15. Is online - checking out your website as you read this.

16. Is online buying tickets, hotel rooms, books, computers and just about everything without ever talking to a sales person in the process.

17. Is redefining what it means to be social.

18. Is blogging about his experiences with you, for thousands to read (Dell, are you listening?).

19. Is listening to people who "interpret" the news for them more than ever.

20. Is YouTubing about his experiences with you for the world to watch - by the millions (See the viral video about United Airlines).

21. Is "Googling," not yellow-paging/yellow-booking.

22. Is more likely to buy music online or off the sound system in their auto – not in a store.

23. Is saving more files electronically… and going paperless.

24. Is more conscious of "green" products, organic foods and is willing to pay *more* to be healthy and environmentally sound.

25. Is using their smart phone to do more than banking: score-keeping, home security checks, unlock their car, and almost any other "apps" they can find.

26. Expects FREE WiFi in their hotel room, on the airplane, in Starbucks, at Barnes and Noble, in the auto service department and at their home. They want it from you, too.

27. Is more likely to get most of their news from the internet.

28. Reads labels and knows all of your ingredients and nutrition facts. And knows the restaurants who won't share this information.

29. Isn't keeping your 9-5 hours of business operation to buy from you.

30. Is recording how you treat them with their flip phone or other device. It will be on YouTube in less than an hour (TSA take note).

31. Doesn't care for your company policies that favor *you*, not *them*.

32. Will only settle for a cheaper price if there is no perceived value from you.

33. Is less certain about the stability of the economy, their currency, savings and their future.

34. Wants to trust you, but feels betrayed by so many false promises in the past.

35. Is looking for a CONNECTIONwith you that relates to them.

36. Expects great service before and after doing business with you (so they will do more).

37. Does not want to wait long for anything or anyone to look something up.

38. Is looking for solutions to their problems…not products or services.

39. Can check your price and your facts in seconds on the internet.

40. Knows as much about your company as you do (and a few things you probably DON'T know).

41. Knows all about what your competitor offers for them and will do.

42. Can pay right now IF you can handle it in a few clicks.

43. No longer trusts big institutions they used to trust – banks, government, health care, etc.

44. Needs to be addressed as an intelligent person – not from your script.

45. Will drive farther and go out of their way if the product or service is valuable enough for them.

46. Isn't bound by your time constraints to make a decision.

47. Goes to Craig's list or Angie's list, YouTube, Consumer Reports online, Google or their friends for referrals and information. Looks at you last.

48. Is uncertain of what will happen to their retirement in the wake of new laws about health care.

49. Is less likely to give you a second chance if you blow the first one.

50. Won't wait ask for a supervisor if your customer service person treats them badly.

51. Add yours here: _____.

ABOUT THE AUTHOR

Jim Mathis, CSP is the Reinvention Strategist. An international certified speaking Professional, author and founder of J&L Mathis Group, Inc., an Atlanta-based group providing products and services that drive market leadership. The author of *Reaching Beyond Excellence* and *Reinvention 101: Bold Ideas on Reinventing Yourself,* he presents internationally on maintaining leadership in challenging economies and competing in the global marketplace.

Jim believes that the economy isn't down; it's different.

As one of the busiest speakers and strategists, Jim is in high demand presenting and strategizing with groups, associations and corporations around the world about his philosophy and business and marketing. He works across industry lines to use common-sense approaches to solving the challenges that companies and organizations face in the New World of Work.

Jim has applied his strategies across numerous industries. He helps you discover indisputable truths and realities about your organization that you can't see on your own and solve the loser to leader problems that you can't solve.

His delivery style has you laughing one minute, writing down a thought the next and thinking your way out of the room. He is both humorous and provocative. He is anything but dull and boring!

CPSIA information can be obtained
at www.ICGtesting.com
Printed in the USA
FFOW04n0654090715
14846FF